MW00717105

"*The Fragrance of His Grace* speaks c wounded heart through a healing process—providing grace, and renewed hope and peace."

CRAIG ELLISON, PhD
Alliance Seminary, Nyack, New York
Founder and former Director of the Alliance Graduate School of Counseling
Nyack Seminary, Nyack, New York

"God's grace is so evident in this book! I have read every page. Couldn't put it down! It speaks to a vast audience of women who have carried the emotional stress of maltreatment for far too many years. I express my gratitude to Jan for persevering through the pain, so that these words have the opportunity to touch many distressed hearts. Read about her pathway to grace."

SHARON ELLISON, BSN
Wayne State University,
Detroit, Michigan

"This book is a fantastic work! As I read *The Fragrance of His Grace*, I was deeply moved by the way Jan Johansson presented such an emotionally challenging journey. Most books that are presented from a personal and Christian perspective do not encourage me to look deep within as this book has. By sharing intimate and personal details of her own life experiences, Jan encourages all who are enveloped in darkness and despair to choose a course of action which will deliver them into the hands of a wise and gracious God. Allowing God to work in our lives produces fruit that He can use for His glory to help others. Jan's book is full of hope, forgiveness and instruction."

MARIE WHITE, PhD
Assistant Professor and Department Chair, Childhood Education
Deputy Chair, Adolescent Education
Nyack School of Education, Manhattan Campus
Nyack College, New York City, New York

"Jan Johansson writes a very personal and poignant book about life lessons in her journey with God. From the soil of many diverse encounters ranging from the tragic to the joyful, the author provides a window into the ways of God. I strongly recommend this book."

DR. MAC PIER
President, The New York City Leadership Center

"A must-read! As you read this book, God's grace will just seem to jump off the pages and touch you deep within. Jan surprised me with her boldness to share openly about her life's journey. She addresses, with amazing authenticity, her struggle to keep her spiritual life, her family life, and ministry thriving in the midst of emotional and physical challenges. She speaks to wives, mothers, women in leadership and women from all walks of life. She writes of 'learning the unforced rhythms of grace,' and as you read through the pages you sense your own wounded heart reaching upward to join in the cadence of this great grace."

LISA SHOPINSKY
Executive Pastor, Evangel Church
Long Island City, New York

"As I read *The Fragrance of His Grace*, I felt as though I were sitting in the author's living room, listening to her tell me the story of her life's journey with the Lord. Jan is very candid about the intimate, and often challenging, details, which allowed her to grow and eventually blossom into the graceful person He desires for all of us to become. Any woman who reads this book, whether a stay-at-home mom or a high-powered attorney, will find a source of comfort and hope in reading that those difficult experiences she encounters can be used by God to facilitate growth in Him."

BELINDA DELGADO, ESQ.
Associate Disciplinary Counsel
Bureau of Legal Affairs / Investigations & Trials
New York City Fire Department

"This is a book of promise . . . God's promise to transform our lives. Jan Johansson—in open, honest prose—has written poignantly about her journey into establishing the roots of surrender and trust in her spiritual walk. Although God allows suffering and challenges, Jan explains that trust and surrender of our wills is implicit in this process. Through God's appointed interventions in Jan's life, God's abundant grace was deeply revealed to her."

SANDLIN LOWE, MD

Clinical Assistant Professor at the New York University School of Medicine
Attending Physician at Bellevue Hospital Center
New York City, New York

"Are you afraid you'll never grow in God's grace? Jan Johansson poignantly expresses a hopeful and fruitful way through this process. In this tender yet revealing book, Jan opens her heart and invites you to share her life's journey of trust and obedience with the Lord. She speaks from experience to address a wide range of faith challenges, including:

Trust and obedience when life throws us curves.

Discontentment vs. surrendering to the will of God.

Godly submission and leadership.

Coping with tragic loss.

Surviving the memory of past maltreatment.

Renewing the mind.

Spiritual warfare.

Growing in the Fruit of the Spirit.

Jan treats these topics with the wise touch of an experienced gardener—gently handling the flower and their fruit, honest and resolute when dealing with the weeds. And she assures us that growth and victory are ours for the taking: '. . . and you will be like a well-watered garden' (Isaiah 58:11 TLB)."

REV. GARY FROST

Pastor, Evergreen Baptist Church, Brooklyn, New York
President, Concerts of Prayer Greater New York
Former Home Missions Director of the Southern Baptist Convention

"Jan Johansson invites you to join her on a beautiful and powerful journey. She vividly relates this journey via a tandem bicycle ride with Jesus —through joy and pain, trials and healing—as He brings about the Fruit of His Spirit in her life. Jan grew up in a Christian home, dedicated herself to serving the Lord, lovingly gave of herself as a pastor's wife, and raised her children to love and serve the Lord. Yet none of these things made her immune from profoundly painful struggles that sought to rob her of her faith, joy, and peace in her life. Her honesty and vulnerability will encourage you to expose the hidden areas in your own life to Jesus' healing balm."

INES M. MIYARES, PhD
Professor, Hunter College – City University of New York
New York City, New York

THE
Fragrance
OF HIS
Grace

JAN JOHANSSON

Lightning
Source™

The Fragrance of His Grace
© Copyright 2010 by Jan Johansson
Evangel Church
39-20 27th Street
Long Island City, New York 11101
718-361-5454

Scripture references are from the King James Bible unless otherwise noted.

Scripture quotations marked "NIV" are taken from the HOLY BIBLE, NEW INTERNATIONAL VERSION®. NIV®. Copyright © 1973, 1978, 1984 by International Bible Society. Used by permission of Zondervan. All rights reserved.

Scripture quotations marked "TLB" are taken from the Holy Bible, New Living Translation, copyright © 1996, 2004. Used by permission of Tyndale House Publishers, Inc., Carol Stream, Illinois 60188. All rights reserved.

Scripture quotations marked "MSG" are taken from The Message. Copyright © 1993, 1994, 1995, 1996, 2000, 2001, 2002. Used by permission of NavPress Publishing Group.

All rights reserved. This book or parts thereof may not be reproduced in any form, except for brief quotations in reviews, without the express permission of the publisher.

Cover and interior layout by David Danglis
Assistant publisher: David Danglis
Cover photo: jwinney / www.istockphoto.com
Diagrams by Andrew Marko

Printed in the United States of America
Library of Congress Control Number: 2010904599
International Standard Book Number: 978-0-615-36426-1

Dedication

To my husband Rob:
You are my Hero,
My Rock,
My Spiritual Advisor,
and the Wind Beneath my Wings.

To my three children: Carolyn, Brian and Stephen
You are the lights of my life,
and the ever-present joy on my journey.

To my four grandchildren: Andrew, Jessica, Emma and Nathan
May your future blessings be as bright
and as numerous as the stars in
God's heaven.

To our heavenly grandchildren: Ethan and Jonathan
You are loved,
You are missed,
You will forever be remembered.

Foreword

For over 36 years I have had the pleasure of knowing Jan Johansson . . . a mature, caring, loving Christian woman. I have been a witness to the life she has lived—a life absolutely dripping with grace from a great and magnificent God. Her inspiring story illustrates the beauty and strength of a godly woman that has spent 48 years faithfully loving and serving God through her relationships with her husband, family and church. I have had the privilege of observing Jan's journey and in the process have been able to bask in the sweet fragrance of God's grace poured into her life.

Her stories will grip your soul and even pull at each one of your heartstrings. At times you may find yourself moved to tears. Yet through it all, the evident steadfastness of God—and His distinct answers to the raw cries of Jan's heart—will encourage and strengthen you. Her journey is described in such honest and poignant words—yet, at the same time, offers practical tools, biblical truths and personal accounts aimed at helping you, the reader, on your own journey.

Be ready to be challenged! Jan's inspiring journey will stress the need for obedience, submission and trust in the Lord. You will be exposed to an understanding of the need for pain, and will be confronted with truths and disciplines that may seem hard to grasp. But as Jan's life can testify . . . as more pain is experienced, an even greater portion of God's love and grace is poured out.

No matter where you are in your walk with the Lord, I pray that the courage and compassion that Jan communicates in this revealing book will bless you and inspire you to grow and become a fragrance of

His grace to others. My hope is this: may Jan's journey inspire all of us to become beautiful flourishing flowers to bring the sweet aroma of God's grace to the world

MIRIAM VELEZ, MSED

(Bilingual Urban Education)
Assistant Professor of Childhood Education,
Student Teaching Coordinator
Nyack College, New York City, NY

Preface

I am first and foremost a child of God
I am a wife
I am a Pastor's wife
I am a mother of three
I am a school counselor

BUT MOST APPARENT

I am an unfinished book in need of His continual Grace

*"And God is able to make all grace abound toward you;
that ye, always having all sufficiency in all things,
may abound to every good work."*
II CORINTHIANS 9:8 NIV

Acknowledgments

The Fragrance of His Grace was formulated years ago as a result of a class I taught, titled, *The Gracious Woman*. It was a 13-week course that I developed due to the cries of so many women who desired healing, spiritual growth and spiritual enlightenment.

While teaching, I was prompted to evaluate, with much introspection, my own walk with the Lord. I've often heard it said that the one who teaches sometimes learns more than the listener. That may be true! I do know that while teaching, I became acutely aware of my own spiritual flaws and thus, the Lord and I began the journey that you will read about in this book.

Many who took that course encouraged me to put my thoughts into book form. I replied: "No, I'm not an author." Again and again, others would ask if I was writing the book. My answer was always the same: "No I'm not an author." Then I began to hear the Lord whisper in my ear: "Write the book!" "Really? For sure, Lord?" I whispered back. I think I thought of every possible avenue to discourage the idea of writing. I said, "Lord, I'm not a scholar, I'm not a theologian, I'm not eloquent," and on and on went the excuses. I felt like Moses waiting for an Aaron to be my mouthpiece. What would I say? Still I heard the Lord say: "Write the book."

So, I did begin, maybe eight years or so ago. I would write a small portion and then put it aside for many months. I wrote some more and then put it aside for years. I believe I put the book to rest at different times because I may have been in the throes of a difficult learning process; or being disciplined and chastised; or, perhaps, in the course of grasping a spiritual truth due to God's spiritual intervention on my behalf. You see, "words" alone are really empty! Oh, the principles are there, but they lack "life" when conveyed without having first experienced their life-changing affects. The Lord knew I needed to differentiate between "telling/teaching" and having the ability to "show" as I actually lived through a particular spiritual development.

I said all that so you, the reader, would understand my deep expression of gratitude to those who relentlessly encouraged me to keep writing. Thank you, ladies of Evangel Church, for your love, your encouraging words and intercessory prayers while I grappled with illness due to a great deal of spiritual warfare. I especially thank the Lord, Whose vigilant watch over my spiritual progress was able to finally say to me: "You started this project and now, at this time, you are ready to finish this book and pass along to others the abundant grace that I have showered on you." There is a season for all things, and this was my season to finish the book. Thank you, Lord, for your patience!

Secondly, where would I be without my husband? His bold faith has forever bolstered mine. His belief in the message of this book was a joy I cherished. He is a stalwart Christian on whose strength I've often leaned, and still do for that matter. Next year will be our golden anniversary. Where did the years go? Thank you for "pushing me onward," and giving me the courage to keep writing.

Thirdly, a very, very special thank you to my daughter, Carolyn. She received many phone calls from me due to my sickness while writing this book and also due to my very limited computer savvy. I am rather quite technologically challenged, and several times thought I had lost the complete manuscript. It was not to be found in the computer (at least, not by me). She walked me through the process of retrieving what I thought was lost forever, and was instrumental in bringing me back to a state of sanity once again. She has patience like no one else I know. Thank you for believing in me. Thank you for your gentleness when I needed a caring touch. Thank you, also, to my two sons, Brian and

Steve, who often called and asked: "Hi Mom, how's the book coming?" The three of you bring much joy into my life.

Fourthly, let me introduce you to Mr. Dave Danglis. He is the former Director of Communications at Elim Bible Institute. But to me, he is an angel is disguise. He was editor, proofreader, graphic designer, graphic artist, layout designer and coach all blended into one package. He calls himself a freelancer, but I call him a "miracle worker." He took the words from my written pages and made *The Fragrance of His Grace* come alive. What a talent! Thank you, Dave, for handling this project with such care and respect. May your many abilities bless those who read these pages!

Fifthly, I am so humbled by those who so graciously endorsed this work. A special thank you to Miriam Velez for writing the foreword and gracing her remarks with such kindness. Thank you all for blessing me!

There are so many exemplary Christians whose lives have impacted mine. They, in particular, are long-time friends, family members, college professors and especially prayer warriors who have deposited their faith into my spirit and soul. Many have invested heavily in my spiritual walk and I am grateful, beyond words, for their gifts of grace and love extended on my behalf.

Above all, there is a great cloud of witnesses and angels who have cheered me on these past 45 years in New York City. Without them, there would not be a book titled: *The Fragrance of His Grace*. Thank You, Lord, for their comfort, and for your beloved Holy Spirit, the greatest Comforter of all.

Thank You, Lord, for Your abundant grace poured into a little girl's heart many years ago. In retrospect, I realize that my family, my college education, my marriage, my career and spiritual makeovers were all predestined and planned by Your masterful hands. Thank You for journeying with me and creating in me Your "Life." I stand before You today, and bow my head in reverence to Your holiness.

The Fragrance of His Grace

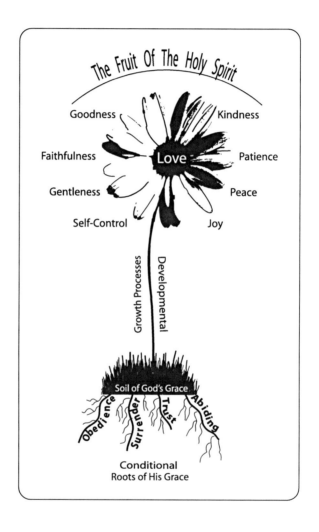

Introduction

A gracious woman retaineth honor . . .

PROVERBS 11:16 KJV

My name, Janice, means "Gracious One." Now isn't that a title to live up to!? Oh, that I could say that I have always been gracious, compassionate, kind and perpetually endued with favor toward others. I know that I have always desired to attain those attributes of God, and so perhaps because of that, the door was opened to venture into the meaning of my name and the graciousness of God. Thus began my journey and discovery of the road map, which led to many years of learning the truths that enable all of us, as women, to become more gracious. Knowing full well that it is "God which worketh in you (and me) both to **will** and to **do** of his good pleasure" (Philippians 2:13 KJV), I remain ever grateful for His unconditional love and unmerited favor extended and re-extended on my behalf as I began my journey.

When I was young, it was paramount that manners were learned and practiced in our household. I did practice those ever-important manners and was always rewarded with praise by others for my attention to "thank yous," and "no thank yous." However, as one progresses toward adulthood, gracious manners, pleasantries, kindness toward others, long-suffering, love and grace require a resource—a well to draw from. We soon learn that drawing from the well of self-help, and childhood learned behaviors, no longer enable us to maintain graciousness in a world of sin and a world that challenges our spiritual character.

One thing is certain; God is an enabler! He is a source that never fails and a well that never runs dry. I'm sure I tried His patience on many occasions over the years (and most likely still do), but He was and is forever a willing participant in all the affairs of my life. Spiritual growth is a process and, for sure, we will always be a ***work in progress,*** but He assures us that we can be "confident of this very thing, that he who hath begun a good work in you will perform it until the day of Jesus Christ" (Philippians 1:6 KJV). The Living Bible states this passage more vividly: "And I am sure, that God who began the good work within you will keep right on helping you **grow in his grace** until His task within you is finally finished on that day when Jesus Christ returns." He simply requests that we willingly put what little we possess together with the vast array of strengths and teachings He offers and He will enable us to succeed. What love! What grace! It is this grace that becomes the soil for the flower explained below.

The flower at the beginning of the book illustrates the progression of my journey, and the pathway to the development God had planned for my life as I learned to travel *with* Him rather than just *for* Him (in my own strength, that is). The journey the Lord takes you on may not be similar to mine, or be in the same order. Nonetheless, God uses the principles presented to shape all our lives and to make us more like Him.

You will notice that the flower progressively grows from chapter to chapter before it blossoms. My prayer it that you also may progressively grow in your journey toward becoming a gracious, fragrant flower and fruitful person, full of praise to the Lord.

As you venture through the pages of this book and encounter the **Roots of His Grace,** which I found to be *conditional* for spiritual growth, don't become discouraged. Remember, God's timetable is not the same as ours. Learning spiritual principles such as obedience, surrender of our wills, trust and abiding in Him, are ongoing—and more often, life-long learning processes. All that God asks is that we possess a willing heart. It is so very important that you become rooted for growth to take place! Keep abiding . . . you *will* see growth!

Then, as you progress up the stem of the flower, you will become acquainted with the **Developmental aspects of His Grace** such as emotional health, as well as discipline and renewal of the mind. If you've made it to the developmental stage of your journey, you're making tremendous progress. Hang in there, because you're about to blossom into a beautiful flower that God can use again and again.

The third part of this book deals with the **Outgrowth of His Grace.** Your spiritual growth will blossom into the fruit of the Spirit as stated in Galatians 5:22 in the NIV Bible. It will be an outgrowth of your abiding in Him. As Love becomes the central part of your life, the remaining fruit of Joy, Peace, Patience, Kindness, Goodness, Faithfulness, Gentleness, and Self-control will follow.

You will also notice that, in chapters I - VI, I have chosen to express my journey with the Lord via a tandem bike illustration. My journey could have been expressed via many different avenues, but the bike illustration is just that . . . an illustration. It was chosen to allow you, the reader, to more readily grasp the intensity of the conversation and togetherness the Lord and I experienced. It is meant to enhance the understanding for the need to establish a relationship with the Lord that will essentially lead to growth. The ultimate goal is to grow into a flower that produces His fruit. "As far as God is concerned there is a sweet, wholesome fragrance in our lives. It is the fragrance of Christ within us, an aroma to both the saved and the unsaved all around us" (II Corinthians 2:15 TLB).

May these chapters be an open door for you to discover the graciousness of our God and His ever-present help in time of trouble; and may you grasp hold of the abundant life He so freely offers. As you read on, I pray you will continue your own journey into gracious living by learning from the *Author of grace* . . . our Lord Himself. I trust His indwelling Spirit will empower you and allow you the wonderful opportunity of retaining the honor He longs to bestow upon His daughters as you graciously live your life for others. I pray you will "BLOSSOM" into graciousness and fulfill the plan that God has ordained for your life.

FOR APPLICATION AND REVIEW

In this second edition, I have included review guides and personal application questions to give you an opportunity to ponder, and more easily review, the progress of your spiritual walk with the Lord. These have been included at the request of many who have found the teaching elements of the book very useful. I trust the study guides will bring more insight as you look at your own life with more introspection, and study portions of His Word for enlightenment. Studying provides "a more excellent way" into the matters of the heart. To read is good, but to study and grasp the true meaning of His word and apply the knowledge gained, is far more admirable.

The Roots spoken of in this book—such as Obedience, Submission, Trust, and Abiding—are all nourished in the soil of His grace. I have found, as I journeyed through each root, that my faith and commitment to establishing a relationship with the Lord were greatly enhanced and I was encouraged to learn the life-lessons He had for me. May the same be true for you!

As I traveled up the stem of my flower, I was faced with deep hindrances to my spiritual development and with great pain, yet also with determination, I persevered to reach wholeness by His Grace. I thank Jesus for journeying with me as I progressed through these impediments to healing in Him. I trust these study guides will help you face your own shortcomings and give you confidence to reach for wholeness, both emotional and mental.

As I approached the blossom of my flower, I was completely enthralled that—finally—I felt I had reached a "right of passage" to the Fruit of the Spirit. I experienced the doors to the Fruit opening as God said to me: *"You have now grown full term . . . it is now time to blossom."* I say that very reverently, for I know beyond a shadow of a doubt that growth and progress would not have been mine without His Grace. I want to be a Fragrance of His Grace, and the Lord wants the same for you. May you find, as you study from the personal guides, that your blossom is flourishing and being filled with the essence of His Fragrance.

> *Study to show thyself approved unto God,*
> *a workman that needeth not to be ashamed,*
> *rightly dividing the Word of God.*
>
> II TIMOTHY 2:15 KJV

PART ONE

Roots of His Grace

Conditional aspects pertaining to learning grace

...

. . . I know thee by name,
and thou hast found grace in my sight.

EXODUS 33:12 KJV

CHAPTER I

The Root of Obedience

*For as by one man's disobedience many were made sinners,
so by the obedience of one shall many be made righteous.*

ROMANS 5:19 KJV

CHAPTER I

The Root of Obedience

Obedience >>>>>> "Take my yoke upon you . . ."

When I began my journey into becoming more scholarly regarding His grace, I was in awe when contemplating that God **knew me by name;** knew the number of hairs on my head; understood the hurts in my life that were responsible for framing my patterns of thinking and responding; knew my weaknesses and strengths; had a plan for me and in retrospect could see His guiding hand on my life; and above all, knew the desires of my heart.

One implicit desire of my heart, as I began this journey, was to truly live a victorious Christian life by His grace. Sounds good. Seems like a noble aspiration. But I have found over the years that it is "easier said than done." Being the idealist that I am, I went into this adventure of victorious, gracious living with the aspiration and the determination to be the best pastor's wife ever. No problem, right? Wrong! After graduating from college, marrying the love of my life and becoming pregnant all in the same year, reality soon became a constant reminder that perhaps I should re-evaluate my ideals. After our first child was born, he was greeted, 18 months later, by a sister. Reality really began to set in then. In fact, I began to dislike that word. Reality! Who wants to face reality every minute of every day? A little break here and there from reality would be nice, wouldn't it? Of course, children don't stop in their growth process to question if the adult is living in a real world or a world of *perfectionistic ideals.* Their needs are ever-present and ever-demanding. However, this being said, it is not to diminish my role of motherhood. I loved being a mother and love my children with every fiber in me. ***The real truth is, my world of idealism and my world of*** *realism were beginning to clash—and I needed answers.*

It was so grand to live in a world of idealism where all seemed perfect and rosy. But, in a real world of responsibility, all is not perfect and all is not rosy; and whatever a person possesses spiritually, will be tested. Together with home responsibilities and church responsibilities, I was becoming weary . . . too weary to be everything to everyone. I was not actually failing, but I wasn't actually succeeding, either; at least, not to my ideal way of thinking. I was in that carry-on, do-your-best, hang-in-there state of mind. I had traveled far from that victorious, best-pastor's-wife-ever state of mind.

Then, we were blessed with a third child. I was excited! As I have said, I loved being a mother. I feel I was an effective mother. And, good! For this, I will be forever grateful. For, when our third child came along, what energy I had left went into trying to be the best mother possible. Most other aspirations in my life were put on hold. But, I was determined to raise great kids, as an offering to the Lord, if I did nothing else. However, just raising my children became a challenge because of several living conditions. Number one, we were living in an apartment attached to the church. This alone was difficult and presented many privacy issues for us as a family. Secondly, the church could not, at that juncture, afford a secretary. That title was given to me. For many years, I answered the church phone from my apartment, typed the church bulletin and performed all responsibilities that pertain to a secretarial position. I also played the piano for church services and taught Sunday school as well as presided over the Women's Ministry. At times, I was barely hanging on . . . I was on the wrong side of the cliff, hoping I could still hold on. I found myself under much duress. I suppose at that point in my life, I had several options. I could have gone into denial and said I was just imagining a clash between my real world and my ideal world. Or, I could have just lived in a fantasy world of idealistic make-believe and pretend. Or, I could have allowed my circumstances to overwhelm me, and fallen into a state of disarray. However, all I did was "hold on" and hope for the best.

In the midst of all this, God—looking down from heaven—assessed my life and decided He needed to make something abundantly clear to me. He wanted me to understand that I could do *all* things through Christ who strengthens me . . . not just be a good mother. His desire was that I would come to the end of myself and begin to understand that I could never do all things in my OWN STRENGTH. The self-determined spirit I possessed was good, but I was leaving out a key element. To truly live a victorious and gracious life, I needed more. **He and I were meant to accomplish tasks and become successful, together, through Him.** I honestly thought I had understood that! In college, our class verse was Philippians 1:21: "For me, to live is Christ—His life in me . . ." (Amplified Bible). But, it is obvious I was thinking in an idealistic frame of mind *("I" will serve God)* and was unable to transfer the knowledge of that verse to a realistic frame of mind *(God and I together)*.

It was not until the truth of the concept of "togetherness" was put to the test, in the trenches, that I began to realize and grasp what a Spirit-filled life was. What the life of Christ *in me* could accomplish! How His power could transform one's thinking. Here I was, wanting so much to please God, but struggling to serve Him on my own . . . all alone. Time and time again, I would launch into a project and forget God and I were supposed to be partners, then wonder why I was literally running out of steam. I often wondered why God wasn't blessing my efforts! But, how could He, if I had not included Him? Believe me when I say that being a partner with God is very different from solely trying to serve God alone. I know this, for I have experienced both! It is impossible to fight the forces of evil on our own. It is impossible to face a world of sin on our own with our human weaknesses. We need to *be connected* to *THE SOURCE OF LIFE*, our Lord and Savior, Jesus Christ, and allow His life to live through us. He is truly a gracious and patient God and His grace will flow through us if we allow Him entry into our lives. So began my journey . . .

🌾

THE CART BEFORE THE HORSE

That Houghton College class verse: "For me to live is Christ—His life in me," was to be the theme of my future. However, learning and understanding that it is His life in me that enables me, was to become a slow line-upon-line and sometimes agonizing journey. It sounds so pragmatic, and yet simple . . . His life in me . . . in you. But, if you have always been a self-directed person like myself, it does not come natural to allow another entry into your life and dictate the outcomes. I can honestly say, I was afraid to hand over the reins and allow Him complete access. For evidential reasons (explained later in the book), I thought I needed to be in control. I'd assumed that being in control meant avoiding any uncomfortable inevitables—whatever those may present themselves to be in my life. Somehow, I must have thought I could wave a magic wand and I would then be eternally happy. Of course, now I know that being in His control and resting in the hollow of His hand is the safest place I could ever remain (especially if I desire the assurance of happiness and the absence of fear). However, at that time in my life, I sure needed an awakening.

The joy, the peace, and patience . . . all the fruit of the Spirit I so longed for escaped me. I guess you could say I was simply putting the "cart before the horse" . . . in other words, striving for the fruit of the Spirit before comprehending the concept of "His life in me," the concept of abiding in Him, the concept of His power working through me, which would enable me to serve Him and exhibit His fruit.

I can recall that in high school (back in the '50s), it was extremely important to succeed in everything. **I** was the head Drum Majorette; **I** was the captain of the cheerleading squad; **I** was the captain of the girl's basketball team; and **I** was the pianist for chorus. **I** was also chosen as the only soloist to attend the All State Chorus from my county and **I** worked hard for those As and Bs. As you can see, the central figure in all these activities is **"I."** It sounds very much like a self-absorbed person speaking, but as I have already stated, being a self-determined, self-directed personality does not easily lend itself to dependence on God and an understanding that "connection" and "abiding" are paramount in serving Him. **I was of the philosophy that if I were going to succeed, (I) would have to make it happen.** I was also of the philosophy that **I** would serve the Lord and if the Lord needed something done, **I** would do it. How wrong that was! The "cart before the horse syndrome!" I truly loved the Lord and I truly wanted to serve Him; but, I didn't know Him, nor had I learned the concept of inclusion. I didn't have an intimate relationship of dependence on Him. I was just going about it in the wrong way. My self-help operation back in high school and college would not work while serving Him in the ministry.

God was challenging me and calling me to climb higher mountains; to cross wider rivers and I was always willing to continue to try. However, I hadn't found the secret to the new strength I would need. Try as He might, I couldn't seem to grasp the "His-life-in-me" concept. I became tired climbing the mountains and I was truly drowning in the rivers. He whispered in my ear and said: **"You are about to venture into a process to get from what you are in your own strength and self-effort as a Christian, to what I (Christ) can offer you simply by walking with Me."** I would eventually learn that the fruit of the Spirit is a natural outgrowth . . . it is not something I can produce by myself. He wanted me to understand that it was **Christ** in me . . . not the **"I"** in me.

The following parable aptly portrays how I began to connect, to abide, to trust, to allow Him access into my life and let Him lead:

At first I saw Christ as my observer, my judge, keeping track of the things I did wrong, so as to know whether I merited heaven or hell when I die. He was out there, sort of like the president. I recognized His picture when I saw it, but I really didn't know Him.

*But later on, when I recognized His presence, it seemed as though life was rather like a bike ride, but it was a **tandem bike,*** *and I noticed that Christ was in the back helping me pedal.*

I don't know just when it was that He suggested we change places, but life hasn't been the same since. When I had control, I knew the way. It was rather boring but predictable. It was the shortest distance between two points.

*But when **He took the lead,** He knew delightful long cuts, up mountains and through rocky places and at breakneck speeds. It was all I could do to hang on! Even though it looked like madness, He said, "Pedal!"*

*I worried and was anxious and asked, "Where are You taking me?" He laughed and didn't answer, and **I started to learn to trust.***

I forgot my boring life and entered into the adventure. When I'd say, "I'm scared," He'd lean back and touch my hand.

*He took me to people who had gifts I needed . . . gifts of healing, acceptance, and joy. They gave me their gifts to take on my journey, **Christ's and mine.***

*And **we** were off again. He said, "Give the gifts away; they're extra baggage, too much weight." So I did, to the people we met, and I found that in giving I received, and still our burden was light.*

*I didn't trust Him at first, **in control of my life.** I thought He'd wreck it. But He knows bike secrets, knows how to make it bend to take sharp corners, jump to clear high rocks, fly to shorten scary passages.*

*And I'm learning to be quiet and pedal in the strangest places, and I'm beginning to enjoy the view and the cool breeze on my face with my delightful **constant companion.***

And when I'm sure I just can't do it any more, He just smiles and says, "Pedal."[1] — AUTHOR UNKNOWN

My Lord and I started our tandem bike ride with a mutual understanding that I had much to learn and comprehend about myself, about the workings of His Spirit in my life, about establishing roots, and about His priceless presence.

GOD'S PLAN

Amidst this struggle and dilemma I was experiencing, I remember having heard my husband speak to a group of ministers and say the following: "God will never ask you to do anything that you can do by yourself. God does this for two reasons."

1) He wants us to learn to depend on *His* strength.
2) More importantly, God's desire has always been for fellowship with Him. If we can do something ourselves, we will not learn to fellowship or learn to ask for instruction. However if we need to ask, we will also need to depend on Him. He wants us to attempt something large enough that failure is guaranteed unless God steps in. He knew that what He was asking me to do, and what I was attempting to do, I could never do by myself. He knew that I would fail. The author John Piper once prayed: "Lord, let me make a difference for you, that is utterly disproportionate to who I am."[2] "*And that, Lord, is our prayer; but we will greatly need your assistance as you take us beyond ourselves to reach what only you can accomplish through us. Amen.*"

That bicycle built for two was going to take us both on a long spiritual adventure into His grace.

It all started when our third child was unable to sleep. It wasn't his fault! He was born a borderline hyperkinetic child. He was perpetual motion and required very little sleep. That's not a good combination! I won't elaborate on this experience and have you think he was a horrible child to raise. Just the opposite! He was marvelous. All three children were marvelous.

Suffice it to say that because my child didn't sleep, I didn't sleep. When that kind of tiredness set in, I lost my appetite and that resulted in becoming anemic and seriously run down physically. Being in that

❧

state led to depression and extreme fatigue. It's not that my husband and two other children weren't helping. They were! In fact, even my in-laws assisted, and a very sincere and helpful lady, named Irma Pilli, came to my rescue whenever I called her. I am so grateful for her endless hours of care given to my son. In fact, I have often told her that my son is partly hers because she gave so much of herself to him. It's just that . . . during this time . . . we didn't exactly see where I was headed —physically, emotionally and spiritually—because this took place slowly over a period of four years. My strength s-l-o-w-l-y eroded away and I woke up one day totally depleted.

My son finally started to sleep through the night at age four and a half. By that time though, I was spent. If you saw him today, you would never believe he had been a hyperkinetic child. I'm sure he could sleep most any place, any time. He still has an intense, energetic personality, but sleep is no longer a problem.

God had a plan! God took advantage of my "spent" condition, and He began to call me into fellowship with Himself in a new way . . . in a way I had never before experienced. Our tandem bike had been taken to the bike shop and was in top condition . . . just waiting for us to begin our bike ride together. My first lesson and root in my flower was **obedience . . . to obediently learn to rest in Him.**

> *Come unto me, all ye that labor, and are heavy laden,*
> *and I will give you rest.*
> *Take my yoke upon you, **and learn of me;***
> *for I am meek and lowly in heart:*
> *and ye shall find rest unto your souls.*
> MATTHEW 11:28,29 KJV

Read the same verses from *The Message,* the Bible in contemporary language by Eugene Peterson: *"Are you tired? Worn out? Burned out on religion? Come to me. Get away with me and you'll recover your life. I'll show you how to take a real rest. Walk with me and work with me . . . watch how I do it. Learn the unforced rhythms of* **grace.** *I won't lay anything heavy or ill-fitting on you. Keep company with me and you'll learn to live freely and lightly."*

Oh, my!! How gracious He was to invite and call me to Himself. And, there was that word again! "Grace." He wanted me to learn the *unforced rhythms of grace.* When I started on this journey, my desire was to look into the meaning of my name. What did it mean to be gracious? He began by teaching me the meaning of **His** grace. He started with obedience . . . **obedience** to His call to fellowship and to His call for togetherness. He wanted me to walk **with** Him, work **with** Him, and keep company **with** Him. He wanted me to learn that when we become "spent," our days become forced; but the secret of resting in Him, staying connected, of abiding, allows for unforced graciousness because of His power, His strength in me. My Father wanted me to learn more concerning this unmerited favor and love, so freely given by His Son, called "grace." **To offer grace and become endued with favor toward others, I first needed to sit at His feet and learn.**

Resting in His gentleness, I felt safe, and I began to tarry in His presence. Waiting on the Lord is a good thing. "My soul, wait thou only upon God: for my expectation is from him" (Psalm 62:5 KJV). After coming to the end of my strength and my resources, I wanted so much to learn this "togetherness" thing. I had, for so long, depended on self. While *waiting,* God began to teach me about the Spirit-filled life.

> *But they that wait upon the Lord shall renew their strength;*
> *they shall mount up with wings as eagles;*
> *they shall run, and not be weary;*
> *and they shall walk, and not faint.*
>
> ISAIAH 40:31 KJV

Let me share the above verse, along with Matthew 11:28-29, through the following diagram, because this is the pathway that the Lord and I traveled. Over the years, I began to learn what **obedience, surrender,**

❧

trust and *abiding* were all about. You will see parts of this diagram at the top of chapters I-IV as it explains the continuing learning process and journey God had for me as we traveled together.

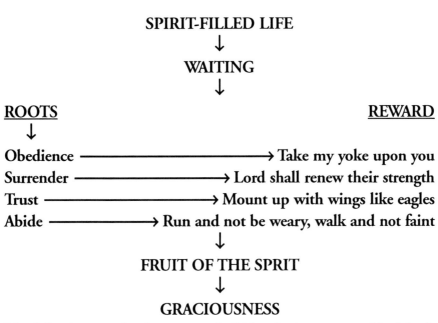

SPIRIT-FILLED LIFE
↓
WAITING
↓

ROOTS   **REWARD**
↓

Obedience ————————————→ Take my yoke upon you
Surrender ————————————→ Lord shall renew their strength
Trust ————————————————→ Mount up with wings like eagles
Abide ————————→ Run and not be weary, walk and not faint
↓
FRUIT OF THE SPRIT
↓
GRACIOUSNESS

The following song has been a wonderful inspiration to me as I look back on this "waiting" journey I have taken with the Lord. It is a confirmation of His faithfulness and the truthfulness of Isaiah 40:31 in my life.

THE POWER OF HIS LOVE

Lord I come to You,
Let my heart be changed, renewed;
Flowing from the **grace** that I found in You.
And Lord I've come to know the **weaknesses** I see in me,
Will be stripped away,
By the power of Your love.

Lord unveil my eyes,
Let me see You face to face,

The knowledge of Your love, **as You live in me.**
Lord renew my mind,
As Your will unfolds in my life,
In living every day,
By the power of Your love.

Chorus:
Hold me close; let Your love surround me,
Bring me near; draw me to Your side.
And as I wait, I rise up like the eagle
And as I soar with You,
Your Spirit leads me on,
By the power of Your love.[3]

WORDS AND MUSIC BY GEOFF BULLOCK

Eventually I would learn to have my strength renewed, mount up with wings as eagles and run and not be weary . . . but not yet! Eventually, I would grasp the meaning of obedience, surrender, trust and abiding . . . but not yet! Eventually, I would come to grips with His grace through the process of just waiting in His presence. The journey was just beginning into the truth of this song as well as Matthew 11:28, 29 and Isaiah 40:31.

OBEDIENCE AS A ROOT OF GRACE

The Lord was at that time, and will always remain, a tender, loving instructor. I am truly grateful He held my hand as He graciously taught and kindly embraced me; especially when I was slow to learn. I can be very stubborn, but He already knew that! I experienced how important it is to establish a relationship with God and to obediently listen for His still small voice. I learned how to take time to worship Him as I waited in His presence and I'm overjoyed that the Bible states the following: "He inhabits the praises of His people" (Psalm 22:3).

God's desire for obedience stems from His deep love for us. He looks down upon us lovingly and understands the effect that disobedience can bring to our souls. Obeying Him is paramount to pleasing Him, and as we establish this root in our lives, we begin to build a principle of trust that we can live by. Before we, as Christians, can live a gracious life and extend grace to others, we need to embrace His command to obediently listen to His voice as we wait in His presence. As we send this root deeper into the grace of God, we experience His blessing and His fruit that He can use to reach and bless others.

The Lord was explicitly interested in establishing more roots in my life and I waited apprehensively for the next lesson. Growth is difficult, and sometimes the root system in our spiritual lives becomes the most thorny and prickly of all the processes of development. However, it is the most vital! Without a root system, plants die; without a spiritual root system, we may not die spiritually, but we surely will not produce fruit. I braced myself!!! But He is such a gentle Jesus, as Matthew says: "Wear my yoke—for it fits perfectly—and let me teach you; for I am gentle and humble, and you shall find rest for your souls; for I give you only light burdens" (Matthew 11:30).

Read on for more exploits into building my root system . . .

CHAPTER I

Application & Review

Obedience always brings blessings, because it is the key to God's heart. The Bible teaches that we will reap what we sow. In light of that, when we obey God, His best will always be ours. When we don't, life may turn out to be much harder. In disobedience, His mercy does abound; however, if you are obedient, you will unquestionably reap His rewards.

1. Explain the meaning of Romans 6:16 as it relates to obedience and disobedience.

2. On a scale of one to ten (ten being the most obedient), how would you rate your obedience to God? Why?

3. Write those obstacles that are preventing you from being obedient. Please be specific.

4. In Matthew 11:28-29, what does Jesus mean when He says: *Take my yoke upon you and learn of me?*

5. What is the primary message of Isaiah 40:31?

CHAPTER II

The Root of Surrender

Submit yourselves therefore to God.

JAMES 4:7

CHAPTER II

The Root of Surrender

Surrender/Submission >>>>>> "The Lord shall renew their strength."

My second lesson on this tandem bike ride, that the Lord and I were venturing on jointly, was that of surrender. From obediently waiting on God, I learned to surrender. He wanted me to grasp how surrendering to Him would renew my strength; how surrendering would make me free to be all that He planned. And so, our journey continued.

An important aspect of waiting on God is a silent *surrendering* of the soul—and this, I knew, was going to be a long journey. I'm a "fighter," and the word "surrender" sounded like weakness to me. To be intimate enough with God to throw one's self upon the mercy of God, in complete surrender of the soul, is something many of us never attain or even attempt. I know I didn't. It was a somewhat unknown factor in my spiritual walk. But God is a God of grace, and He kept reaching out to me in love. Before this intimacy took place—this complete surrendering of the soul, that is—let me start from the very beginning.

OUR JOURNEY INTO SUBMISSION

It was August 5, 1961. My husband Rob and I had just said "I do." I was so elated. I thought I would walk on rose petals for the rest of my life. And to tell you the truth, I pretty much have . . . except for a few bumps in the road while riding that tandem bike with the Lord, when He chose to take me on some rough roads for my own education and spiritual growth.

I had just graduated from Houghton College in May of '61 with a degree in Christian Education, and my husband, Rob, had previously graduated from Elim Bible Institute and had one more year at Roberts Wesleyan College before he got his degree in History. (He later went on to get his Masters in Religion from NYU in New York City. He now has a doctorate from Nyack College. But here I am, getting ahead of myself.)

Rob had previously pastored two churches in Waverly, New York, before he took a position as assistant pastor to Rev. Philip Wannamacher at Bethel Church in Rochester, New York. This position gave him the opportunity to attend Roberts Wesleyan College, and it was during this time his sister, Marilyn, thought it was "of God" that Rob and I meet. I was a senior at Houghton College when Marilyn (who also attended Houghton) invited me to Rochester to meet her brother. That meeting led to another meeting and another and another, which eventually led to 8/5/61 (our wedding) at Bethel Church, and our journey together began. Guess it was "of God" after all! Thank you, Marilyn, for introducing me to the love of my life. Because of him, I *have* been walking on rose petals ever since.

After we were married, we moved into a renovated house (renovated by my husband, who built a new bathroom and kitchen) that was located behind Bethel Church at 7 Anson Place. Those were good years! We brought our son, Brian, to this apartment in June of '62, and our daughter, Carolyn, in December of '63. What wonderful memories we have of that apartment, even though there were big rats in the basement. We just took care of the rats and didn't think too much about it. Today, I would probably "flip out."

From Anson Place, we bought a house in Irondequoit, a suburb of Rochester, and again Rob renovated. It was a dream house for us, with a huge fenced-in back lawn, swings for the children, wonderful neighbors and a barbeque. Rob was still pastoring at Bethel Church, and I was teaching Sunday School and playing the piano for church and cantatas. The fellowship we shared with so many, in those early "Bethel days," remains unparalleled to this day. Many have remained cherished, life-long friends, and the memories we accumulated will endure and never be forgotten. During this stay in Rochester, from 1961 to 1965, we also had such a grand time enjoying our small children, which is obvious from the thousands of slides and pictures we took of them . . . **and then, it happened!!!**

GOD SPOKE!

It was one of those days! "Hurry up kids, Daddy will be home in two minutes." You know how those days go: you need six hands, four sets of eyes and enough energy to start a steam engine . . . especially when you have two little ones. We had one hour to eat, clean up and arrive at church in time for choir practice. I heard the car door slam. "Daddy's home, wash your hands." I brought the small step stool to the sink so that my two little ones could wash up. Out of the corner of my eye, I caught the expression on my husband's face . . . a very serious expression. Our eyes met and he said: "We need to talk."

Now, I was worried. What had happened?

Clean hands would have to wait. Supper would have to wait. We would obviously be late for choir. I placed my 11-month-old in the playpen and gave my 2½-year-old some toys and said: "Mommy needs to talk with Daddy for a minute." That minute was one of the longest in history.

"I need you to pray, and carefully consider what I'm about to say."

"Okay, but you're scaring me, what is it?"

"I feel God is calling us to pastor my grandfather's church in New York City."

"You're kidding, right?"

"No, I'm very serious."

"But we just moved into this house—you just finished renovating."

I sat stunned! I sat in silence and then finally found my voice and squeaked out: "When are we leaving?" as I contemplated all that we would have to leave behind, including friends, our home, security and Bethel Church.

"Probably some time in October. I'm flying down to speak with gramps and then I'll have a better idea of the time schedule. In the meantime, I want you to pray."

Never in a million years would I have thought that the serious expression on my husband's face would have carried such weight. And never in a million years would I have been able to ponder the import of such a move. The summer of '65 was more than a memorable time in our journey—it was life-changing!

We were to sell our dream house and move to New York City. This is a chapter about surrender, and there we were, happily serving God in Rochester, and we were to "submit" to the will of God and journey to New York City. I did pray, and I said to the Lord: "God, this is *me*; do you really want *me* in New York? I'm from a little town, I don't know anything about BIG cities . . . I'll be lost; not only will I be lost, I'll **get** lost. How will I ever find my way around?" It was hard enough acclimating to the "Little Big City of Rochester." Forget about New York City!! God had an answer: it was going to be one of those tandem bike rides. But, at that time in my journey, I didn't know about sharing a bike and I was pedaling in my own strength. One thing was for certain, though: God was graciously steering (albeit form the back seat). I had not yet learned to surrender and allow God to "renew my strength." Even though I knew I would always go wherever God sent me, I still had not learned to do things **with** Him. That personal pronoun "I" was still in place, and "I" would serve God. So, I guess you could say that I was hindering God from renewing my strength. It is amazing what one can do in their own strength but, believe me, that human endurance will soon run out.

My husband's grandfather, Rev. Evan Williams, had pastored a church in Long Island City for 30-some years and was retiring. He had fasted for 40 days and 40 nights and during that fast he prayed for a "Joshua" to take his place. In February of 1965, Rev. Williams copied the following poem from the *Bridegroom's Messenger* Magazine (which later became the *Pentecostal Witness* Magazine). He prayed diligently and took this poem to heart:

GOD ANSWERS PRAYER

I know not by what methods rare,
But this I know, God answers prayer.
I know that He has given His Word,
Which tells me prayer is always heard,
And will be answered, soon or late,
And so I pray and calmly wait.
I know not if the blessing sought,
Will come in just the way I thought,
But leave my prayers with Him alone,
Whose will is wiser than my own,
Assured that He will grant my quest,
Or send some answer far more blest.[1]

ANONYMOUS

My husband was to be that "Joshua." God had spoken and we were to make Long Island City our home! In retrospect, Rev. Williams' prayer and my husband's calling were simultaneous. Both the prayer and the calling were in February of '65. That confirmation was quite amazing in itself. We arrived in Long Island City on October of 1965. That was eight months after Rev. Williams read the poem and absolutely believed every word. God sometimes works at a slower pace, but in this case, He decided to work in a more speedy fashion. We packed our belongings, placed our two small children in our Volkswagen, pulled a trailer from Rochester to New York City, and never looked back. Can you imagine? In my marriage vow I remember saying: "Where thou goeth, I will go, and where thou lodgest, I will lodge," and so I never questioned God's involvement in my husband's decision. But, I sure was scared!

Now, Long Island City was not as threatening as New York City. I later learned that Long Island City was located in a borough called Queens. It turned out that New York City had *five* boroughs. Well, I guess I could handle one borough! Little did I know, though, that these five boroughs were all joined together by bridges and I would, therefore, have to learn to travel from one borough to another by crossing all those crowded bridges. If you know the traffic in New York City, then you understand the fear and trepidation that overcame me. I was a little hick girl from the sticks and New York City appeared to be a monster to conquer back then. Where I was raised, there were just a few cars on the road, but in New York all you see are cars and more cars . . . trucks and more trucks. Being the adventurous type that I am, I did venture onto the Grand Central Parkway soon after arriving, but I thought I was going to have a major heart attack when I saw the multiple lanes and the massive amount of cars I had to wind through. I was literally panic-stricken. God didn't leave me alone, though. He was graciously steering all the way, and at every turn in the road, I said: "Thank you, Lord." But I still had not *invited* Him to ride with me . . . we were still not doing this "togetherness" thing yet. **In a practical sense, I was serving God and He, in turn, was there helping—but I did not know of the fellowship that I was missing.**

Rev. William's church had dwindled down to a few people due to his ill health and missionary work in Haiti. Thus, we began our journey in the BIG CITY with approximately 20 people or so. This was my husband's home church. He had grown up here, and it's not always easy to become the pastor of your home church. People knew him as "twinnie" because he had a twin brother. So, decidedly, it was important that we, as a family, start calling him "pastor" in hopes that the rest of the congregation would catch on. When we first arrived, our salary was $25 a week, and included the use of the apartment attached to the church. The stove in the kitchen was inoperable, so I cooked on a hot plate for many months until the church could afford a new stove. I also washed out diapers by hand for many months until my husband was able to attach a laundry room next to the kitchen area. Those were the days before disposable diapers. Yuck!! Once again, Rob had to renovate, but I had no complaints because he always made our homes special with his God-given talents.

My only protest, during this "stretching" time in my life, was that my two small children were deprived of a grassy area to play in. And stretching, I learned, certainly will test your mettle. Where I was raised, I could roam the fields and pick wild berries or wild flowers and, best of all, sit in or by a crystal clear creek. Grass equals fun, cement equals scraped knees! New York City is called "cement city" and that was truly the case where we lived. The only space to play in was the church parking lot. It was impossible to take them to a city park every day. Besides, most parks within walking distance did not have grass. They just had more cement, a few swings and basketball courts. We decided, together, to enroll them in Queensview Nursery School. Here, there was a grassy play yard, plenty of room to exercise in, playground equipment and companions to play with. We had absolutely no money, but prayed and asked the Lord to provide. It was several weeks after enrollment when the owner approached me and inquired if I knew of someone who would consider driving six children to their homes in the afternoon. Parents would pay whoever was willing to drive. I said, "I'm willing," and found myself thanking God, all the way home, that He had provided so that my little ones could play in the grass and not on the cement. When I look back on this experience, I can't believe I packed all six children (including my two) in our car, and not one wore a seat belt. In the late '60s, seat belts were not required. I'm thankful that I did not have one speck of trouble and God helped me deliver every one safely home for several years. God is good!

THEN, the projects began! The projects continued for over a period of approximately 12 years. As the church began to grow, the new funds allowed us to rebuild the interior of the sanctuary and finally buy a stove I could cook on. Now, Rob's grandfather was a builder before

❧❦❧

becoming a pastor, and he had built this church. He had built the original building in the '30s, but in the '50s there was need to expand the sanctuary, and his lack of funds didn't hinder him in the least. Since Rev. Williams was a very frugal man, he decided to build the walls of the sanctuary with the wood from old mahogany telephone booths that he had confiscated from the dump. It gave the sanctuary a warm atmosphere, but the mahogany also made it dark inside. The seats were original, too! My husband's grandfather found old theater seats that were being disposed of, and decided they would make great pew seats. They were also dark and dingy-looking. Now this is not to say that Rev. Williams had poor taste in décor. *He was a builder.* But in the '30s and in the '50s money was not as readily available as it is today. So he built with what he had or could appropriate.

The building that we came to in 1965 had been built by Rev. Williams in 1934 and was already 31 years old (aside from the "fix-ups" in the '50s). So it was in need of repairs, a good deal of renovating, and a lot of "sprucing up." Thus, the **first project** began. The telephone booth paneling came out and sheet rock and paint took its place. The old theater seats were removed and padded oak pew seats were installed. The sanctuary took on such a bright, cheery atmosphere. Wouldn't it have been nice if Rev. Williams could have seen the new sanctuary! But then, I'm sure he was looking down from his heavenly palace in heaven taking in the handiwork of his grandson. (Shortly after we came to New York City, Rev. Williams passed away while ministering at an orphanage in Haiti. I'm sorry I never had an opportunity to become better acquainted with him. However, I have reaped the benefits of his influence on my husband. He passed his building skills to his grandson and, everywhere I look in my home, I am reminded of Rev. William's legacy. I am also reminded of his spiritual legacy each time I hear my husband's sermons.) **Project two** was the re-facing of the front of the church, and this made it look more like a modern building. **Project three** was the purchase of the apartment building that was adjoined to

🌿

the church building. This was renovated and used for Sunday school classrooms, a bookstore and apartments. **Project four** involved the purchase of the property next to the apartment building and, in 1979, we built a multipurpose building and a gymnasium.

The story of these projects is a book in itself, and I have greatly diluted the information regarding this period in our lives. I'll reserve the embellished venture into these developments for another time. (We have since moved from this property and have built a 2,000-seat sanctuary, an apartment tower, a gymnasium and fellowship hall on a new location in Long Island City. On the same property was a public school building; we have renovated this building and now have a school with an enrollment of over 500. The next project is to build more classrooms on top of the gymnasium for our growing high school. However, for the sake of continuity in this book, I will continue in the theme of surrender and what God was trying to patiently teach me, and save the embellishment of all these building adventures for my husband's book.)

During all of these previous projects, and the birth of my third child in 1971, I was still pedaling my bike alone. When would I learn the "togetherness" idea? As I stated in chapter I, it commenced when I came to the end of my strength; but I hadn't yet reached that point. I had submitted to God's will as far as "I'll go where you want me to go, dear Lord." But, working WITH the Lord still eluded me. I became weary, rather disillusioned, physically spent, emotionally spent and discontented. I longed for those ideals I had while in college . . . those somewhat "fantasy" ideals I had. But this was reality, and I remember writing the following poem in 1973.

DISCONTENTMENT

Oh restless heart of mine,
Your desires are not for this time,
I find they are out of season
And who can find their reason?

You look to the left and then to the right,
But your contentment is nowhere in sight,
Rather, plant firm your feet on the ground where you stand,
And He will straightway lead you with a helping hand.

Take stock, look around and see
Thy tasks, what they be,
Precious, important, rewarding and blest,
Why not *trust* your all to His best?

Fulfillment is here, right at your door,
Give this your life, you will want no more,
Rest, oh weary and anxious heart,
For He has been with you from the very start.

What can a discontented heart gain?
Nothing! So, *yield* and let Him have the rein,
He has ordered thy steps thus far,
And in mercy, covered sin's great mar.

Oh discontented heart, be free!
For life is so very short, you see!
Open your heart and live life now,
The Lord has promised to show you how.

Oh restless heart, you should learn to *trust,*
For abundant life this is a "must."
Learn to *obey,* for this is the way,
For contentment to come in your heart to stay.

Accept what He's placed in your hands to do,
For this is required and long overdue.
Thus, in all of life you will learn to say,
"Contentment reigns in my heart today."

JJ

🌿

It seems I was rather preaching to myself and didn't know it. It is interesting that the words mingling together in this poem, such as **trust, yield, obey** and **fulfillment,** became lessons I would learn later on. The Lord knew! For now, God was only asking for intimacy and the surrender of my heart.

BECOMING

After three children and four projects, God began to draw me to Himself and He not only wanted me to DO for Him, but it was time to BECOME . . . to become better acquainted with the Person I was serving . . . to spend time getting to know Him. To submit! So, I waited and waited and waited! In my discontentment, I waited before the Lord. It was a time to become spiritually educated and I learned the following as I obediently surrendered during this time of struggle:

1) I became aware that to silently remain in His presence demanded my sharpest attention, my every attention.

2) I found there can be no day dreaming, no thought for myself, but waiting demanded my complete devotion to remain silent as I began to love God while He loved me. I simply began to surrender my heart to the Lord in love! I thought I had previously done that, but I was mistaken. He wanted more . . . *He wanted intimacy.*

3) I learned that the knowledge of God, who He is, His character and attributes were greatly revealed as I silently waited before Him.

4) I realized that to surrender my soul, and become wholly taken up with the Lord, is the most intimate form of communion with God.

5) And most of all, I learned that God just wants to have fellowship with us. I was humbled, and still am, that God would want this kind of relationship with me and pursued my presence. It's not so much what we DO for Him, rather that we BECOME more intimately acquainted while sitting in His presence . . . enjoying fellowship together.

6) As I sat in His presence, I was awestruck by His holiness. Conversely, I saw my lack of holiness.

7) I learned that as I began to **surrender,** I was no longer weak . . . **my strength was renewed. My soul was restored. I was no longer alone. I had a constant friend. I wondered how I had ever managed without this togetherness, this closeness.** Learning from the Lord is usually a line-upon-line process rather than a rapid revelation. I have heard of those rapid revelations but unfortunately for me, it was line-upon-line. But I didn't complain! I was, instead, becoming excited about the intimate relationship I was experiencing with the Lord.

I was also made aware, as I began an intimate relationship with my Creator, that it was my responsibility to invite Him to ride this tandem bike with me—and not only ride, **but take the reins (handlebars) . . . to sit in the front seat . . . to steer.** And so I did! He waits for our invitations. He never imposes Himself on us, but He always stands ready to reach out His hand when we extend ours to Him. I'm still learning to ride with a partner but it is far better, far easier and far more exciting than pedaling all on my own. I'm learning to be kind and considerate to Him. Finally, I understand . . . it's not just about *serving* God, it's about having a relationship with God . . . it's about working together . . . it's about communion . . . it's about Him loving me and me loving Him . . . it's about inviting Him into every aspect of my life . . . it's sharing, giving, asking and receiving . . . it's fellowship . . . it's intimacy . . . it's relinquishing our wills to a caring and loving shepherd . . . IT IS GOD'S GRACE EXTENDED TO US.

> *Anyone who intends to come with me*
> *has to let me lead.*
> *You're not in the driver's seat; I am.*
> *Self-help is no help at all.*
> MATTHEW 16:23-26 MSG

TANDEM BIKE RIDES

I began to understand the following from a new perspective:

1) That I no longer receive praise for accomplishments. This, to me, is not necessarily a pride issue but, rather, an "expected" outcome from an effort expended. But let's look at this clearly! If God is riding in the front, if He is dictating the outcomes, then you and I both know WHO should receive the praise. Oh, there are the occasional accolades and satisfaction of a job well done; but let's face it, without God, my meager efforts would never be anything but meager efforts. The "I" that wanted to serve God had to take a back seat. **It's not about what I can do for God but what we together can accomplish and what He can do through me.**

2) Secondly, I became aware that it is easy to fail. My strength will fail. My love will fail. My service to Him will fail. So many times I wanted to get off that ol' bike. "Just drop me off at the next corner would be fine," I'd say. However, I knew that *unless* I had His stamp on my life . . . *unless* He was in charge . . . and *unless* He had the liberty to fully use my yielded life, I would fail. Surrender became a huge word in my vocabulary. I knew that failure was not a word in God's vocabulary, so if surrender was the key to our success together, than surrender it would be. **I stayed on the bike!**

3) Thirdly, I am not as physically spent as I used to be. I'm tired, but not drained; weak, but not overcome; burdened, at times, with cares, but not cast down. Those are big differences.

4) Fourthly, He has chosen to bless. His blessings are innumerable and I am learning how to receive from Him in countless ways.

5) Fifthly, His grace extended to me is overwhelming . . . His kindness, His patience, His presence, and His continual pursuit of a relationship all speak of His unconditional love.

❧❦⋰

The following best expresses God's heart and His grace to us. It explains quite aptly how God and I were conversing at this time in my life:

THE FATHER AND THE CHILD

The child spoke:

Father, I am overwhelmed by your grace.

That is as it should be. May you always stand in awe of My Grace. What has meant the most to you?

I think I see for the first time how truly helpless I am. **It is the height of presumption to try to rely on myself; my strength, my performance, my flesh.** *Only in understanding how totally dependent I must be, do I experience Your presence and Your grace. The more I see my need for* **grace,** *the more* **grace** *I receive.*

You have begun well, My child. How will you continue to grow in My grace?

As You instructed me in the beginning . . . by continuing to listen carefully to Your Word, drawing close to You in prayer, and walking daily in Your Holy Spirit.

Good. My body needs women who exemplify My grace. Remember that **My grace is never-ending,** and that I delight in lavishing it on My children who **walk** with Me.

I can think of no greater blessing, Father.

There is none . . . for I desire that you always know deep within your heart that **I am the God of all grace.**[2]

— CYNTHIA HEALD

Therefore the Lord longs to be gracious to you,
and therefore He waits on high to have
compassion on you.

ISAIAH 30:18 NASB

AN UMBRELLA OF PROTECTION

Surrender/Submission takes on a new perspective as it pertains to wives and husbands plus those in authority over us.

The words "surrender" and "submission" are synonymous in meaning. They are two words that reflect the responsibility to which every Christian should adhere. The admonition is not only to be in submission to God, but also to each other: "Submitting yourselves one to another . . ." (Ephesians 5:21 KJV).

In the first chapter, I spoke of obedience and how God wanted me to obediently wait in His presence. The word "obedience" and the words "surrender" and "submission" are somewhat contrary in that it is possible to be obedient and not submissive. In truth, obedience is an act of the will, while submission is an attitude of the heart. So, it is possible to obey God but have a defiant attitude while doing so. We, as women, are responsible for our attitudes, and the word "submission" can conjure up a few misunderstandings.

A WOMAN'S ROLE

Submission! Where do we stand as women on this subject, as it relates to marriage? Horror of horrors!! For so many women, it has become the dreaded word. However, it's not really that offensive or difficult if understood.

First, let's catch a picture of what submission IS and what submission IS NOT. The following best illustrates the biblical pattern:

❧

UMBRELLA OF PROTECTION

GOD

CHRIST

HUSBAND

WIFE

SUBMISSION IS:	SUBMISSION IS NOT:
A wife's responsibility	An exclusive concept
A matter of the heart	An enslavement concept
An obedient response	A controlling concept
A positive concept	A wallflower concept
An attitude of the heart	An inferior position

The biblical order is as follows: "But I would have you know that the head of every man is Christ; and the head of the woman is man; and the head of Christ is God" (I Corinthians 11:3 KJV).

WHAT SUBMISSION IS

A Wife's Responsibility:

"Wives submit to your husbands, as to the Lord" (Ephesians 5:22 NIV).

"Wives, understand and support your husbands in ways that show your support for Christ" (Ephesians 5:22 MSG).

"You wives must submit to your husband's leadership in the same way you submit to the Lord" (Ephesians 5:22 TLB).

The scripture seems quite clear that submission is to be a woman's deliberate and voluntary response to her husband. It is never, however, to be the result of a husband's imposed authority. It is an admonition from Christ to a woman. It becomes an act of worship to God when a woman voluntarily chooses to submit to her husband.

A Matter of the Heart:

Submission is to be a continuous, on-going frame of mind. In other words, it is not a conditional response, or a response to a particular circumstance, but a life-long unquestioned attitude expressed by your heart. Our hearts can very easily deceive us and, for that reason, the Lord admonishes us to: "Keep thy heart with all diligence; for out of it are the issues of life" (Proverbs 4:23 KJV).

An Obedient Response:

"If you love me, you will keep my commandments" (John 14:15 KJV).

In essence, submission is a command, and a refusal to submit would be equivalent to an act of rebellion. It sounds very cut-and-dried, doesn't it? Never fear; there are rewards, which we'll discuss later. Submission is simply a willingness to obey . . . a cheerful response, not a grudging response. Keep reading for a discussion of attitudes.

A Positive Concept:

Let's look at this clearly . . . there are positive results when the biblical pattern is followed.

"Honor Christ by submitting to each other" (Ephesians 5:21 TLB).

"Out of respect for Christ, be courteously reverent to one another" (Ephesians 5:21 MSG).

In other words, you and your husband are a team. You, as a woman, are to be your husband's teammate, working toward the same goals. You

❦

are to submit to each other and be courteously reverent to one another. Of course, as on any team, someone has to make the final decisions. In that case, the wife as a team member supports the team leader. If not, goals will be thwarted and confusion plus frustration will result. If this pattern is followed God will honor you, bless you and praise you. Submission, therefore, becomes a positive concept, not a negative concept, as many believe.

An Attitude of the Heart:
This topic is revealed further on in the chapter!

WHAT SUBMISSION IS NOT

Not An Exclusive Concept:
Submission is a concept for all Christians, as the following verses will reveal.

"Submitting yourselves one to another in the fear of God" (Ephesians 5:21 KJV).

"Everyone must submit himself to the governing authorities for there is no authority except that which God has established" (Romans 13:1 NIV).

As women, we can become so absorbed in feeling that the word "submission" is directed at us that we can very easily develop an attitude. But, as you can see from the above verses, surrendering ourselves and submitting to authority is a commandment for all human beings. Don't let Satan deceive you and rob you of the joy that comes from submission. It is truly a blessing in disguise.

Not An Enslavement Concept:
Because a woman must submit to her husband, it in no way connotes a slave position. Her only responsibility is to obey and respect her husband. She is no less than her mate, but remains an equal.

As you serve and help your husband and family (not as a slave), a positive reward follows: "Her children arise and call her blessed; her husband also and he praises her" (Proverbs 31:38 NIV).

Not a Controlling Concept:

Somehow, many women assume that if they submit, they automatically lose the ability to be an individual . . . that they cease to have an opinion, can never open their mouths or give advice, or pursue a career. I have spoken to many who feel like second-class citizens—who have expressed that their only purpose is to support their husbands. The opposite is true! I don't want women to have a misguided conception of what true surrender/submission is. Remember, you are a wonderful woman who was created by God with a particular purpose in mind, and that one purpose is not to just serve your husband. He is not to become a controlling, authoritative figure in your life. Submission, under God's plan, is to free you to become what God has in mind, not what your husband has in mind. You are to serve and support each other in whatever plan God has for each of you. Period!

Always remember, as a woman, you are an equal, and under the umbrella of protection, you are blessed with the freedom to have an opinion and **respectfully** voice your opinion, give advice where needed and develop a career according to His wishes. **Respect** is a key word here.

Not a Wallflower Concept:

A woman does not become a wallflower when she submits. You are not meant to sit along the sidelines and watch life go by. God has endowed each woman with abilities and talents, and submission does not prevent her from developing those gifts. Read Proverbs 31:10-31. This ideal woman of the Bible made the most of every gift God gave her. She certainly did not just sit on the side lines and watch. She was created for a purpose and she fulfilled that purpose. Remember, God speaks to women as well as men. You should feel free to openly share those moments with your husband and ask for his covering in all your endeavors.

Not an Inferior Position:

Submission is definitely not a status of inferiority. If Christ was submissive to His Father, certainly we as women should and can be submissive to our husbands. Christ did not feel inferior to God. He simply knew there was a necessity for order, structure, a division of responsibilities and a chain of command. The same plan applies to husbands and wives. Christ and God are equal and one. Husband and wife are equal and one. However, in God's design, one person is to be in charge . . . the husband. The two should compliment each other by working together . . . not compete. Christ certainly never competed with God. In John 5:30 (KJV) Jesus stated: ". . . I seek not mine own will, but the will of the Father which hath sent me." He knew that His Father was in charge. Neither should we, as women, compete with our husbands. The chain of command is Father – Christ – Husband – Wife. Christ is not superior to God, nor is the husband superior to the wife. "Let this mind be in you, which was also in Christ Jesus: Who being in the form of God, thought it not robbery to be equal with God" (Philippians 2:6 KJV).

FOUR ESSENTIAL ATTITUDES OF THE HEART

Some women, who are submissive, are not submissive in attitude. Their outward appearance is one of compliance but they still possess a defiant, begrudging attitude inwardly. My mother used to say: "Janice, you may be sitting down on the outside, but I know you're standing up on the inside." I knew exactly what she meant . . . I wasn't being submissive. I'm sure there were many times when I didn't have an attitude of submission, but just a plain old "attitude." I think I got punished more for that than anything else.

According to God's word, He is asking us to display four important attitudes in submitting to Him and to those in authority. That includes your husband, for He is the authority in your home.

A Respectful Attitude:

Always remember that God works through authorities. Respect for all authority is an essential attitude. Respect for elders, deacons, as well as government officials, is a command, not a choice.

"Everyone must submit himself to the governing authorities" (Romans 13:1 NIV).

"Remind the people to be subject to rulers and authorities" (Titus 3:1 NIV).

If we, as women, are not able to subject ourselves to civil authority, how will we be able to submit to our husbands? Do whatever you do "as unto the Lord" (Ephesians 5:22 KJV); a respectful attitude is included in that command.

A Grateful Attitude:

"Let us come before Him with Thanksgiving" (Psalm 95:2 NIV).

"Give thanks to the Lord, for He is good" (Psalm 107:1 NIV).

It is so true that how we think affects how we behave. In light of that, it is essential that our minds be controlled by the Spirit of God and not "self." A negative thought-life and our flesh can greatly reduce our ability to have a joyful, thankful and submissive spirit. It is difficult to be grateful at times—especially when life deals a deadly blow. Giving our cares to Him lightens our burdens, and for that we surely can be thankful.

". . . those who live in accordance with the Spirit have their minds set on what the Spirit desires." ". . . the sinful mind is hostile to God. It does not submit to God's law, nor can it" (Romans 8:5,7 NIV).

A Teachable Attitude:

"Show me thy ways, O Lord, teach me thy paths" (Psalms 25:4 KJV).

"Lead me in thy truth, and teach me . . ." (Psalms 25:5 KJV).

"Pride goeth before destruction, and an haughty spirit before a fall" (Proverbs 16:18 KJV).

❧

It is so hard to say we are wrong, isn't it? We like to think we "know it all" and we have everything under control. Wish that were true!! Guess we just have to admit it's time for all of us to grow up, to mature, to allow God entrance into our lives and give Him the opportunity He's asking for . . . to teach us, change us and mold us into fit vessels He can use for His good pleasure. Submitting our spirit to His Spirit allows the Lord to teach us. Let's all be obedient and give Him permission to help us.

A Calm Attitude:

Are you constantly in turmoil? Are you stressed to the max? Do anger and a critical spirit rule your life? Are you fatigued beyond words? God admonishes us through the following verse: ". . . in quietness and confidence shall be your strength" (Isaiah 30:15 KJV).

> In this verse, God is simply giving us His good counsel to repent of our sinful ways and rest in Him . . . to stop struggling. Our strength will come as we become completely dependent upon Him. Our confidence, our trust, is in His guidance, His protection, His help and His counsel . . . not in ourselves.[3]
>
> — WAYNE MACK

Our responsibilities as loving wives are as follows:
1) To "do him good and not evil all the days of his life" (Proverbs 31:12).
2) Make the home a safe place for him. A place where he finds comfort, encouragement, understanding and a place of refuge (Proverbs 31:11,27).
3) Maintain good attitudes (Philippians 4:4).
4) Maintain a submissive heart (I Peter 3:1).
5) Have a grateful heart toward him (Romans 13:7).
6) Show confidence in his decisions (Corinthians 13:4-8).
   (The above scriptures taken from the KJV)

OUR REWARDS

Submission to our husbands does bring us considerable rewards. First and foremost, the husband is commanded "to love his wife as Christ loved the church and gave himself for it" (Ephesians 5:25 TLB). Does a husband fully understand how Christ loved the church? I think not! He can only gauge his responses to his wife according to scripture:

1) Christ's love is unconditional (Romans 5:8).
2) It is a decisive love. He chooses to love us (Ephesians 1:6,7).
3) It is a love that never ends (Romans 8:35-39).
4) His love is a purely unselfish love (Philippians 2:6,7).
5) It is a sacrificial love (I Peter 3:18).
6) It is definitely a manifested love (Romans 8:32).
   (The above scriptures taken from the KJV version)

It behooves us, as wives, to respect and appreciate our husband's desire to love us as Christ loved the church. This is a tall order for sure, but a rich benefit for us. Since you and your children are the unique responsibility of the husband, he is to express his love in the following areas:

Security/Protection:

He is responsible for the physical provisions of his family, which includes food, shelter and clothing. Of course, in today's economy, we see many mothers sharing in this responsibility. This also includes social and emotional aspects of life as well. The security and protection we all so long for comes out of love.

"Love is patient, love is kind. It does not envy, it does not boast, it is not proud. It is not rude, it is not self-seeking, it is not easily angered, it keeps no record of wrongs. Love does not delight in evil but rejoices with the truth. It always **protects**, always trusts, always hopes, always perseveres" (I Corinthians 13:4 NIV).

❦

"For the Lord loves the just and will not forsake his faithful ones. They will be **protected** forever" (Psalm 37:28 NIV).

If your husband follows the biblical rules and obeys God's laws, you *will* be under the umbrella of His protection.

Priesthood:

The husband is to be the priest in his home and is responsible for the spiritual welfare and spiritual direction of his family. He is to model true Christian behavior in every sense of those words. He is to stand between his family and the influences of the world, and create an atmosphere of spirituality that aids in wholesome Christian development of each member.

"For it is declared: You are a priest forever, in the order of Melchizedek" (Hebrews 7:17 NIV).

"Blessed is the man who does not walk in the counsel of the wicked or stand in the way of sinners or sit in the seat of mockers. But his delight is in the law of the Lord, and on his law he meditates day and night" (Psalm 1:1,2 NIV).

Partner:

He is to be a partner . . . not an authoritarian figure. He has authority, but he should never misuse it and become a dictator. "Together" is a key word here. The husband is to be a friend to his wife and share all things together . . . including home responsibilities and care for the children.

"For His Holy Spirit speaks to us deep in our hearts, and tells us that we really are God's children. And since we are his children, *we will share* his treasures . . . for all God gives to his Son Jesus is now ours too" (Romans 8:17 TLB).

"Remember that you and your wife are *partners* in receiving God's blessings, and if you don't treat her as you should, your prayers will not get ready answers" (I Peter 3:7 TLB).

The Head of the Home:

"Now the overseer must be above reproach, the husband of but one wife, temperate, self-controlled, respectable, hospitable, able to teach, not given to drunkenness, not violent but gentle, not quarrelsome, not a lover of money" (I Timothy 3:2,3 NIV).

"He must **manage** his own family well and see that his children obey him with proper respect" (I Timothy 3:4 NIV).

The word "manage" literally means to supervise, preside over and lead. A good manager of his home does not destroy or neglect his wife's talents. Instead, he will use them to full measure. He does not think of her as someone who needs to be dragged along but rather a partner, an advisor and a wonderful blessing from God. He should count it a privilege to consider her a friend

Peter also contributes his admonitions to husbands in the following verse: "Be good husbands to your wives. Honor them, delight in them. Treat your wives as *equals*" (I Peter 3:7 MSG).

ROLES

The roles of submission and helpmate (for women) and the role of leadership (for men) have been greatly diminished in our 21st century. The culture of today frowns on women who submit, calling them weak and insecure, while men are considered "beasts" who tout their authority ruthlessly. There is also such role reversal in our society that neither men nor women are aware that there is a useful biblical standard they can utilize for guidance. Today, the husband's role of protector and provider has been gravely undermined and threatened as women compete with men in the work force. On the other hand, women who are stay-at-home moms are considered oppressed and . . . excuse the expression, "dumb," who simply desire to raise their children. I must be "dumb," then, because I was a "mere" housewife until my last child moved out from under my roof. Then, I was a school counselor for 20 years. I never once, while at home, felt oppressed or stupid. I had completed college degrees just as other women had. However, it was important to me to be a mom, and it was my choice to remain at home. Never, not even once, have I regretted that decision. I do understand, though, that for many moms, financial circumstances do not allow them to stay home. Nevertheless, it is a detriment to our society that the role of "homemaker" is considered an outmoded responsibility. What about the children? Conversely, it is a detriment to our society that this culture considers a woman successful only if she has a prominent position in the business world. For men, if their identity is inextricably connected to their responsibility of provider and protector, how must they feel in a society that has greatly discredited them? For me, radical feminism is a failure today and will remain a failure in the future. The way I see it, surrendering ourselves to the Lord and submitting ourselves to our husbands does not leave us weak, inferior individuals. It strengthens us and frees us to be all that God has planned because we are obediently operating within the rules God has established and ordained.

If, however, you are married to an unreasonable or abusive husband, then my only suggestion is to seek counsel, for the biblical pattern of submission would then require review. If you are married to a good man who is a non-Christian, the biblical pattern applies. You should be an example and submit. Through prayer, he can be won to the Lord.

SUBMISSION AS A ROOT OF HIS GRACE

One of the most marvelous revelations regarding the love of God is that it never, ever stops. When we decide not to submit to His will, He just continues to love us. It's not so much that God needs us. Oh, there's definitely the fellowship aspect of our relationship with Him, but He has all the resources of heaven to get a job done. So, it's not so much that He needs us, but rather that He wants us and loves us. A more emphatic statement is that *we* need *Him*. We need His love, His grace,

His salvation, His righteousness and His holiness. That's the clearer picture; and as we submit ourselves to Him, we have access to all of that.

Years ago, I read an article by Bob Benson that told the story about a young man who attended an old-fashioned Sunday school picnic. The following is his tale and what he learned:

THE BALONEY SANDWICH

Do you remember when they had old-fashioned Sunday school picnics? I do. As I recall, it was back in the "olden days," as my kids would say, back before they had air conditioning.

They said, "We'll all meet at the Sycamore Lodge in Shelby Park at four-thirty on Saturday. You bring your supper, and we'll furnish the iced tea."

But if you were like me, you came home at the last minute. When you got ready to pack your picnic, all you could find in the refrigerator was one dried up piece of baloney and just enough mustard in the bottom of the jar so that you got it all over your knuckles trying to get to it. And just two slices of stale bread to go with it. So you made your baloney sandwich and wrapped it in an old brown bag and went to the picnic.

When it came time to eat, you sat at the end of the table and spread out your sandwich. But the folks who sat next to you brought a feast. The lady was a good cook and she had worked hard all day to get ready for the picnic. And she had fried chicken and baked beans and potato salad and homemade rolls and sliced tomatoes and pickles and olives and celery. And two big homemade chocolate pies to top it off. That's what they spread out there next to you while you sat with your baloney sandwich.

But they said to you, "Why don't we just put it all together?"

"No, I couldn't do that. I couldn't even think of it," you murmured in embarrassment, with one eye on the chicken.

❧

"Oh, come on, there's plenty of chicken and plenty of pie and plenty of everything. And we just love baloney sandwiches. Let's just put it all together." And so you did and there you sat, eating like a king when you came like a pauper.

One day, it dawned on me that God had been saying that sort of thing to me. "Why don't you take what you have and what you are, and I will take what I have and what I am, and we'll share it together." I began to see that when I put what I had and was and am and hope to be with what He is, I had stumbled upon the bargain of a lifetime.

I get to thinking sometimes, thinking of me sharing with God. When I think of how little I bring, and how much He brings and invites me to share, I know that I should be shouting to the housetops, but I am so filled with awe and wonder that I can hardly speak. I know that I don't have enough love or faith or grace or mercy or wisdom, but He does. He has all of those things in abundance, and He says, "Let's just put it all together."

Consecration, denial, sacrifice, commitment, crosses—were all kind of hard words to me, until I saw them in the light of sharing. It isn't just a case of me kicking in what I have because God is the biggest kid in the neighborhood and He wants it all for Himself. He is saying, "Everything that I possess is available to you. Everything that I am and can be to a person, I will be to you."

When I think about it like that, it really amuses me to see somebody running along through life hanging on to their dumb bag with that stale baloney sandwich in it saying, "God's not going to get my sandwich! No, siree, this is mine!" Did you ever see anybody like that—so needy—just about half-starved to death, yet hanging on for dear life. It's not that God needs your sandwich. The fact is, you need His chicken.

Well, go ahead—eat your baloney sandwich, as long as you can. But when you can't stand its tastelessness or drabness any longer, *when you get so tired of running your own life by yourself and doing it your way and figuring out all the answers with no one to help, when trying to accumulate, hold, grasp, and keep everything together in your own strength gets to be too big a load; when you begin to realize that by yourself you're never going to be able to fulfill your dreams, I hope you'll remember that it doesn't have to be that way.*

You have been invited to something better, you know. You have been invited to share in the very being of God.[4]

— BOB BENSON

Benson so clearly depicts this "togetherness" idea I have been attempting to explain. We are so fearful to let go. Fearful that there will be nothing else to take its place. But, clearly, what we hold on to is so meager in the light of what He offers. This togetherness erases all fear of failure as we join forces with Him and continue to hold His hand. Our strength will be renewed as we submit, surrender and give to Him whatever we possess. His strength becomes our strength, His joy becomes our joy, His desire becomes our desire as we learn to share with Him and He shares with us. I think we get the better part of the bargain for sure! What do you say?

It has been said of surrender that it's the same as signing your name at the bottom of a blank sheet of paper and then handing that paper to God with the following statement: "Here is my blank sheet . . . Lord, you fill it in and my name will always remain signed at the bottom." Whew!! That is so permanent, so binding . . . there's no wiggle room, that's for certain. This, however, is God's prerequisite to establishing a strong root of submission.

Sending a root of surrender deep into the soil of His grace will keep us in good stead! When the winds of despair try to rip us from His presence . . . when trials seem unbearable . . . when we can't see beyond our need and when we don't understand; we will still be strong, because we are rooted and "renewed" in His strength. Not renewed in our own strength, but in a powerful, beyond belief, heavenly "renewal" supplied by God Himself. I've seen it happen and so will you. **JUST GIVE HIM THE OPPORTUNITY . . . SURRENDER!**

In my next adventure, I begin to learn to Trust . . . .

CHAPTER II
Application & Review

One of the most marvelous things about the love of God is that it never stops: whether we submit to His will or remain self-absorbed, He still loves. The reward of surrender, however, is freedom. We are no longer bound to self, but free to accomplish the purposes for which we were created.

1. List areas where you have learned to surrender.

2. List the hindrances and struggles that are keeping you from surrendering.

3. Is surrender/submission a concept for all Christians? Explain by reading Ephesians 5:21 and Romans 13:1. Express your opinion.

4. What are the four essential attitudes of the heart contained in this Chapter (see pages 43-45)? Obedience is an _____ of the will and submission is an _____ of the heart.

5. Why should your husband be the head of your home? Use I Corinthians 11:3 and I Timothy 3:4-5 as your guide.

6. What is the role of women in submission? Based on Ephesians 5:22-23, and the contents of this chapter, give your response.

7. What is the chain of authority, according to I Corinthians 11:3?

❧

CHAPTER III

The Root of Trust

Trust in the Lord with all thine heart,
and lean not unto thine own understanding.

PROVERBS 3:5 KJV

CHAPTER III

The Root of Trust

Trust >>>>>> "Mount up with wings like eagles."

It was 8:45 A.M. Clearwater, Florida time. The sun was streaming through the curtains in our bedroom. It was a beautiful, balmy central Florida morning. The birds were joining all nature in a chorus that only God could create. It promised to be a glorious day. We were sleeping in, but it was time to rise and shine. We had plans . . . my husband and I were looking forward to our vacation and time together.

The phone rang! My husband sleepily answered. Then, he sat up. Silence permeated the room and I knew. Something was wrong! He hung up the phone and lay back down. The bed began to shake . . . his body had gone into shock. I said: "What is it?" He replied: "Stephen **thinks** Ethan is dead."

"NO, Noooooooooo," I said.

"We just saw him, he was fine," I cried. "Oh God, you raised Lazarus from the dead, surely you can raise Ethan," I pleaded. "Please don't take our little grandson!"

But, the heavens were silent. The room was silent. I couldn't hear the birds any more. I couldn't hear the busyness of the day beyond our door. All I could hear was silence and the small pendulum clock in the living room ticking . . . swaying back and forth with a rhythmic: "Ethan is dead, Ethan is dead." Time seemed to stand still. Was our second grandson really gone? Ethan had been born premature and after a short stay in the hospital was progressing nicely at home. We were, therefore, more than shocked when we received the phone call. In our minds "all was well" or we would never have gone on vacation.

We would not know the truth or full impact of this phone call to our condo in Florida until we arrived in New Jersey 20-some hours later. We closed up the condo, packed the car, said goodbye to our friends in Florida and started the venture back home. Had we used our heads, we would have called the airlines and flown home. In retrospect, my husband and I concluded that shock had set in and we were operating by simply placing one foot in front of the other . . . our reasoning capacity had taken flight instead. All of our thought processes and movements were seemingly in slow motion.

I cried: "God, where are you?" No answer! However, I don't think my listening skills were in operation. I know I probably didn't want to know the truth of what God wanted to say. As we journeyed to New Jersey, where our son lived, I finally got up enough nerve to ask my husband what he was hearing from the Lord. He very simply and very quietly said: "Suffer the little children to come unto me . . ." and then I knew. Jesus was preparing to take Ethan home to live with him.

WHERE WAS GOD, ANYWAY?

We called several times on our way home and the diagnosis for Ethan had not changed. We were told that the emergency phone call placed to 911 by my daughter-in-law was the result of SIDS (Sudden Infant Death Syndrome). We learned that the emergency personnel revived Ethan but the hospital's prognosis was not a welcome message . . . they did not find sufficient brain waves to allow Ethan the ability to live. He was living temporarily on life support. We had sent our daughter Carolyn, from Long Island City, to be with Steve and Jen until we arrived. Later, our son Brian arrived from Pennsylvania with much love and comfort as well. When we arrived, we learned that all the relatives were graciously waiting for us. They wanted us to have an opportunity to say goodbye to Ethan.

The life support was disconnected and it was at that very moment that Ethan was carried to heaven on angel's wings and ushered into the presence of God. Where was God, anyway? Why hadn't He heard our plea? Why hadn't He come to Ethan's rescue? Why did He think it was better for my son and his wife to suffer than to give Ethan back to them?

It took me a year to work through those questions. I wish I could say that I was able to implicitly TRUST God's decision with unquestionable certainty. However, that was not the case. Trust equals the ability to mount up with wings as eagles. I wasn't mounting up . . . I wasn't soaring. I was, instead, descending into the depths of despair. I didn't agree with His decision. I didn't want to see my son and daughter-in-law suffer. I wanted to hold that beautiful baby and watch him grow up to be a man of God. That obviously was not what God wanted. I went into seclusion with my anger and overwhelming sadness and tried to work through the grieving process.

ONE YEAR LATER

I must tell you that during that entire, heart-rending year, I grappled with the attribute of TRUST that is supposed to be so characteristic of believing Christians. All of those "why" questions just kept chasing each other around in my brain and I couldn't reconcile the suffering that was taking place in our family.

It was on a Monday afternoon, around 2:15, almost a year later when I finally said to God: "I give up, I surrender . . . I can't fight you anymore . . . you win." Well now, isn't that a miracle? . . . it only took a year! I'm sure God was thinking the same thing! You know, and I know, that there are times when God asks us to trust Him, but we choose instead to have deaf ears and wallow in self-pity. God so willingly and compassionately gave me time to grieve, but there was no allowance for pity. I know that I chafed at that. I wanted to feel sorry for myself, and for everyone in my family who was experiencing this anguish. That was such a long year . . . a painful year . . . a year of learning that to question is acceptable, but to trust is better . . . that God

knows best . . . that He stands ready to walk through the pain with us
. . . that He has a reason for all experiences in our lives, but we just may
not understand it all on this side of heaven.

During my darkest hours (even through the anger—for I truly was
angry with God), I hung onto God's love so graciously expressed
through others. When I could not see the light at the end of the tunnel, when darkness embraced and engulfed my entire being, I clung to
that ray of hope that **God makes no mistakes,** and to the certainty that
God would only bring good from this seeming tragedy. The following
poem by A.M. Overton, written in 1932 after the death of his wife,
clearly expresses this thought:

HE MAKETH NO MISTAKE

My Father's way may twist and turn,
My heart may throb and ache,
But in my soul I'm glad I know,
He maketh no mistake.

My cherished plans may go astray,
My hopes may fade away,
But still I'll trust my Lord to lead,
For He doth know the way.

Tho' night be dark and it may seem
That day will never break;
I'll pin my faith, my all in Him,
He maketh no mistake.

There's so much now I cannot see,
My eyesight's far too dim,
But come what may, I'll simply trust
And leave it all to Him.

For by and by the mist will lift
And plain it all He'll make.
Through all the way, tho' dark to me,
He made not one mistake.[1]

TO TRUST

As soon as I decided to surrender and as soon as I began to endeavor to trust the wisdom of God, the cloud of despair began to lift, peace slowly began to envelop my soul, and I started to gain a new perspective. I can't say that I suddenly graduated to full-blown trust in God—do any of us have that?—but it was a beginning. I had been reading many verses on what trust actually is, and the truth of each one began to find lodging in my troubled soul.

"Commit your way to the Lord; trust also in Him . . ."
PSALM 37:5

Trust is the firm belief in . . .

The *Honesty* of God (Numbers 23:19):
   "God is not a man that He should lie."
The *Justice* of God (Psalm 25:2):
   "Let not mine enemies triumph over me."
The *Truthfulness* of God (John 14:6):
   "I am the Way, the Truth and the Life."
The *Power* of God (Isaiah 40:29):
   "He giveth power to the faint."
The *Mercy* of God (Ephesians 2:4):
   "God who is rich in mercy . . ."
The *Goodness* of God (Romans 11:22):
   "Behold the goodness of God."

The *Grace* of God (II Corinthians 12:9):
    "My grace is sufficient for thee."
The *Sovereignty* of God (Isaiah 40:10 NIV):
    "The Sovereign Lord comes with power."
The *Kindness* of God (Jeremiah 9:24):
    "I am the Lord who exercises kindness."
The *Love* of God (Jeremiah 31:3):
    "Yea, I have loved thee with an everlasting love."
        (The above scriptures are taken from the King James Version
                    unless otherwise noted.)

However, during those months of seclusion, when despair gripped my heart, Satan whispered many lies in my ear. Whenever tragedy strikes or when difficulties come, Satan takes advantage of our weakness and, in my case, he tried to convince me that to trust God was sheer foolishness.

I kept telling myself that if I were God I would not do such things to humanity. But I'm not God. He sees the larger picture . . . I see through a glass darkly. His love is immeasurable, mine is finite . . . so conditional. His grace, His mercy is boundless . . . mine is so human. Yet, during that long year I did listen to Satan's lies.

The first lie he presented went something like this: "See, you and your husband **can't really trust God!**" And, I must admit, there were times when I felt God had abandoned us, that He was a "child abuser" —we were His children and He was abusing us; He had let us down. But if we can't trust the wisdom of God, what do we really have? I was slowly becoming aware that if Satan can't have our souls, he tries to steal *our trust, our joy and our happiness.* He tries to make us unfruitful, unproductive Christians. It was at this point that I gained new strength and a new perspective, and began to start the process of mounting up with wings like eagles. I began to shift my anger from God to Satan. I began to "stand up" and face the real enemy . . . Satan.

When you have an opportunity, read I Samuel chapter 30. It tells the story of David's return home after the Amalekites had raided his land. They took all the women, young and old. The Amalekites had burned David's village and the entire population of wives, sons, and daughters were all taken prisoner. Then, *David prayed to God, "Shall I go after these raiders: Can I catch them?" The answer came, "Go after them! Yes, you'll catch them! Yes, you'll make the rescue!"* (I Samuel 30:8 MSG).

David did pursue the Amalekites, and this is his tale: *"David pounced. He fought them from before sunrise until evening of the next day. None got away except for four hundred of the younger men who escaped by riding off on camels. David rescued everything the Amalekites had taken. And he rescued his two wives! Nothing and no one was missing—young or old, son or daughter, plunder or whatever." **David recovered the whole lot*** (I Samuel 30:17-20 MSG).

David went into the enemy's camp and he recaptured all that the enemy had taken from him, and this story became very real to me. I felt, during that long year of grieving, that Satan (the enemy of my soul) had snuck into my life and carried away my trust. I decided, like David, that I would march into Satan's camp and take back what he stole from me.

And that is exactly what I did! I made a little trip into the enemy's camp . . . and I took back my **trust.** Did I suddenly agree with God's decision to take Ethan? No! But I was more willing to trust His wisdom, for I knew that in His panoramic view, He could see the larger and more complete picture where all the pieces fit together. In my finite mind, I could only see the loss and pain.

But that's not all. There were more lies. Satan said: "Look how hard your husband has labored to build a new sanctuary, and this is the thanks he receives from God . . . He takes your grandson?" Here we go again! I had to march into the enemy's camp a second time and, when I got there, I said: "Satan, God may have taken our grandson, but the God I know doesn't make any mistakes . . . plus, the gratitude for my husband's labor is waiting for him in heaven." Even though I knew God makes no mistakes, I still labored to understand. But I also knew that I needed to set aside the fact that I did not understand, and make an effort to take back my **joy.** Believe me when I say I didn't sing and dance, but I did feel those dark clouds of oppression start to leave me. God had given me the ability to "stand" again . . . to stand against the enemy of my soul.

Then there was a third lie. This was a direct hit. It was personal. I heard Satan say: "Look how you have sacrificed and spent so many hours alone so that your husband could minister to others, and this is your **reward** . . . He takes your grandson?" You guessed it! For the third time, I marched into the enemy's camp and we had a little discussion. I heard him say: "Are you here again? What do you want this time?" I said: "I'm not finished with you yet. You told me another lie and I want to respond. Yes, I have spent many hours alone, but I'm waiting for heaven to receive my rewards, and one of my rewards will be the joy of seeing my grandson once again. Therefore, I'm taking back my **happiness.**" The old saying—"only one life, 'twill soon be past; only what's done for Christ will last"—sustained me whenever I thought of this lie. Satan truly is a deceiver and would rob us of all trust, joy and happiness in our Christian walk. **But I'm so grateful we have such a God of grace who gently swoops us up into His loving arms and clothes us in His righteousness to withstand the wiles of Satan.**

After this encounter with Satan, I took my grieving process into God's camp where I began to heal and gain a new perspective. As I sought for answers as to why Ethan's death had affected me so deeply, I concluded that it had touched the very heart of a mother in me . . . that mother's heart that wants to protect, to care for, to keep out of harm's way. And since I love my grandchildren just as though they were my own—just like I love my own children—the fact that I couldn't help Ethan affected me greatly. I had prayed for a miracle, but God had a larger plan and the miracle didn't take place. I couldn't protect my grandson and even my prayers couldn't save him. I took his death very personally.

However, I had to make a choice. The only wise option was to give my pain back to God and understand that it was God, in His wisdom, who chose not to heal Ethan. I didn't know why He had taken my precious grandson, but I understood that I had to let God be God—to reign sovereign in this event in our lives. Essentially, I had to trust Him and trust His decision without having rancor in my heart. I came to realize that it had very, very little to do with the mother's heart in me and my longings, but everything to do with God's heart and what God wanted.

Needless to say, I wanted my son and my daughter-in-law to enjoy this baby. But I soon recognized that they were more courageous than I, and accepted God's answer of "No" more readily than I. How proud I am of them! However, as grandparents, it was a double whammy. Not only did we lose a grandson—we also had to witness our son and his wife suffer as well, and experience their loss.

Regardless, I have to say that I am richer for having gone through this experience. Even though I have lost, I have also gained. God's love, especially, is more real to me. In every tragedy or difficult moment I have experienced, I have always heard God whisper: "Remember, daughter, I love you." And each time, His love grows richer and richer. But I'm about filled up! (Just kidding!!) I guess we can all say we don't want more pain to experience more love, but that's for God to decide isn't it? I am so grateful, though, that God always chooses to love me, no matter my state of being . . . even if, at times, I remain more inflexible than God would prefer when calling upon me to trust. **Trust**—it's such a complicated concept to learn . . . but not as complicated with a loving God.

During this long year, I also gained a new perspective on heaven. I once read a story that depicted heaven as the horizon. It was an allegory and, at the time, very comforting and enlightening. If my memory serves me correctly, the story involved a ship and its journey to the horizon. I had noted the following in my notebook of clippings: Rossiter Worthington Raymond once said, "Life is eternal and love is immortal, and death is only a horizon; and a horizon is nothing save the limit of our sight."

This ship, it seems, was opulent, with large sails that were spread wide by the breezes. The people who remained on the seashore watched as this ship, with all its beauty and elegant lines, sailed for the ocean. As the ship began its journey, those who remained to watch realized it had quickly become a small speck on the horizon and eventually the people dispersed, saying: "She is gone."

The question many asked was: "Gone where?" That's a fair question! That magnificent ship is only gone from our sight, not really gone. And then, it seems that as the ship reached its destination, there were other people on another shore who were watching the ship approach and said: "Here she comes." And if you think about it, that is what death is: those that we love are just out of our sight, not really gone but waiting over on the horizon.

When Ethan died, our daughter-in-law came to us and said: "It's over . . . he's gone." But we knew at that same moment . . . over on the horizon, where the sea and the sky come to mingle with one another . . . there were other eyes watching and the angels were saying: "Here he comes," and the rejoicing began that a little one was being ushered into the presence of God. And the hope that we have, this comfort, is that we will see our loved ones in heaven. They're not that far away. Just over the horizon.

During my process of accepting God's will in taking Ethan, I expressed my love to our sweet grandson in the following poem:

TO ETHAN

The Trace of His Hand

Weeping May Endure For A Night . . .
But this storm passed through our lives with such a fright,
Our grief-stricken souls had to embrace unrelenting sorrow,
Which found no relief in our tomorrow.

How we loved you! "A second grandson," we gratefully said,

While caressing our hearts with your presence,
    how could we know that tears would soon be shed?
You came to us as a precious jewel, a treasure beyond compare,
You carried the fragrance of heaven . . . of this, we were well aware.

Ethan Shropshire Johansson . . . in you,
    we saw the trace of His mighty hand,
You arrived as a gift from above . . . an angel unaware,
    to grace our weary land.
It remains God's great mystery why He took you home to His love,
But we give Him our terrible grief, and release you to His care above.

Yet, it's still so hard to let you go, we want you here for us to hold.
But we know how very special you were made . . .
    spun from the finest gold,
So, when God saw what a wonder He had made . . .
    so beautiful to behold,
He must have decided He needed you more than we did . . .
    a story yet to be told.

So now, *Joy Cometh In The Morning* . . . the winter is past,
    the rain is over and gone,
And we rejoice in knowing that you, dear Ethan,
    have filled God's heart with song.
The flowers appear on the earth . . . the time of singing of birds is come,
You, our beloved grandson, are pleasing the heart of God and then some.

Your Daddy had a vision of Jesus holding you
    in His strong and gentle arms,
How encouraging it was to know that God
    had embraced your many charms,
But now, we see you differently as you run
    through the fields of flowers,
Playing catch with God for hours and hours.

❧⟡

We see your big blue eyes, your sun-kissed hair,
    your freckled nose, your sunburned face,
And there in the distance, a rainbow radiantly glows . . .
    a symbol of His never-ending assurance of mercy and grace.
Yes, the winter is gone, our heavy hearts can once again sing,
For God never sends the winter, without the joy of spring.

How well we remember the day you walked into our lives . . .
    do you know you left your footprints on all our hearts?
But we know that God will not fail us . . .
    we will trust His love to help us while we're apart.
I heard you say, "I'm an angel, grandma; I'm having fun up here;
    I've been playing catch with God . . .
so please don't cry anymore, grandma, okay?"
So . . . we give our tears to God in heaven,
and know He will give His blessings on each and every new day.

Oh . . . and while you're there, don't forget to grow me
    a grand field of Daffodils . . . you know I love them so,
And when we get there, grandpa, you and I will admire the show.
Until that day when we will all be together,
Remember that we love you, always and forever.

We love you Ethan!!!   — GRANDMA JOHANSSON
(Scripture references in this poem were taken from Psalm 30:5 and Song of Solomon 2:11,12 KJV)

FINDING MY WAY/INSIGHTS GAINED

1) It was clear that the exasperating wiles of SATAN can greatly diminish our success as Christians if we allow him entry. It is Satan's plan to call into question every motive of our heavenly Father and undermine our trust. He wants us to have the perception that if God real-

ly loved us, He wouldn't allow such tragedies. I became abundantly aware of the stipulation to put on the full armor of God, as Paul so aptly states in Ephesians 6:11, and stand against this enemy who desires to destroy me. However, I would not learn to apply this heeding until later on.

2) It became very evident to me that I was dealing with a SOVEREIGN God. He had created me. I had given my life to Him and He was to be in control . . . He was to call the shots . . . He was to direct my path. As a sovereign God, He governs . . . He rules and overrules and, most importantly, allows nothing in my life outside of His will and control. His love is perfect. End of sentence!! But, so hard to grasp when in pain.

3) I began to understand that in His WISDOM, He sees the end from the beginning, and He knows exactly which fruit He wishes to produce in my life through painful experiences. I can't say that I saw the wisdom in God's decision to take Ethan. But, I **was** willing to learn to trust Him and begin to learn that difficulties in my life in no way indicate that God is anything but a good God, and that the fruit from this experience would be used to glorify Him.

4) I learned that His CARE for me is so gracious that, one day, I will no longer see through a glass darkly. He will roll out the scroll that contains my journey, and lovingly explain each phase . . . how mercy and grace was applied at every turn in the road . . . how He kept me from dashing my foot against a rock, and all the "whys" to my many questions will have answers. Best of all, I will understand the answers because I will then understand the purpose for the pain.

5) Lastly and most importantly, I learned that God is too GOOD to be unkind. A song that sustained me during this painful time is entitled "Trust His Heart," sung by the Legacy Five Singers:

❧❧

TRUST HIS HEART

CHORUS

God is too wise to be mistaken
God is too good to be unkind.
So when you don't understand,
When you don't see His plan,
When you can't trace His hand,
TRUST HIS HEART.

VERSE 1

He sees the master plan,
He holds the future in His hands.
So don't live as though you have no hope,
Our hope is found in Him.

VERSE 2

We see the present clearly,
But He sees the first and the last,
And like a tapestry, he's weaving you and me,
To someday, be just like Him.

CHORUS

God is too wise to be mistaken,
God is too good to be unkind.
So when you don't understand,
When you can't trace His hand,
TRUST HIS HEART[2]

BABBIE MASON / EDDIE CARSWELL

A GRACIOUS GOD INDEED!

As an addendum to this story, my son (Steve) and daughter-in-law (Jen) experienced another loss. Jen gave birth to 4-month-old Jonathan Gabriel a short time after losing Ethan. It seemed that sorrow was a constant foe for a while and trust a foreign word. How little did we know that joy was awaiting us around the corner!

In God's gracious mercy, on March 3rd of 2001 Jen gave birth to Nathan . . . a premature but very healthy baby. We rejoiced! They rejoiced! God rejoiced! They also have a beautiful (almost) teenager, Emma Leigh. She will probably be a teenager when this book goes to print. God is Good! And one thing is certain, another joy awaits us in heaven, for there, both Ethan and Jonathan will greet us and we will rejoice for all eternity. Isn't God good to always counter our pain with joy? Joy cometh in the morning!

FROM YOUR PERSPECTIVE

As some of you were reading this chapter on trust, I'm sure that you were saying: "I've suffered worse than that; I've seen worse than that; I've heard worse than that." And I, for one, do not doubt that. As a pastor's wife for 48 years, I have seen raw pain many, many times over. But in loving kindness, I will give you this assurance: if you contact me, I will hold you up in prayer, for there is no greater power on this earth than the power of speaking to our Creator on behalf of others.

As war rages in Iraq and Afghanistan, many have lost sons, husbands, daughters, wives and close relatives. There is absolutely no description for that kind of loss and anguish. Some of you may have terminal illnesses and have lost hope. I have no idea how I would respond to either of those scenarios in our society, or the many others that are so very excruciating. However, deep in my soul, I do know that

He loves me and He loves you. He can be trusted to help us from the beginning to the end of difficulties and the unbearable moments in our lives. He said He would not only be with us during the pain but also see us through. When we come to turbulent waters, we will not go down but we will GO THROUGH. Sorrow may envelope our souls, but He will see us THROUGH. Doubts and fears may cloud our sight, but He will see us THROUGH. And waiting on the other side are the welcome arms of Jesus, ready to embrace us with His welcome words: "See, we made it through together!"

When thou passest through the waters . . .
they shall not overflow thee . . .
ISAIAH 43:2 KJV

The Lord is good, a refuge in time of trouble,
He cares for those who trust in Him.
NAHUM 1:7 NIV

GOD'S PROTECTION

There are so many ways we must **trust** God with our lives, and one is His never-ending protection over each one of us. How many times do we ask God for His protection, and trust He will give His angels charge over us? As mothers, how many times do we entrust our children to God's care? How many times have we taken a trip and asked God for His protection? How many times have we trusted God to intervene on our behalf and keep evil far from us? How often have we asked God to strengthen and renew our bodies . . . to protect us from innumerable diseases, germs, viruses and terminal illnesses? God certainly must be busy because we do a great deal of "asking," and I'm hoping there is an even greater amount of "thanking." However, we also need to thank Him for the many, many times that He has protected us when we haven't thought to ask. Only heaven will reveal the countless times God, in His grace and mercy, has protected each one of us . . . even when we were not aware of it.

> *For He shall give His angels charge over thee,*
> *to keep thee in all thy ways.*
> PSALM 91:11 KJV

That brings me to a missionary's story of God's protection that I recently read from an old and very enlightening book entitled *Stories Worth Rereading*. The following occurrence was related by missionary von Asselt while on a visit to Lubeck, Germany . . . God protects when we are unaware!

When I first went to Sumatra, Malaysia in the year of 1856, I was the first European missionary to go among the wild Battas. Twenty years prior, two American missionaries had come to them with the gospel; but they had been killed and eaten. Since then no effort had been made to bring the gospel to these people, and naturally they had remained the same cruel savages.

What it means for one to stand alone among a savage people, unable to make himself understood, not understanding a single sound of their language, but whose suspicious, hostile looks and gestures speak only a too-well-understood language . . . yes, it is hard for one to realize that. The first two years that I spent among the Battas, at first all alone and afterward with my wife, were so hard that it makes me shudder even now when I think of them. Often it seemed as if we were not only encompassed by hostile men, but also hostile powers of darkness; for often an inexplicable, unutterable fear would come over us, so that we had to get up at night and go on our knees to pray or read the Word of God, in order to find relief.

After we had lived in this place for two years, we moved several hours' journey inland, among a tribe somewhat civilized, who received us more kindly. There we built a small house with three rooms . . . a living room, a bedroom, and a small reception room,

❧

and life for us became a little more easy and cheerful.

When we had been in this new place for some months, a man came to me from the district where we had been, and whom I had known there. I was sitting on the bench in front of our house, and he sat down beside me, and for a while talked of this, that, and the other. Finally he began, "Now tuan (teacher), I have yet one request."

"And what is that?"

"I should like to have a look at your watchmen close at hand."

"What watchmen do you mean? I do not have any."

"I mean the watchmen whom you station around your house at night, to protect you."

"But I have no watchmen," I said again; "I have only a little herds boy and a little cook, and they would make poor watchmen." Then he asked, "May I look through your house, to see if they are hid there?"

"Yes, certainly," I said, laughing; "look through it; you will not find anybody." So he went in and searched in every corner, even through the beds, but came to me very much disappointed.

Then I began a little probing myself, and requested him to tell me the circumstances about those watchmen of whom he spoke. And this is what he related to me: "When you first came to us, tuan, we were very angry at you. We did not want you to live among us; we did not trust you, and believed you had some design against us. Therefore, we came together, and resolved to kill you and your wife. Accordingly, we went to your house night after night; but when we came near, there stood always, close around the house, a double row of watchmen with glittering weapons, and we did not venture to attack them to get into your house. But we were not willing to abandon our plan, so we went to a professional assassin (there still was among the savage Battas at that time a special guild of assassins, who killed for hire any one whom it was desired to get out of the way), and asked him if he would undertake to kill you and your *wife. He laughed at us because of our cowardice, and said: 'I fear no God, and no devil, I will get through those watchmen easily.' So we came all together in the evening, and the assassin, swinging his weapon about his head, went courageously on before us. As we neared your house, we remained behind, and let him go on alone. But in a short time he came running back hastily, and said, 'No, I dare not risk it to go through alone; two rows of big, strong men stand there, very close together, shoulder to shoulder, and their weapons shine like fire.' Then we gave it up to kill you. But now, tell me, tuan, who are these watchmen? Have you never seen them?"*

"No, I have never seen them."

"And your wife did not see them also?"

"No, my wife did not see them."

"But yet we have all seen them; how is that?"

Then I went in, and brought a Bible from our house, and holding it open before him, said: "See here; this book is the Word of our great God, in which He promises to guard and defend us, and we firmly believe that Word; therefore we need not to see the watchmen; but you do not believe, therefore the great God has to show you the watchmen, in order that you may learn to believe." [3]

— VON ASSELT

One day after reading this story, I was riding in the car listening to music and the following song made me appreciate, once again, how very faithful God is and how appropriate the song was to the missionary's story. It has become one of my very favorite songs, sung by my most favorite group, The Legacy Five Singers. I find myself singing it often throughout the day.

THE STORMS I NEVER SEE

VERSE 1

Lord sometimes you call upon the wind and the waves to cease,
And there are times when in the storm,
you calm my heart with peace.
But only you will ever know what never comes my way,
All because your unseen hand has kept the storm at bay.

VERSE 2

I believe that angel's swords rebuke some deathly blows,
When Satan comes in fury and you simply tell him "no."
Lord every trial of my life is subject to your will,
These earthy eyes can't see the times you keep the water still.

CHORUS

So thank you Lord for safety when the winds begin to blow,
And for the times you keep me, when I never even know.
In troubled, stormy weather, you always shelter me,
But Lord I'm also grateful for the storms I never see.[4]

CINDI BALLARD / TWILA LABAR

TRUST AS A ROOT OF HIS GRACE

Distrust can make us suspicious . . . suspicious of others and suspicious of God. You and I will almost always be "on our guard" and defensive if our souls are devoid of trust. We will never truly allow others or God into our innermost beings. We will question motives, take personally things which are said, question God's decisions, open ourselves up to Satan's lies, become filled with anxiety and, above all, have zero amount of peace.

It is absolutely essential, therefore, to establish a strong root of trust, if we ever hope to flourish and grow as Christians. We must send that root of trust deep into God's unconditional love and grace, and allow nothing to uproot it. Winds will blow, hardships will come, but if we hold on and stand resolute, God will not fail us . . . He will hold us up with His right hand of righteousness. "Fear thou not; for I am with thee: be not dismayed: for I am thy God: I will strengthen thee; yea, I will uphold thee with the right hand of my righteousness" (Isaiah 41:10 KJV).

I suppose I could write a book just on TRUST; for there have been so many happenings, experiences, events, and occasions, where trusting and believing in His sovereignty was an issue. And I am sure, this admission is the same for you; unless, of course, you are a more trusting person than I, and have arrived at a spiritual plane that allows you this unequivocal acceptance of His will and control in your life. You are to be admired if that is the case. I surely am trying to learn to trust in all things and send that root deep into His grace. May you desire the same (if you are like me) and may you "mount up with wings as eagles" as you place your trust in His unfailing love. I pray He will continually bless all of us with that needed wind and breeze of His presence to keep us ever "soaring" and "mounting up."

When it comes to trust, I find that I am leaning very heavily on the Lord but, even so, I find He has mercy on me as we continue our tandem bike ride together. He graciously pedals a little stronger to keep me topside, for there have been a few times when it seemed so much easier to just stop the bike and get off . . . to give up. But that's when I would hear Him say: "Keep pedaling, hold on, the race isn't over yet . . . take my strength, take my joy, take my peace, we'll make it together." And I do! And we will! By His grace!

The Lord and I journey on to the root of abiding . . . 🚲

CHAPTER III
Application & Review

If we place our trust in God, He will move heaven and earth to accomplish His purposes through us. We can freely put our trust in the nobleness and character of a God Who will never leave us nor forsake us. Let Him fold you in His strong arms . . . He is waiting to hold you—even carry you, if need be. Trust Him!

1. What does God say in Psalm 46:1-2 and 50:15?
   Can we trust Him?

2. What is the hardest thing you have had to trust God for? Give details.

3. Explain the sovereignty of God in your life.

4. Read Isaiah 40:10 and 61:10-11. How do these verses relate to trust and His sovereignty?

5. Name the basis for our trust: It is the firm belief in what?
   See pages 60-61.

6. What hinders you from fully trusting God? Explain.

7. What is stopping you from completely trusting Him?

CHAPTER IV

The Root of Abiding

I am the vine, ye are the branches: He that abideth in me, and I in him,
the same bringeth forth much fruit: for without me ye can do nothing.

JOHN 15:1 KJV

CHAPTER IV

The Root of Abiding

Abiding >>>>>> "They shall run and not be weary,
and they shall walk and not faint"

Webster's dictionary describes the word *abide* in the following manner: to remain; to continue; to stay; to dwell; to reside, and to remain steadfast, and faithful. Jesus describes the word *abide* according to His Word: "I am the vine, ye are the branches: He that abideth in me, and I in him, the same bringeth for much fruit: for without me ye can do nothing" (John 15:5 KJV). We, as Christians, are to make a conscious decision to remain in Him—and everything that is of Christ is ours as we abide.

"Abiding in Him is our responsibility.
His abiding in us is His grace personified.
The result of our togetherness is fruit.
Without Him we can do nothing."

JJ

So far, as I have traveled on this tandem bike ride with the Lord, He has asked me to obediently wait in His presence; to submit my soul, my very being and all that life involves and entails to His keeping; and to learn and capture the meaning of the word "trust." The Lord is encouraging me (and He will forever encourage me) to stay on the bike with Him, to continue this journey steadfastly connected to Him, and to learn to walk in His Spirit—to abide. This is exactly what He meant way back in chapter one: to "come unto me, to rest, for my yoke is easy and my burden is light" (Matthew 11:28,29 KJV). Abiding provides all of this. If we are abiding, we will "run and not be weary, we will walk and not faint."

❧

A TAPROOT

What is a taproot? In scientific terms, the taproot of a tree is that root which runs straight down from the trunk into the deepest soil, "anchoring" the tree against storms and providing nurture from the very deepest of sources. There may be hundreds of secondary roots, but it is the taproot that is most necessary for the tree to survive and thrive.

Abiding is like the taproot of a great old tree. Just as a taproot anchors a tree by searching deep in the earth for water and nutrients, abiding anchors us, as Christians, by putting us in touch with the "Living Water" of God's grace. Being anchored in Christ gives us continual nutrients so that we can reach out our limbs, mature, bear fruit and be useful to the Kingdom of God.

In the book of Jeremiah, the prophet offers us an encouraging picture of those who trust and abide in the Lord: "He will be like a tree planted by the water that sends out its roots by the stream. It does not fear when heat comes; its leaves are always green. It has no worries in the year of drought and never fails to bear fruit" (Jeremiah 17:8 NIV). It's not that we won't face crises in life and dry spells, but if we have sent a taproot of abiding into the grace of God, we are anchored, we are safe, we are secure and fruit will remain in our lives.

The previous roots of obedience, surrender, and trust all mingle together and become strengthened in this taproot of "abiding." **Abiding then becomes a central source for growth and development.** Metaphorically speaking, the taproot of abiding is a root established deep in the grace and love of Jesus. It is to be a strong root (a taproot), which will stabilize and strengthen other roots. Abiding reaches deep into His grace and drinks lavishly of His spiritual nutrients. In my estimation, abiding then becomes a paramount root in a Christian's spiritual root system. The main cause of damage, or that which will inhibit the growth of this spiritual root of abiding in the life of a Christian, is sin. When sin enters our lives, withdrawal from abiding most likely will occur, and an unhealthy root system will develop and destroy spiritual progress. Those important roots of obedience, submission and trust will soon be struggling to stay alive.

Abiding, therefore, is an essential root for all Christians. Out of abiding we are more readily able to remain obedient, surrender our desires to His desires and trust in His wisdom. Just as a tree needs a tap-root to survive and thrive, so the Christian needs the taproot of abiding to survive and thrive.

A SENSE OF BELONGING

God's desire for us is to fulfill that sense of belonging that each and every one of us was created to experience. We were made such that our souls long for oneness with others. God's plan is for humans to belong to a larger framework of goodness . . . to think beyond ourselves . . . to belong to a kingdom that uses our gifts and talents . . . to belong to a kingdom that enables us to have purpose in our lives as we serve and care for each other. In other words: "The purpose of life is to have a life of purpose."

There is no other format where this sense of belonging and purpose can be so completely experienced and fulfilled than being a member of the Kingdom of God. The culture of this world also allows people to feel one with others, to serve others, to give of their talents, to show forth goodness, and to experience a sense of belonging. But only a member of the Kingdom of God can introduce another to eternal life through Jesus Christ where they will "belong" forever . . . where there is a forever lifetime membership to His unconditional love . . . where they will abide in His presence for eternity. So, that sense of belonging that God placed in our hearts enables us to understand, and help us to more easily grasp the importance of "abiding" as it relates to our spiritual health and as it relates to helping others. That sense of belonging places in our heart a desire to experience a oneness with Him and a desire to remain, to stay, to dwell, to continue, to abide in His presence.

> *You are members of God's very own family,*
> *citizens of God's country, and you belong in God's*
> *household with every other Christian.*
>
> EPHESIANS 2:19 TLB

CHRISTIAN HERITAGE

Christian heritage is that which is passed down from generation to generation and provides the recipient a wonderful sense of belonging. My Christian heritage began in a small town in upstate New York. We all attended church, we were taught values and morals at home and in church, we were taught and given a work ethic . . . we were a family. We vacationed together, we sang together, we enjoyed sports together . . . we were a family. We attended reunions, we visited grandparents, we went to camp meetings . . . we were a family. My **sense of belonging** came from my earliest recollections of family life. Being a member of a family was where I connected, where I was accepted, where I resided, where I dwelt, where I stayed . . . it was my abiding place. It was my "home." I felt safe there. I was loved and strengthened there. It gave my life meaning.

My mother passed away in April of 2006. She was three months shy of being 95 years old. My father, a sweet, rather emotionally aloof and fearful man, had died 30 years earlier. He was a dedicated father and a wonderful provider for his family. It was my mother, however, who had the greatest influence on my life.

When the hospital called and informed me that my mother may not last the night, I wanted to travel to her bedside, but knew I would probably never make the 8-hour trip before she passed away. It was disconcerting, to say the least, that the hospital had waited so long to notify me of her condition. What to do? Since her hearing was so poor, I knew a phone call would be useless and, at that point, her condition was such that she was heavily sedated and unable to respond well enough to use a phone. My only recourse was to write her a poem, fax it to the hospital and have a nurse read it to her . . . hoping all along that she would be alert enough to understand the poem. I wanted her to know of my appreciation for the years she devoted to me as a child, a teenager, a college student and as a married person. Even though I had praised her many times for her devotion to our family, I wanted her to hear, just once more, of my love. My poem to my mommy follows:

ON THAT GREAT DAY

She was born a tiny, gently little girl,
And her Mommy named her "Janice"—she said she was her pearl.
"So sweet, so cute," so everyone said,
And she was "Daddy's little girl" in all the days ahead.
    "Dear Jesus . . .
    Would you remind my Mommy, that I love her so?
    And let her know I'm thankful that she carefully helped me grow.
    May she always understand that I wish she'd forever stay?
    But to please have no fear, for we'll all meet in heaven . . .
    on that great day."

This little girl became her mother's pride and joy,
As she imparted musical talent, that her daughter could employ.
Playing the piano and singing would become life-long gifts,
That God would use for His glory to encourage and uplift.
    "Dear Jesus . . .
    Would you remind my Mommy that I love her so?
    That teaching me piano has blessed others I know.
    May she always understand I wish she'd forever stay?
    But to please have no fear, for we'll all meet in heaven . . .
    on that great day."

As a teen, this daughter, was taught by example,
For her Mom's service to her family was more than ample.
Domestic skills were taught, observed and passed along,
A legacy for future generations, who would then belong.
   "Dear Jesus . . .
   Would you remind my Mommy that I love her so?
   That her home was my pride to always show.
   May she always understand I wish she'd forever stay?
   But to please have no fear, for we'll all meet in heaven . . .
   on that great day."

Graduations, marriage and births have all come and gone,
Church work and building a church now make each day long.
Your daughter now takes pride in her family . . . a joy fulfilled,
And is thankful for strength to accomplish His will.
   "Dear Jesus . . .
   Would you remind my Mommy that I love her so?
   That showing me how to be a Christian is a blessing bestowed.
   May she always understand, I wish she'd forever stay?
   But to please have no fear, for we'll all meet in heaven . . .
   on that great day."

Your daughter is safe; she's happy, and well taken care of,
For her husband has surely loved her, with gifts from above.
She wants her mother to now quietly rest,
Knowing her daughter has been greatly blest.
   "Dear Jesus . . .
   Would you remind my Mommy that I love her so?
   That her prayers for a husband were answered, I know!!!
   May she always understand I wish she'd forever stay?
   But to please have no fear, for we'll all meet in heaven . . .
   on that great day."

Our future is His to do as He wills,
And we remain faithful—God's plans to fulfill.
His love is gentle, strong, faithful and wise,
And our devotion to Him could never be compromised.

"Dear Jesus . . .
Would you remind my Mommy that it is her I adore?
And thank her for giving me 'life' to explore.
May she always understand that I wish she'd forever stay?
But to please have no fear, for we'll all meet in heaven . . .
on that great day."[1]

I love you Mom, Your loving daughter, Jan

APRIL, 2006 (INSPIRED BY CHERYL KIRKING)

It was two hours after the poem was read to my mother that she went to her eternal reward. The nurse who cared for my mother said she was waiting to hear from me before she would let go of her hold on this earth. It seems that the Lord opened her ears enough to hear my words as the nurse gently read them to her. She responded very positively and I'm so very thrilled that I didn't fail her. However, I do wish I had been with her to hold her hand as she went to see Jesus. I will always regret that she was alone at this time. But I know, over on the horizon, other eyes were welcoming her home and saying: "Here comes Jan's Mom." That's a grand assurance!

MY MEMORIES

A little girl when asked where her home was,
replied: "Where Mother is."

KEITH L. BROOKS

My mother was to me (when I was young) the personification of the perfect homemaker. Her tiled floors sparkled. She got on her hands and knees and applied a paste wax to the tile and then shined them with a machine. In fact, her whole house sparkled and gleamed. There was very little money in those days (the late '30s, '40s and into the '50s) and my mother would either take in washing and ironing for neighbors, clean rich, affluent people's homes or bake bread to sell to supplement my father's income. I used to go from door to door and sell her wonderful bread. There was no bakery in our small town, so my mother's bread was in great demand. She never charged much. It was more of a service to others. But the little she did make helped put food on our table, helped pay a bill or gave her a little extra spending money. However, she very rarely spent money on herself. She would always ask her children what they needed. I know that my shoes got pretty worn down, many times, before my parents were able to buy me a new pair. Somehow, my Mom would always scrape together enough of her saved pennies to buy new shoes. She is to be commended. She made the best of her lot in life and I don't ever remember her complaining. Instead of complaining, she would find a way to make life for her children better.

One of my mother's greatest talents was playing the piano. In fact, she was so proficient that she gave piano lessons to other children when she was only 12 years old. My grandmother's desire was for my mother to be a concert pianist. She was a skilled classical pianist and would very often perform for her family and friends. Instead of following her mother's desire, however, she gave her talent to the Lord and played the piano in church for years and years. A fond remembrance for me was camp meeting. Every summer, my Mom was the pianist for the Lamoka Bible Camp located on Lamoka Lake in the Finger Lakes region of upstate New York. It was always just she and I. To think that I had my Mom all to myself for several weeks was heaven on earth. I used to sit in the front row of the tabernacle and watch her play . . . I was so proud! As I grew older, my Mom said it was time for me to learn to play. And I did. History repeated itself, because I was the church pianist for many years after I married. My mom not only taught me, but I taught my daughter and son (with a little help later on from the Brooklyn Conservatory of Music and several local teachers) and now they both play in church. I thank her for taking the time to fill my heart with music, which allowed me to pass the talent along to my children. Thanks, Mom!!

My very fondest memory of my mother was of her baking skills. She would take a whole day and bake for her family of five. The breads, pies, cookies, donuts and cakes were to last for a week, but rarely did. Coming home from school to the aroma of baked goods is a memory I will treasure always. In fact, all of our yesterdays, when combined, include wonderful memories that we can store in our hearts for future recollection. They are there to bring sweet remembrances of our loved ones and very often we use those remembrances to encourage our hearts, or to heal the pain of loss, or just to help us smile again. So, for me, yesterday is a **sacred room** in my heart where I keep fond memories and I will cherish them forever. And in that sacred room in my heart, I cherish the memory of the aroma of my mother's baking (as well as her musical talent) and her labor of love for her family. It was a time in history when women always cooked meals, baked goodies, wore dresses and aprons, stayed home (very few worked), did their own cleaning, washing and ironing and were just contented raising a family. I am so happy my mother was there when I came home. And, not only there, but she taught, disciplined, loved unconditionally and gave me that needed sense of belonging and Christian heritage that is missing from many homes today.

In those early days of my childhood, freezers were not available, and my mother canned just about every thing she could get her hands on. My father's blue ribbon garden gave her plenty of produce to keep her busy canning. Such delights as corn, green beans, peas, tomatoes, beets, squash and cucumbers (made into pickles) graced our table all winter. She also canned pears, peaches, cherries, apples, applesauce, and made many berries into jams and jellies. It used to take many weeks to can all that was needed for the winter. I know, because I prepared many fruits and vegetables to ready them for the canner. We very rarely bought canned foods from the grocery store. Later, in my teenage years, my mother was able to purchase a freezer. Hallelujah! We were then able to take all the produce, prepare them for the freezer (each produce required a different process), place them in plastic bags or containers and put them in the freezer. Freezing was a much easier and less time-consuming process than canning and greatly reduced the labor involved. We never had gourmet meals, but we ate healthy and always had plenty. Between all the animals my father brought home from hunting (such as rabbit, deer, pheasant, duck, etc.; fish from his many fishing expeditions), and his fabulous garden, my Mom was able to make delicious, hearty meals for all of us (and sometimes the neighbors who had less than we).

I am so blessed to have been able to live in a home where I had such a superb **sense of belonging.** Not everyone has been or will be that fortunate. I am a school counselor, and it is quite astonishing to hear the stories of some of the children I counsel. Over the years, many children have told me of their sadness and how lonely their lives are because their parents do not (or are unable to) spend enough time with them. Very frequently two parents are working to make ends meet, and this does not allow for quality time to be given to their children. Consequently, children do not have that "sense of belonging" which is so essential in a home, and some begin to look elsewhere for a connection. It breaks my heart to see so many children hurting in such an unnecessary way. Parents today are giving their children money to ease their guilt, or they have chosen to replace their presence with video games, computers and "things." How sad is that!? Parents must find quality time somewhere, or change their priorities so that children feel important and wanted.

Times have certainly changed from when I grew up. I didn't have an allowance; in fact, my parents never had extra money to give me (maybe a quarter for a hot lunch at school sometimes), but I did have a home where I knew I belonged, and a home where I felt important because my parents had time for me. Our entertainment wasn't video games; it was board games or puzzles and a bowl of popcorn with my parents. That's a treasure! That's a memory that has helped me in life— one I have stored in my sacred room of yesterday's memories.

You may be saying: "I'm so happy you had a good home, but what does that have to do with the topic of abiding?" Let me tell you! Not everything was perfect in my home, but that feeling and experience of being a part of a family gave me a template, a chart, a road map that has given me the ability to transfer my sense of belonging and abiding in my home to a sense of belonging and abiding in the Kingdom of God. My family experience has allowed me to realize how very important the root of abiding is. I want to feel a part of His Kingdom. "For the kingdom of God is not meat and drink; but righteousness, peace, and joy in the Holy Ghost" (Romans 14:17 KJV). And just as I desired to please my parents, I desire to please my heavenly Father. God is my parent now. I belong to His family. I belong to His Kingdom and it is my responsibility to **remain,** to stay, to dwell, and to accept His teaching and discipline if there is to be fruit in my life. I must remain connected to the vine.

Take care to live in me, and let me live in you.
For a branch can't produce fruit, when severed from the vine.
Nor can you be fruitful apart from me.
JOHN 15:4 TLB

AREAS OF ABIDING

WALKING:

How does one walk with God? By abiding! When I first started serving the Lord, I thought "I" could do most anything **for** Him. Now that I am learning to "abide," I don't think there is anything I can do

without Him. It's that simple. I need Him by my side. But, if you are like me, walking is so boring! I'd rather skip, hop, jump, fly, swim, jog or ride. Anything, but walk! I'd rather be soaring: "mounting up with wings as eagles" (Isaiah 40:31). But walking? Where does that lead? What does that produce? It's just walking. When we stopped the bike to rest, the Lord and I often strolled. We walked and I continued to learn. I have found that as I abide and continue to "walk" with Him, I have been led to several experiences. And, I'm afraid, if I had been traveling at any other speed, I would have surely missed out on the following:

1) The exchange of my weakness for His strength . . . the strength that Paul speaks of in II Corinthians 12:9: ". . . for my strength is made perfect in your weakness." As the Lord and I walked and talked, it has been a joy to empty all the junk drawers of my spirit, which have only created weaknesses and wrong thinking in my life. I said: "Here Lord, I give them to You." All those preconceived ideas and hurts from the past had to go. They had to be emptied out!

As the Lord and I walk together, I am experiencing that process of being emptied of my beliefs, my will, and my desires . . . just emptied of plain old "me." But also, I am experiencing that process of being filled. Filled with His beliefs, His desire, His Spirit and His life. What an exchange! If you have encountered this exchange like I have, then you and I need to remove our shoes, bow our heads and kneel before Him because He has given us a holy gift. A gift of ABUNDANT GRACE!

2) Gaining a new perspective on how to listen . . . to hear His still small voice saying some of the same things He spoke to Solomon. "And if thou wilt walk in my ways, to keep my statutes and my commandments, as thy father David did walk, then I will lengthen thy days" (I Kings 3:14 KJV). **In many of God's words to Solomon, He pledged success, lengthened days, a promise to dwell with His people, and a promise to never forsake them.** I'll take all that! The condition then and the condition now is the same: to *walk* in His ways and to keep His commandments. In light of that, you and I need to continue abiding and maintaining a forever relationship with He who loves us beyond what we will ever be able to comprehend. His promises are continual if we are obedient and listen for His voice and walk in His ways.

3) Discipline! Pruning! They are not words I like. They are not processes I enjoy going through, any more than other Christians. According to the Bible and the verse "I am the vine and you are the branches," John uses the metaphorical words "prune" and "discipline" to refer to spiritual growth in our lives. All our branches need pruning! There is only one reason God has left us on this earth, and that is His desire for us to bear fruit that He can use. And the only way for us to bear fruit is for the painful process of pruning and discipline to take place.

Discipline is usually what takes place when God desires to help us with our waywardness. Your sin is not too great for His grace, but very often, He needs to bring us back to that place of confession, to that place where we know we need His forgiveness. "If we confess our sins, he is faithful and just to forgive us our sins, and to cleanse us from all unrighteousness" (I John 1:9 KJV).

> *When I kept silent, my bones wasted away*
> *through my groaning all day long.*
> *For night and day your hand was heavy upon me;*
> *my strength was sapped as in the heat of summer.*
> *Then I acknowledged my sin to you*
> *and did not cover up my iniquity.*
> *I said "I will confess my transgressions to the Lord"*
> *and you forgave the guilt of my sin.*
> PSALM 32:3-5 NIV

Pruning, on the other hand, takes place when God wants to help us rid ourselves of those things that prevent us from fully doing His will, such as our immaturity, selfishness, or anything that pertains to "self." In discipline, the Christian is to repent. However, in pruning, the Christian is simply to release or give to God those things which keep that person from growing and producing more fruit. Have you ever seen a rose bush or grape vines pruned? I have! They look destroyed after pruning. What a surprise when springtime and summertime yields baskets of fragrant roses or luscious grapes. It is a needful process and you may feel destroyed, shattered or damaged as well. Fear not—if you cooperate, fruit will surprise you and give your Father joy. It is never His desire to harm His children. But, He sees the end from the beginning and knows of the prosperous results of His pruning. Our main purpose will always remain the same, to live an abundant and fruitful life that will glorify Him. When we walk with Him, God is able to speak to those issues in our lives that need improvement. It is our responsibility to respond accordingly . . . to abide.

> *I am the true vine,*
> *and my Father is the gardener.*
> *He cuts off every (undesirable) branch*
> *That does not bear fruit.*
>
> JOHN 15:1,2 NIV

PRAYING:

How does one learn to pray? By abiding! For me, prayer is friendship. God is my friend. My earthly friends, I would either write to, talk to, commune with, fellowship with, help, and most importantly, spend time with. Should I do any less with God? To my chagrin, God, at times, takes second place when I so unkindly leave Him out. I'm learning, though! I know how very much I need His friendship, how very much I need His guidance and help. More than any of that, though, I want to be kind; to show my gratitude, to worship, to give Him that place in my life He is so deserving of. After all, He gave His life for me! He asks for so little in return . . . just that I abide, remain, stay, commune, fellowship and treat Him as a friend. That is truly a bargain. And, it is also truly mystifying. Not only did He save us from sin, but He wants a relationship, too? Totally incomprehensible! But true! They say that we most surely become like those with whom we keep company. If that is true, my desire is to keep company with Jesus, always! His words to us are as follows:

> *I no longer call you servants, because a servant*
> *does not know his master's business.*
> *Instead, I have called you friends,*
> *for everything that I learned from my Father*
> *I have made known to you.*
>
> JOHN 15:15 NIV

The following are some notes on prayer that I have taken as I traveled on this *abiding journey* with the Lord. He was so willing to stay on this tandem bike ride and help me understand how very essential talking to Him was. He taught me how vital abiding was to a vigorous and healthy spiritual root system. And I have stayed on the bike . . . learning how to pray.

Speaking of learning how to pray, Corrie Ten Boom once told the following humorous story:

> *A mother I met told me that she saw her little boy sitting in a corner of the room, saying "A-B-C-D-E-F-G . . ."*
> *"What are you doing?" she asked.*
> *"Mom, you told me I should pray, but I have never prayed in my life and I don't know how. So I gave God the whole alphabet and asked Him to make a good prayer of it."* [2]
>
> — CORRIE TEN BOON

I believe I've found a better way . . . not as humorous, but better. I love the innocence of children, though. They simply believe. And, if they don't know how to pray, then what's better than giving the whole alphabet to God to make a prayer of? We adults are so complicated. "... and a little child shall lead them" (Isaiah 11:6b KJV).

Years ago, I came across an outline that contained a method of praying that has been an immense help to me. I don't know where I found it, so I am unable to give credit where credit is due. We, so very often, pray when there is a need in our lives and just leave it at that. There is no communion, no fellowship and no friendship involved. However, the method I am referring to is called "ACTS," and it greatly helps in maintaining a relationship with the Lord. Prayer is so much more than supplication, so much more than just asking. It is also listening, worshipping, becoming prayer warriors on behalf of others and possessing the knowledge that He answers our prayers before we even ask.

I. A-C-T-S – A Guide To Prayer

"A" - The letter A represents **Adoration**. Prayer should open in worship and praise. There are so many ways to praise. For example, I have gone through the entire alphabet to find a word that begins with each letter to describe an attribute of the Lord, and used this method in worship to Him. I have often sung a praise song. Or, I have read a psalm or a scripture that may more appropriately express Adoration. I take my time. It is part of "abiding" ... not rushing into God's presence just to make my requests known. I certainly wouldn't rush into my earthy friend's home and begin to make requests. So, why should I rush into God's presence? That is equivalent to being rude. Of course, there are times when emergencies arise and all we have time for is "Jesus, help me." And He does. I remember the time I went to visit my mother in Pennsylvania and arrived late in the evening in total pitch-blackness. Before I realized, I had come upon a sharp curve and I knew I wasn't going to make it. It became one of those "Jesus, help me" moments and instead of braking, which is a normal reaction, I believe there was an angel sitting beside me who pressed on the accelerator pedal and I quickly and neatly projected straight out over a 4-foot embankment into a field. I was flying through the air and landed on all four tires. I know for certain that if I had braked on the curve, the car would have turned over and it would have been an entirely different outcome. There was no time for adoration . . . I needed help, pronto! But He already knew that! He had already sent one of His angels on a mercy mission. Generally speaking, however, we are to be respectful in prayer. This is a holy God we are speaking to . . . not someone off the street! We need to take the time to give Him the honor He is due. "Be thou exalted, O God, above the heavens: let thy glory be above all the earth" (Psalm 57:11 KJV).

"C" - The letter C represents **Confession**. Taking the time to confess our sins, whether they be sins of commission or sins of omission, helps wipe the slate clean and cleanses the soul and the heart. God, in His mercy, is ready to forgive, but He can't forgive what we don't confess. "Create in me a clean heart, O God; and renew a right spirit within me" (Psalms 51:10 KJV).

"T" - T is for **Thanksgiving** . . . having a thankful heart. God knows our hearts. He knows if we are thankful or not thankful. The whole point in thanking Him becomes the fact that He loves to hear it. And it creates within us a gratefulness that robs selfishness from taking root in our lives. It expresses our appreciation and our high regard for His goodness to us. He doesn't have to give us His grace, joy, peace, righteousness and happiness, but He delights in giving His children good gifts. Not only does He give us spiritual gifts, but just think of the temporal gifts He pours out upon us, such as food, clothing, shelter, transportation, etc. He surely is a good God. His protection is also evident in each of our lives every day. Thank Him for it. Don't take His goodness for granted. Thank Him for your salvation. He didn't have to die for you. He chose to! His gifts to us are too innumerable to count, both spiritual and temporal. "Enter into his gates with thanksgiving, and into his courts with praise: be thankful unto him, and bless his name" (Psalm 100:4 KJV).

"S" - The letter S represents **Supplication**. My list is usually long, but I'm glad that in this prayer model, it's last. Adoration, confession and a thankful heart are far more important to the Lord than my requests because our needs are always before Him. Since we serve an omniscient God, He is well aware of all our human situations. However, due to the fact that adoration, confession and thankfulness are an act of the will, He highly treasures those expressions. "Be careful for nothing; but in every thing by prayer and supplication with thanksgiving let your requests be made known unto God" (Philippians 4:6 KJV).

There are exceptions to the prayer model, however. Especially if I am praying very specifically for another's need . . . if someone is sick, is having emergency surgery or any number of unforeseen occurrences or emergency scenarios that I may have to encounter. Then, there's no waiting . . . it's straight to the throne of God to intercede on their behalf. And, He is never offended! He understands the human heart. Make it a practice however, that before you ask: adore, confess and offer up your gratefulness.

I sincerely hope this model facilitates a more meaningful prayer life for you; it has certainly become a blessing in mine. Aside from this formal venture into prayer, I often find myself talking to the Lord all day . . . friend to friend. And, He graciously listens! *"Thank you Jesus for your friendship!"*

II. LISTENING

Another aspect to prayer is listening. Sometimes, we just need to sit and hear Him speak to us. It is a special time of fellowship and not necessarily a time to listen for answers to requests. I actually enjoy this part of prayer . . . waiting in anticipation . . . curious as to what gem will be revealed to me. Sometimes I like what I hear and sometimes I don't. It depends on whether discipline or pruning are part of the revelation or not. Regardless, it's wonderful communication and communion with a God whose greatest attribute is love. Love for you and love for me. Love so great,

He desires to talk to us . . . to have fellowship with us. Truly amazing!!

Many years ago, I was faced with a situation that was heart-rending. There were no answers, no solutions to ease the pain. In harmony with what all Christians do in such a crisis, I cried out to God, I read every psalm over and over, I prayed endlessly, I worshipped, but . . . I did not listen! It occurred to me one day that God was waiting for me to just sit in His presence and calmly wait. To my astonishment the following took place: As I closed my eyes, I was spiritually transported before the throne of God. I saw myself running and kneeling at the feet of God and then bowing my head in His lap. He tenderly placed His hand on top of my head and said: "Daughter, it is almost over . . . the end is near." Had I not waited in His presence, I never would have encountered such precious love that our Father wants to bestow upon His children. I sat stunned! Literally stunned! It was exactly two weeks after that encounter that the Lord graciously solved the crisis. Listen! Wait! Hear Him speak to your longing heart! Listening reaps a renewed Spirit.

III. PRAYER WARRIORS

We are also to be prayer warriors . . . to stand against the wiles of Satan: "For the weapons of our warfare are not carnal, but mighty through God to the pulling down of strongholds" (II Corinthians 10:4 KJV). Isaiah also states: "No weapon formed against thee shall prosper" (Isaiah 54:17 KJV). God calls upon us to stand in the gap for others . . . to pray against the powers of darkness that would rob all of us of a fruitful life. The Christian is the enemy of Satan and he wants to keep you and I from the truth. Satan's primary focal point is the mind, which we will discuss in another chapter. Keep vigilant, and pray against the forces of evil that want you to despair and relinquish your faith. "Be on your guard; stand firm in the faith; be men of courage, be strong" (I Corinthians 16:13 NIV).

IV. THE KINDNESS OF GOD

There is yet another aspect to prayer as it pertains to "abiding," and that is the kindness of God to answer our prayers of supplication. "And it shall come to pass that before they call I will answer . . ." (Isaiah 65:24 KJV). God does know the desires of our hearts before we even utter a word to Him and He graciously has an answer ready. (Sometimes He answer, "Yes." Sometimes, "No." And then, there are times He simply asks us to wait). Asking, however, is part of the fellowship, the friendship, and the acknowledgement that He, and only He, has the right answers. Looking back over the years, many prayers have ascended to the throne of God and I know that our heavenly Father had the answers already planned before we even asked. Many times we had to wait, but He always answered! He is truly a gracious God. To abide, to remain, to stay, to continue on, to be steadfast and faithful have brought about some wonderful answers to prayer:

In 1980, we as a congregation began to pray for another location for our church. We were bursting at the seams. In those projects I mentioned in chapter two (location, 41st Street, Long Island City), we had used every available inch of land and it was just impossible to expand any more. We were already holding two services. Where would we go? Property in New York is expensive . . . it is calculated by the square foot. A city lot equals 2500 square feet. In 1980, a lot of 2500 square feet was worth $150,000, and we surely would need more than one lot. Of course, today a city lot would cost approximately $700,000. Where would we find that kind of money needed to purchase a parcel of land large enough to build on and accommodate our ever-growing congregation? Or, if not build, where would we find a building suitable for expansion, plus affordable? It seemed impossible, but we held on to Matthew 19:26 KJV: ". . . but with God all things are possible." God can move mountains and has all the resources of heaven at His disposal, so we waited in anticipation to see what miracle He would perform. In the meantime, it was our responsibility to pray and believe.

We had also started a private Christian school and progressing beyond a 3rd or 4th grade was simply beyond our capability space-wise. Just across the border of Queens into Greenpoint, Brooklyn, we located a large parcel of land (five acres) that had a hospital and several smaller buildings owned by the city. Could we convert *this* into a school and church? Much to our dismay, this property was being used to house the "homeless" of New York City, and the residents of this area were quite "up-in-arms" over their presence. Would the city sell to us? When it was time to meet with the community board in Greenpoint to state our case, the community did not welcome us with open arms. It seemed that certain groups were against us as well as against the homeless. In fact, some were rather irate in expressing their opinion of a school and church relocating to this particular piece of property. It appeared that this door was closing. The door was closing for another reason also. After some deliberation, the city refused to relocate the homeless and it was therefore not interested in selling.

What next? God had an answer, but it was another seven years before the door was opened to 39-21 Crescent Street, Long Island City, New York. Here, we had finally found a home for Evangel Church and School. Public School #4 was located on this property, which contained several lots . . . 23 lots to be exact. In fact, this property went through the block to 27th Street, giving us much-needed room to expand into what was formally the school play yards. We not only had a building for our Christian school, but God had so graciously given us plenty of space to build on. While praying, searching and waiting, Evangel had been saving every penny.

When the property on Crescent Street became available, we had saved one million dollars. After serious negotiation, we traded our old church plus one million for the new property. The school building itself had greatly deteriorated as it was formerly being used as a warehouse. It was in need of much repair and we began a project entitled: "The Nehemiah Project." Our oldest son, Brian, became the director of this project and oversaw the installation of a new elevator, 17 new bathrooms, new electric and plumbing, new sheet rock in classrooms, painting, and finally the installation of new windows and a furnace. The work was done by several experienced workmen and many volunteers. For two years, 50-60 church people, every Saturday, worked in demolition, plastering and painting. The cost of the renovation was $2.5 million. These new monies were raised in our first stewardship program for capital improvement. When the Nehemiah Project was completed, all outstanding bills were entirely paid. It was a great day when we moved to our new property in 1989.

When we relocated, the school occupied the first three floors. The church offices and sanctuary were on the 4th floor. We conducted three church services every Sunday morning for ten years. After ten years, the church and the school were again bursting at the seams. Shortly after relocating to this property, we had begun planning for the "mother of all projects." This new endeavor would consist of a new sanctuary for 1800 people, a full-size gymnasium, a fellowship hall and an office/apartment tower to be built on our existing property. The tower was to contain two floors of offices and eight apartments for school and staff housing. After working six years to obtain a variance from the city of New York, we broke ground for this new project in 1996. It was June 5, 1999 that we dedicated our new sanctuary. What a great day of victory! The project was done for $10,000,000. How this was done can only be described as a miracle. **An unmistakable answer to prayer!**

My accolades to my husband on this momentous dedication day, June 5, 1999:

To My Husband, My Pastor and the Love of My Life
Well, here we are . . . 37 years later. Actually 38 years in August and what a journey! . . . somewhat bumpy at times—but a glorious, memorable journey. This is not to say it's over, for I know you (better than any one); and knowing you as I do, there WILL be other

projects in our future journey (if God tarries). This particular project, however, is nearing completion and might I say: "JUST LOOK WHAT YOU'VE DONE." This is a rather major accomplishment no matter how you look at it. I know, I know, I can hear you saying to yourself: "NO, NO, LOOK WHAT GOD HAS DONE." Well, that is absolutely true also. But God, through history, has proven that a special job requires a particular, special person and **He always chose wisely. It is also true that God chose wisely when He directed you to New York City.** *For I can think of no other who could have, or would have, stayed as long, endured as much, persevered as well or cared as greatly as you.*

Over the years, we have both found that it can be difficult to build in New York City. In fact, at times it can be rather irritating to say the least. We both know; you don't just start to build here. There are umpteen permits to file for, too many long lines to stand on when visiting various city departments, too many trips to the building department, phone calls galore and God surely does know "what else." But, on this particular project you stopped counting the irritations and you just kept pressing on toward the vision God gave you.

Harry Emerson Fosdick once wrote: "The most extraordinary thing about the oyster is this: irritations get into his shell. Of course he does not like them. But when he cannot get rid of them, he uses the irritation to do the loveliest thing an oyster ever has a chance to do . . . make a pearl. When there are irritations in our lives, there is only one prescription . . . make a pearl." [3]

LET ME PROCLAIM TO THE WORLD TODAY . . . you have made a pearl. We, the congregation, thank you for this sanctuary . . . this pearl. In fact, in your lifetime, you have created a string of pearls.

YES, GOD CHOSE WISELY when He chose you. In the words of Dwight L. Moody: "Character is what you are in the dark." Let it be know today that during your darkest hours on this project, your character shone the brightest. Faith and faithfulness have always been the hallmarks of your character. Those hours of testing and attacks by Satan only proved the quality of your character to be as pure gold. Your faith has always been like the bird that feels the light and sings when the dawn is still dark. You knew the dawn was coming—you never lost hope . . . never! (Especially on this project.) You made a choice to believe . . . you made a choice to be courageous and determined. Those choices and many other choices have made your character what it is today. You surely could have said many times with just cause: "I give up, it's not worth it." But those words are not in your vocabulary. As we sit in this sanctuary today, we are enjoying the fruit of your faith. That hope, that never gave up, was never discouraged and always remained positive. Faith and faithfulness are the attributes I saw in your parents. But I also know that it is God who gives faith and it is God who aids in our endeavors to remain faithful. So, it is fitting that we, as a congregation, should thank God first and then your parents for this wonderful heritage.

*Of course there have always been a few Nay-Sayers . . . those who said this couldn't be done . . . who said it was unnecessary. Or, there were those who just didn't like your style or didn't catch your vision. That's okay, because you simply chose to ignore the negative and follow the vision God gave you. **I admire you for that!** Where would we all sit today if you hadn't been obedient?" It is said that the difference between listening to Nay-Sayers and holding on to a hurt (or) releasing it with forgiveness . . . is like the difference between laying your head down at night on a pillow full of thorns (or) a pillow full of rose petals. Your pillow has always been filled with rose petals. **I admire you for that also.** What a marvelous example you have been to your family.*

YES, GOD CHOSE WISELY WHEN HE CHOSE YOU . . . for good character is more to be praised than outstanding talent. Oh, but wait a minute . . . am I saying you have talent as well?

🌿

You had better believe it! You and I both know of your desire to be an architect and just look around and see what you have built!! This congregation not only has a caring shepherd but one who can build and design also. I hear you had much to say about all those blueprints up in your office. But, I am also a recipient of your building talent, for my home is full of your inspired touches. You've rebuilt my entire home. **How I thank you.**

There's so much more to your character than faith, faithfulness, courage and determination. Have I mentioned your unconditional love? There's an old Chinese Proverb that goes something like this: "If your vision is for a year, plant wheat. If your vision is for ten years, plant trees . . . but if your vision is for a lifetime, plant people. You, Pastor, have invested a lifetime in loving people, your congregation, your children, your friends, those who once attended our church but are now out on the highways and byways . . . and of course, there's me. What would I have done without you? It is said that a successful marriage requires falling in love many times . . . always with the same person. It is so special that you and I together fall in love again and again every day. How privileged I am . . . how very blessed.

I have no time to mention your other attributes this congregation has been a recipient of—such as your strength, your tenacity, your wisdom, your humility, goodness, godliness, commitment . . . and the list goes on! But God knows all about those character traits and so do your children. For there are many ways to measure a man's success, not the least of which is the way your children describe you to their associates. I know that they would describe you just as I have. I have seen your Christian influence woven into the lives and decisions of all your children. One son, Brian, is the Vice President of Christian Herald and the famed Bowery Mission. Another son, Stephen, has a prominent position in computers with a large Christian corporation called Cardone, and your daughter, Carolyn,

❧

is Evangel School's well known, much loved Principal. To have each child glean from your life and follow your example in leadership positions is truly success personified. How I thank you for your influence on their lives.

Let me end by saying that every man is entitled to be valued by his best moments. **This is one of your moments!** *In your own optimistic words: "It doesn't get any better than this." I know you would agree when I say that no medal, ribbon or accolade (as wonderful and as appreciated as they are) even remotely compares to the deep and abiding love and respect of the Lord, your children, your wife, your congregation and your friends. You deserve this moment . . . you deserve our love and respect.*

There is nothing profound in what I have said . . . just a great deal of love and admiration from my heart to your heart. And, regarding those future projects . . . let's remember that I am 60 and you're 63. Maybe we should shift down some and take life a little slower . . . slipping into neutral would seem even better. Then, we could just coast for a while. Do you remember the poem I wrote for you on your 60th birthday? Let me read a small portion that I have revised:

The angels are singing Hallelujah,
As we dedicate His new Church . . . and Behold!
They are standing with you on this platform, very bold,
As your labor of love unfolds.
For the angels know, as I know,
That God is saying "Well done"
For a very major victory has now been won. JJ

You and I have gone down many roads together and crossed many bridges all of which have brought us to this very moment. And as I ponder on that, I am reminded of the verse God gave to us, separately, just before we were married. Ephesians 3:20 reads like this: "Now unto him that is able to do exceeding abundantly above all that we ask or think, according to the power that worketh in us, unto him be glory in the church by Christ Jesus, throughout all ages, world without end." God has kept His promise . . . He has been more than faithful and He has done exceeding abundantly above all we could have asked or thought.

Yes, God did choose the right person, and so did I.
Congratulations. All my love and respect, Jan

I included this accolade to my husband in this book because there are so few who understand how very difficult it is to establish and build a church in New York City. There are so many hindrances, obstacles, impediments, restrictions, restraints, financial concerns (it cost 3-4 times more to build here than elsewhere), community oppositions, city regulations, etc. to deal with that discouragement is easy to come by. And then, when you factor in the evil forces of darkness with Satan's darts being wielded at you, it takes an immense amount of fortitude and steadfastness to remain at the helm. I can say, unequivocally, that my husband has taken the "high road" in all aspects of his dealings with the city and stood stalwart in his claim that Evangel would stand the test of time. His integrity and uprightness are beyond reproach because he decided a long time ago, in Bible school, that he would serve the Lord regardless of circumstances. I have to admit that there were times when I desired to "jump ship" but I held onto my husband's shirttail . . . I knew he was "going through" and to give up was simply not a thought he ever entertained. I held on to his faith and his vision if ever either of mine started to wane.

Fast forward nearly 10 years, and guess what we're talking about? You guessed it . . . building again! Our growing high school needs more room. The enrollment for the entire school has reached approximately 560 students. So, beginning in the spring of 2010 or '11, we will hopefully begin to build "up." New Yorkers don't build "out," we build in the only direction we usually have available and that is air space. The top floor of this new building will contain a prayer tower that overlooks the beautiful skyline of Manhattan, not only for our congregation, but for all churches in the city to use. I know one thing is certain, I will be holding on tight as the Lord and I continue our tandem bike ride through this, I pray, our last project. It is emphatically true that as "older" age approaches, I need more of every thing that time wants to take away. It requires a great deal more effort to do almost anything! *"Do you think, Lord, that we could contemplate slowing down after this last (I say 'last' cautiously) enterprising endeavor into the building empire again? I would be so grateful!! Amen."*

God has brought to our remembrance the truth of His Word on many occasions as we held on to the visions He gave us and the work He wanted to do through us: "So shall my word be that goeth forth out of my mouth: it shall not return unto me void, but it shall accomplish that which I please, and it shall prosper in the thing whereto I sent it" (Isaiah 55:11 KJV).

HIS WORD IS TRUTH

1) As we abide, His grace abounds more and more. Listen to the words of Jesus:

    If ye abide in me, and my words abide in you,
    ye shall ask what ye will, and it shall be done unto you.

    JOHN 15:7 KJV

2) With God, nothing is impossible:

    And Jesus looking upon them saith,
    with men it is impossible, but not with God;
    for with God all things are possible.

    MARK 10:27 KJV

3) Abiding is a preventative measure. If we constantly and faithfully abide then burnout, discouragement and lack of energy are not as

likely to occur, because we are continually being nurtured and re-
fueled by His grace, His strength and His Life.

> *That He would grant you,*
> *according to the riches of His glory,*
> *to be strengthened with might by His Spirit*
> *in the inner man.*
>
> EPHESIANS 3:16 KJV

4) His power and faith, which dwells within us, enables us to overcome obstacles such as looming mountains.

> *. . . Verily I say unto you, If ye have faith, and doubt not . . .*
> *ye shall say unto this mountain, be thou removed,*
> *and it shall be done.*
>
> MATTHEW 21:21 KJV

**For more accolades that testify to the truth of Ephesians 3:20 and
the abundant blessing and truth that arises from dedicating one's
life to serve and abide in His keeping power, see Appendix B.**

ABIDING AS A ROOT OF HIS GRACE

How would we survive as Christians if we didn't abide? Staying connected gives us life. Without abiding, we would hunger and thirst and
become wilting flowers, producing unproductive fruit. We would become deserts in our souls; always panting for the clear, cleansing water
of righteousness. It would hinder our root system to the point of extinc-
tion, because our remaining roots of obedience, surrender and trust
would not have a resource to draw from. We would pine for a sense of
belonging, and greatly miss out on the friendship and communion of
our Savior. Abiding keeps the door to our heart safe from Satan's ever-
present wiles and sends him "packing." Abiding (as a taproot) helps us
to become steady, strong, stable and fruitful Christians that God can

again and again use for His Kingdom. It allows us to be taught, disciplined and pruned by the greatest and most loving teacher that ever lived. Without abiding, we would become like petrified wood, unable to grow and produce. Abiding is our nourishment, our very "lifeline." As we abide, the Lord has promised the following.

> *And the Lord will guide you continually,*
> *and satisfy you with all good things,*
> *and keep you healthy too;*
> *and you will be like a well-watered garden,*
> *like an ever-flowing spring.*
> ISAIAH 58:11 TLB

CONCLUSION OF PART ONE

Looking back through the previous chapters, which have brought me to this point in my journey, I am quite in awe of His graciousness. While establishing the roots of obedience, surrender, trust and abiding, I know, indisputably, that if I were God I would have "slapped me around" a few times. I have been stubborn, rebellious, a "baby," confrontational, indifferent, angry, resentful, ungrateful, unloving and probably umpteen other adjectives would suffice to exemplify my state of being over the years. To be perfectly honest, I have screamed at God in my moments of unrequited quests as to why I struggled in certain areas, especially with anger. In Part Two, I will explain how God revealed those answers.

Because of His grace, I was able to comprehend and come to grips with God's intervention in my life and the need for the work that He wanted to do. When God wants to do a work in our lives, He doesn't stop because we are whining. As I stated in the introduction, if God begins a work, He plans to continue, to persevere as revealed in Philippians 1:6. **He was determined to help me "grow in grace."**

I am more conscious of the fact that it is possible to have my strength renewed, to mount up with wings as an eagle, and to run and not be weary, to walk and not faint, because I've been able to establish roots. I have a source to draw from . . . living water to nourish my soul. It was a long journey to this point. However, believe me when I say, those established roots will be tested. The secret to remember is that His strength and His grace will sustain us. The bike ride, so far, has been freeing, exhilarating and above all, life-changing.

MAY WE ALL BE *ROOTED* IN HIS GRACE:

Rooted and built up in him and established in the faith,
as ye have been taught, abounding therein with thanksgiving.

COLOSSIANS 2:7 KJV

Let your roots grow down into him and draw up nourishment from him.
See that you go on growing in the Lord, and become strong
and vigorous in the truth you were taught. Let you lives overflow
with joy and thanksgiving for all he has done.

COLOSSIANS 2:7 TLB

AMEN!

As our tandem bike ride continues in Part Two, the Lord and I will need to ride through some rough terrain.

I hold on for dear life!! He remains patient! I tremble! God encourages! I ask for grace! God brings victory! . . .

CHAPTER IV
Application & Review

Abiding is staying linked to Christ. Without it, we would hunger and thirst for righteousness and become unproductive Christians. Abiding provides fulfillment, a sense of belonging, communion, fellowship and friendship with our Savior. Take this root seriously, since the roots we have studied up to this point will find nourishment in Abiding.

1. What is a taproot? Why is it important in our spiritual root system? Read and comment on Colossians 2:6-9 in the Living Bible.

2. According to chapter IV, what are some of the areas in which we must learn to abide?

3. Explain John 15:5, as it is stated on page 80. What is our responsibility?

4. What is the result of abiding, according to Isaiah 58:11?

5. What does Christ call us in John 15:15? Why?

6. What is the difference between pruning and discipline, as stated in this chapter?

PART TWO

The Pathway of His Grace
Developmental aspects to learning grace

❦

But grow in grace, and in the knowledge
of our Lord and Savior Jesus Christ.
II PETER 3:18 KJV

❦

CHAPTER V

The Pathway to Emotional Health

Developing Wholeness

He heals the brokenhearted
and binds up their wounds.

PSALM 147:3 KJV

CHAPTER V

The Pathway to Emotional Health
Developing a strong stem of emotional wholeness

. . . I have heard your prayer
and seen your tears; I will heal you.
II KINGS 20:5 NIV

After establishing some important roots in my spiritual life, the Lord and I took a harrowing and traumatic trip into the intricacies and, at times, discouraging malaise of my emotions. I couldn't pinpoint the rationale for the discomfort I often experienced. What was the reason? To my knowledge, the Lord had always sheltered me under the shadow of His wings, and there protected me from harm, so from where did the occasional emotional discomfort arise? I didn't know. While reminiscing through my childhood, I couldn't trace to a poignant moment in my life when I was traumatized. And yet, there were intermittent times when I felt I was suffering from posttraumatic stress. I had studied psychology while working toward my counseling degree, and it seemed quite obvious that most of my symptoms pointed toward this disorder. The problem was, I didn't know the cause, so I certainly didn't understand the effects and therefore found no solutions. The easiest thing, at that time, was to brush everything under the rug and continue forward in life the best I could. So I thought! The Lord had another strategy. I am so thankful, today, that God knew the entire situation, knew how to solve the problem and wanted me to venture into another bike ride. This time, it was for healing. Our conversation went something like this:

He said: *"It's time to gear up for another journey. We have some business to take care of."*

"Uh oh," I said. I knew, from past adventures, that "business" and the tone of His voice either meant pruning, discipline or something serious! *"What is it for?"*

"Just hold on. This excursion will be for healing," He answered.

I replied: *"Okay, that sounds promising. I'll hold on tight, but please don't let go of me."*

"I won't . . . Never . . . Ever," He answered.

"Okay then, I'm ready to face the music," I said. *"Oh, by the way, is this going to be difficult?"* I queried.

"I'm certain it will be, but we'll go through it together," He answered.

I replied: *"Together is good."*

For the sake of my healing and for the sake of developing His fruit in my life, He very carefully and cautiously steered our tandem bike into:

A PAINFUL DISCLOSURE

I was a happy child. Quiet (that part hasn't changed). Caring. I had a penchant for older people—I always wanted to help them. When I delivered my mother's wonderful homemade bread to our senior neighbors, they would often ask me to run an errand or to come back another day and help them clean their home. I was more than happy to oblige. My little-girl heart loved people, especially the elderly. I also loved school, animals, dolls and teddy bears (still do), hopscotch, marbles, camping, baking with my Mom (I still love to bake), vacation trips, ice skating, skiing on local mountains, biking (I had a beautiful, new 1940s Schwinn bike—what a treat), swimming in the Finger Lakes of upstate New York, apple picking, trips to grandma's house, and countless other childhood memories. I can't ever remember being discontented or unhappy. At least, that was the case until I was around nine or ten. And then, my world changed from light-hearted happiness to dark sadness.

That happy little sparkling star got swallowed up in darkness. The light went out of her little soul. She was a sweet, innocent flower that got crushed amidst evil. She was abused—molested!

To my knowledge, I never said a word of this despicable act to a soul (as a child). Interestingly, there is a phenomenon that often occurs when one is traumatized, and that is a protective formula we all possess called "repression." Those hideous moments in time were allocated to the very recesses of my mind and life went on as usual. From ten years old to adulthood, I was never haunted by a remembrance of this travesty. Repression is that psychological term for depositing and storing information in our unconscious. The information is there but it is kept tightly sealed from our awareness. My mother, who later in my life was privy to these incidents, said the only symptoms of trauma that I exhibited as a child were withdrawal, fear and sadness. To her, those were not excessively unusual behaviors as I was already a quiet, reserved and timid child with a personality that had a propensity toward melancholy. She was not alarmed. So, in the convening years, this trauma in my life went undetected until I became an adult.

As an adult, echoes of the past abuse began to reverberate and filter into my consciousness. One emotion I began to experience was anger. I was not particularly pleased about feeling angry, especially when I didn't know its source. Then, I became filled with anxiety and fear for no apparent reason. There was this niggling thought that somehow I had been hurt by someone. Finally, I had "flashbacks" of those unspeakable acts, which had been perpetrated upon my child's heart and body. As a hurting adult, I became fully conscious that my childhood innocence had been preyed upon. I was unable to point to any particular epiphany moment when that truth was made evident except for the flashbacks. I do know that the certainty of this truth brought absolute shock followed by depression to my troubled soul. Later, this truth was verified by a very reliable source. It had then truly become a fact and not a figment of my imagination.

✤

How could this have happened? In fact, I asked many questions. Why do I have to come to terms with this pain now? What do I do with my anger, anxiety, fear, shock and depression? Where do I go from here? I decided to speak with several psychologists, but they were so "heady" and academic in their responses that help was not forthcoming. I became lost in all their psycho mumbo jumbo. I had studied psychology and counseling—I knew how to interview a client—I knew what was important to ask and most importantly, I was trained to express love and empathy. Even though these were Christian psychologists, they failed the interview test on my first visits. Those main ingredients of love and a caring attitude were omitted. Instead, their egos were being caressed by communicating years of book knowledge. God's knowledge of the human soul took a back seat. I am most certainly not against Christian psychologists, but they are positively not all created equal. Some are good—some are not so good. In my experience . . . not so good!

I went to the Lord! It was clear, as I spoke with the Lord, that healing was His primary focus and, in Him, I found love, care and concern. We stopped the bike for a rest! We began our conversation again:

"Now I know why You said it would be difficult. Is this connection with my past that important? Do I really have to go there?" I queried.

He replied: *"Daughter, if you want to be whole, and I know that you do, then this is the only way."*

"Then I'll need every bit of strength You possess . . . for right now I am faint of heart," I cried.

He said: *"Then you shall have my strength, but remember it's 'together' . . . we will face this together, hand in hand."*

I said: *"Then I place my hand in Yours and now, I'm ready."*

I knew from my psychological training that I needed to revisit this painful experience in my life, and **reclaim this uncultivated part of my soul,** if healing was to take place and if fruit was to abound that God could use. I didn't want to. But, I also knew I didn't want to be angry. I had asked the Lord why I was angry in the conclusion of chapter 4 and He didn't fail me. I now knew, and it was my responsibility to work through this pain to a healing resolution—which, in itself, hardly seemed fair. If some pain in our lives is the fault of another, why is it then our responsibility to work through that pain? I didn't cause this pain in my life. Why did I have to work through this agony? My emotional state was often piqued by those questions. To be irritated and annoyed, on top of every other feeling I was experiencing, was not wise. The simple truth is that, sometimes, life is not fair—it can deal some deadly blows. If, however, the desire is to be whole (and that was my desire), then the answer is to face the problem square on. As unloving and harsh as that sounds, there is no other choice. So, that's what I did. As with all other actions in my life, once I make a decision, determination takes over. And, I was determined to be whole.

LET ME ENCOURAGE YOU

Let me interject a word of encouragement before I continue. If you find yourself in an abusive situation and wonder where to turn, please do not hesitate to seek out any one of the following: Pastoral Counseling, Christian Counseling, Psychological or Psychiatric Care. I have told you my story based on my education, my personality, my readiness for help and my own God-given instincts. Please do not let my encounters with professionals be your guide. However, just because a person has a title with his/her name, it does not automatically endow that person with the ability to "connect" with all patients. It also does not necessarily disqualify his/her ability to express genuine care and concern. When seeking help, each person must feel comfortable in a professional's presence, trust the counsel or care given, and be able to meet financial obligations. Just remember that secular professionals are highly trained but generally lack God's perspective. It's a thought you should ponder when choosing counsel.

For your perusal, the following are considered abusive encounters and if you have found yourself in the midst of any one of these, do not waver in your decision to seek help, advise, or counsel. Childhood abuse affects our adult behaviors and perspective on life and thus requires the painful process of seeking wholeness by reviewing and revisiting the past. Adult abuse, on the other hand, should never be tolerated and requires great courage to face and address the issue(s).

Childhood abuses:
- Neglect of any form
- Verbal abuse
- "Setting up" a child to fail
- Placing a child in dangerous situations
- Withholding food, medical attention and love
- Failing to meet a child's emotional and physical needs
- Teaching a child immoral or illegal behaviors
- Threatening to harm a child
- Rejection of child
- Constant criticism
- Embarrassing a child in public
- Lying to a child
- Verbal, physical or emotional abuse from an alcoholic or drug addicted parent
- Physical abuse in any form
- Molestation
- Self abuse due to low self-esteem or trauma.

There are many diverse abuses that children, unfortunately, encounter in our society. Ultimately, they will carry the repercussions of those abuses into adulthood. It is a sad commentary that adults, then, must process and seek healing for undeserved and cruel treatment as a child.

Adult abuses:
- Verbal abuse from spouse

- Critical, demeaning, debasing or humiliating treatment
- Sexual harassment
- Rape
- Neglect by spouse
- Self abuse such as eating disorders
- Drug or alcohol abuse imposed by self or spouse
- "Battering" such as aggressive, violent behavior from spouse
- Emotional abuse from spouse or boss

There is a long list of abuses in our culture that adults experience also. Please consider counseling with a professional if you find yourself suffering in any one of the above forms of adult abuse or former childhood abuses. Don't allow any maltreatment destroy your personhood and the plans God has for your life. Be set free by His grace and assistance. He won't fail you!

WHY?

Why did God allow this in my life? That's the age-old question that often arises in abusive situations. For some reason, I wasn't angry with God. I was angry with the person who committed this evil, that's for sure. So for me, I didn't become angry and convict God of neglectful commitment to me. As if that would have ever held up in court anyway! I don't know why He allowed this to take place. The only answer I have is that God has used this darkness that was brought upon my soul to minister to others in like situations. So, for that I am grateful. Any other reasons and answers, I leave with Him. I know He loves me. That's enough! "But as for you, ye thought evil against me; but God meant it unto good" (Genesis 50:20 KJV).

He is the source of every mercy, and the one who so wonderfully comforts and strengthens us in our hardships and trials.
And why does he do this? So that when others are troubled,

❧

needing our sympathy and encouragement, we can pass on to them this same help and comfort God has given us.

II CORINTHIANS 1:3,4 TLB

In finding my way through the "why" question, I am blessed to say that I had a source of strength to draw from. And that is to God's credit, for it is He who diligently insisted on establishing roots in my life. The root of abiding began to take on new meaning as it pertained to this new revelation that gripped my soul. That "living water" of my Savior would sustain me as we traveled together to confront this obstacle in my life. Hand in hand, side-by-side, bike seat to bike seat, face to face, arm in arm, the Lord and I would "together" defeat darkness. He promised: ". . . beauty for ashes, the oil of joy for mourning, the garment of praise for the spirit of heaviness; that they might be called trees of righteousness, the planting of the Lord, that he might be glorified" (Isaiah 61:3 KJV). Be glorified, Lord!

TREKKING THROUGH THE MUCK & MIRE: BETRAYAL

How does one describe betrayal? It is such an ugly word. It speaks of such a violation of one's confidence in another. It is so deceitful. I knew the person who hurt me. I trusted him. I suppose that is why I had trouble trusting as an adult. At least, most psychology books will testify to this. My trust in human beings had been injured and not until I realized the full impact of this betrayal was I able to comprehend the damage to my heart. When a person's heart lays shattered, it is quite difficult to pick up those pieces and create wholeness again. The Lord revealed those broken pieces, and gave me His strength to face them. Some of those broken **heart pieces**, which lay shattered in my life, are as follows:

1) A *Protective* Heart Piece: When a heart has been shattered by past abuse, humans develop intricate, self-protective defenses to insure that hurt will never enter their beings again in any form. And that protective stance will, most likely, permeate all aspects of a person's life. The type of choices made in areas such as relationships, friends, career, education, religion, spouse and recreational interests all reflect a need to remain in a defensive position. Hurting people follow their protective heart and make choices that are comfortable and safe. To become "vulnerable" is quite out of the question. And yet, that's exactly what needs to take place in the process of healing.

After the revelation that I had been abused, the Lord and I spent many hours biking through the maze of protective defenses my heart had built. Gradually, I was introduced to the word "vulnerability." I didn't want to hear about being defenseless. No way! However, in spite of all my resistance, His love and persistence prevailed. He said He knew best . . . my heart didn't. At this juncture, my protective heart only wanted to remain in a safe place. Nevertheless, the Lord selected unique, uncomfortable moments and situations where I was forced to make a choice. I could either continue protecting or begin to become whole. I chose wholeness. The healing began!

2) A *Suspicious* Heart Piece: I found myself dealing with another word besides "vulnerability." The Lord would not allow us to skirt around the word "suspicion" with our bike. In fact, we had to stop the bike and examine the word. Suspicion is described as distrust, mistrust, disbelief, and wariness. He made me realize that I was suspicious of most motives of others and that betrayal had fueled the fire for a suspect posture toward the world around me. Suspicion is like an open sore that affects all relationships and leaves a person lonely and standing alone. The Lord took me through a process of why, when and where I became suspicious in any given situation. By doing this, I was able to set aside my preconceived ideas that most people are not worthy of trust, and begin

❦

to engage in analyzing and using deductive reasoning to come up with a counter response. A positive response! People, for the most part, are innately good. They are certainly not scheming and calculating their next offensive moves to prove that we, who are hurting, should never trust. The abused person views life through a filter of suspicion and thus builds walls for protection. But the world doesn't know that, and consequently they have no reason to build on that suspicion. Many times, suspicious people who never break out of their isolationism become trapped in their own thought processes of distrust and wariness. Begin to break out! Each step you take toward trust instead of distrust is freeing. It does take time, but I have found myself enjoying people and relationships without conditions attached. Don't be afraid to open your heart. Oh, there may be some bruises along the way, but the value of possessing a free spirit and wholeness will far outweigh any costs.

The healing continued.

3) A *Controlling* Heart Piece: When a person is abused, they feel powerless. The control over one's life, their heart and their soul has been overpowered and taken away by another person. They feel helpless and out of control. Their life-long goal, then, is to gain back that sense of control. Thus, very often, abused people will place themselves in an environment where control is easily accessible and manipulated. An environment of perfectionism is one form of control. Creating perfect surroundings makes one feel safe, and creates a sense of being in control of their lives. It can also be debilitating. We don't live in a perfect world, and to assume that one can control all aspects of life to perfection is simply an unrelenting task. It will never happen. I am a perfectionist! My perfectionism and control is evidenced in the following ways: I like order, neatness, exactness and precision . . . I am meticulous and particular about most things. It could be termed, in a sense, bondage. However, I do feel more comfortable when I am operating within those parameters. Once again to God's credit, I can forego that need to create a perfect surrounding if need be. Ask my husband! We obviously did not have a perfectly ordered world during those many, many building projects. I'm wondering, is it possible that God could use "perfectionism" that is a part of my shattered heart for good? I pray so! Still working on this area, but 98% there.

4) An *Angry* Heart Piece: Anger, in itself, is not wrong. It is actually sent as a messenger to warn us of a problem in our lives. To heed this message is wise, but very often we don't. Instead, we become entrenched in the emotion of anger until it escalates out of control. Therefore, the way we respond to anger is key to the situation. Simply put, what we do with anger will either cause the anger to become troublesome and problematic, or it can help us in facing the situation and resolving the cause. Uncontrolled anger is definitely a sin.

My anger rose to rage when confronted with the truth of my abuse. As my memory of this event became more lucid, I was slapped with another realization. I was awakened to the fact that sexual verbal abuse was included in this package of pain I had to deal with. Memory after memory came tumbling from the recesses of my brain, and to say it was disconcerting is stating it mildly. It is quite astounding how repressed those memories had become. My rage escalated! I confronted this person and I do believe if I had possessed a gun, I would have shot him, so great was my rage.

As time went on, the tandem bike ride through anger became too bumpy, too rough and potholed for me to hold on. So, He held onto me and He never let go. He encouraged me. He embraced me and said: *"Give me your anger."* Of course, that was asking the impossible. Didn't I have a right to be angry? Didn't I have a right to be filled with hate? Yes and no. Yes, I had a right to experience the anger, but only to the point of facing the problem and working toward a solution. No, I did not have a right to let rage consume my entire being. You see, when we hold onto anger, as a right, we only hurt ourselves. We are not hurting the person who violated us. They simply go on with their lives. We, on the other hand, remain crippled by the sin of unrelinquished anger. I began to see the severity of the damage I was creating for my own soul. I relinquished. Once and for all, I gave my anger, my rage, to the one who calms the seas of life—and healing continued.

5) A *Worthless* Heart Piece: It is an overwhelming fact that when a person is sexually abused, they experience shame. Shame crowds out self-esteem in the abused person and leaves the heart of that person feeling worthless. Very often they feel marked for life . . . stained and damaged. Even though the abuse was no fault of their own, the shame creates feelings of self-contempt. Consequently, rejection then becomes a huge emotion often encountered, especially when the abused reject themselves. And, they automatically assume others reject them as well. When shame and guilt strip away a person's dignity and sense of personhood, they are left feeling worthless. Restoring this shattered piece of an abused heart requires learning to trust again. My bike ride through this open wound in my heart was especially difficult. Trust is the hope that we will never be destructively hurt again and, for me, it meant pulling down all those protective walls as I gave my soul to another. Healing came slowly, but today I believe I can honestly say that the word "worthless" has become a foreign word. God was my refuge and I ran to Him many times for comfort, restoration, fulfillment, encouragement, and healing. It also helped to have the most wonderful husband in the world!

God sees us whole, complete; restored with a purpose so grand that the scope of God's love and confidence in us should thrill us, as stated in Jeremiah 29:11 (NIV): "For I know the plans I have for you, declares the Lord, plans to prosper you and not to harm you, plans to give you hope and a future." How grand is that? I chose to see how God beholds my life and never again give the abuser power to diminish my life in any way. Healing came in the form of warm oil, poured on an open wound in my shattered heart, from my heavenly Father's storehouse of grace and love. He no longer sees a shattered heart but a whole heart. He took my broken heart and mended those scattered and shattered pieces into one complete, whole heart again. I am jubilant that God would care so passionately about my healing.

No matter what the past has held for any one of us, we do have a future in Him. Let Him rejoice over your life! He has promised to!

The Lord your God is with you,
he is mighty to save.
He will take great delight in you,
He will quiet you with his love,
He will rejoice over you with singing.

ZEPHANIAH 3:17 NIV

Whose opinion really counts when it comes to our self-worth anyway? Yours, mine, others' or God's? God bases our worth on Who He is, not on who we are . . . not on *what* we have but *Who* we have, Jesus. Not on past experiences but on a hopeful future. He bases our worth on His grace, His free gift of salvation and the work He accomplishes through His forgiveness. Healing for a worthless heart comes when we begin to realize what we possess through Him and how He views our lives:

We are no longer in condemnation (Romans 8:1).

We are justified (Romans 5:1).

We will never be abandoned (Hebrews 13:5).

We have an abundant, incorruptible inheritance (I Peter 1:4).

We are members of His Kingdom (Colossians 1:13).

We possess every spiritual blessing (Ephesians 1:3).

We are victorious (Revelation 21:7).

We are loved with an everlasting love (Jeremiah 31:3).

We have been set free (John 8:32.36).

We are more than conquerors (Romans 8:37).

We are healed by His stripes (I Peter 2:24).

❧

We are complete in Him (Colossians 2:10).
We are the apple of His eye (Psalm 17:8).
(All verses taken from the Kings James Version)

FORGIVENESS

True healing comes when we forgive! There's no other way. I may fool myself into thinking that the protective, suspicious, controlling, angry and worthless heart pieces are gone, and that healing has taken place, but those shattered pieces will raise their ugly heads when given an opportunity if I have not truly forgiven. ***God heals, but we are the ones who must forgive others.*** Forgiveness is a process of restoration—from a powerless, fragmented and abused soul to the completeness and wholeness that we so desire. How do we get there when the pain is so deep? How do we forgive when the abuse is so unjust?

Most importantly, we need to remind ourselves that forgiveness is a choice, a matter of the will and not our emotions. However, what we do with forgiveness certainly does affect our emotions. As hard as forgiving another is (especially for the pain of abuse), it is a command from our heavenly Father:

> *Then Peter came to Jesus and asked,*
> *"Lord, how many times shall I forgive my brother*
> *when he sins against me?*
> *Up to seven times?"*
> *Jesus answered, "I tell you, not seven times,*
> *but seventy-seven times."*
> MATTHEW 18:21,22 NIV

Whoa! Can it be? Yes! Seventy-seven times puts forgiveness into a whole new perspective, and Jesus doesn't stop there. He also states: "For if you forgive men when they sin against you, your heavenly Father will also forgive you. But if you do not forgive men their sins, your Father will not forgive your sins" (Matthew 6:14 NIV). To forgive is a choice . . . a matter of the will. Forgiveness, in the eyes of Jesus, is not an option, but a command. Conversely, choosing unforgiveness is synonymous with disobedience. Jesus operates within the rules He has forever established. Disobedience equals sin. Obedience equals healing. Becoming defiant and disobeying was not a choice I wanted to make. That would only heap guilt on top of an already emotional struggle to become whole. I chose to forgive . . . unconditionally and wholeheartedly.

In time, I felt my heart returning to completeness. *Those fragments of my crushed flower heart were beginning to meld together and blossom into an emotionally healthy vessel that contained the fragrance of His grace . . . that grace that never let me go while we ventured into this darkness of my soul and brought me to a place of triumph.* Our bike returned from this trek with bike bells ringing and victory flags flying from both handlebars. His grace is more than marvelous; it's awesome. My soul is free.

Max Lucado once wrote:

> "Where the grace of God is missed, bitterness is born.
> But where the grace of God is embraced, forgiveness flourishes.
> You will never be called upon,
> To give anyone more grace than God has already given you."[1]

God is always a ready participant in all our journeys and we have only to look to the sidelines to hear His thunderous ovations and encouraging cheers. He is forever for us, not against us . . . for our healing, our success, our wholeness, our happiness, our joy and especially our fruitfulness that He can use for His glory.

This adventure was over! I never, ever thought I would travel down such an immensely significant, overwhelmingly painful and dreadfully soul-searching process to reach wholeness.

"Thank you Lord for healing my shattered heart. Thank you Lord for blessing my life with your constant presence. Thank you Lord for journeying

"together" with me through the muck and mire of my past. Thank you Lord for taking me out of that darkness and bringing light into my soul. I will forever and ever be grateful to you. Thank you for wholeness . . . thank you for the peace I have received. Thank you for giving me the grace to forgive . . . now I am free."

He replied: *"You are welcome; we did it 'in concert.' "*

"I Love You Lord."

"And I love you, my daughter."

> *You have seen me tossing and turning throughout the night.*
> *You have collected all my tears in your bottle!*
> *You have recorded every one in your book.*
>
> PSALM 56:8 TLB

OUR HEALER

Only a wounded Lord and Savior, because of Calvary and His graciousness, is capable of taking the shattered pieces of a protective, suspicious, controlling, angry and worthless heart to a place of healing and wholeness. Pain and suffering are words that He is familiar with, and the Apostle Paul expresses the following:

> *For we have a high priest*
> *who is touched with the feelings of our infirmities.*
>
> HEBREWS 4:15 KJV

Infirmities. What are infirmities? A good description is weaknesses or lack of strength, physically or emotionally. Not only is Jesus touched by our infirmities—He is also intimately touched by our feelings. Feelings such as anxiety, depression, loneliness, rejection, anger, fear, hurt, pain, or turmoil cause Jesus to be concerned and to be touched by those feelings.

Jesus is able to identify with our humanity for the following reasons. Since He was tempted and tested at every turn of the road, we can be assured that we have a great Savior and advocate who is more than able to understand and feel our infirmities.

1) In the garden of Gethsemane, Jesus was no stranger to sorrow: "My soul is exceeding sorrowful, even unto death" (Matthew 26:37-38 KJV). Those feelings and emotions while praying must have been excruciating. Talk about agony!! He was also no stranger to desertion: After asking His disciples to watch with Him for one hour, ". . . all the disciples forsook Him and eventually fled" (Matthew 26:56 KJV). Remind yourself, when you feel deserted, rejected and lonely, that Jesus suffered the same—and at the hands of His disciples, no less.

2) While our Lord was on trial, listening and enduring false testimony, He endured the following: "They spit in His face and buffeted Him and others smote Him" (Matthew 26:67 KJV). "They mocked Him . . . struck Him on the face" (Luke 22:63 KJV). Debased, demeaned, degraded and humiliated are all words that have caused Jesus much pain and grief. How is it that He suffered this agony alone? How is it that God loved us to such a degree that He would allow His Son to experience this dishonor? Our finite minds are simply powerless to grasp a love so noble.

3) There are no possible words to describe and express the array of powerful emotions Jesus experienced on the cross. I am certainly not theologically qualified to even attempt such a task. However, the disciple Matthew and the prophet Isaiah have given us some insight into His anguish. The crowd mocked, scoffed and derided Him: "If thou be the Son of God, come down from the cross" (Matthew 27:40 KJV). "He was oppressed, and He was afflicted, yet He opened not his mouth: He is brought as a lamb to the slaughter . . ." (Isaiah 53:7 KJV). "He shall see the travail of his soul, and shall be satisfied: by his knowledge shall my righteous servant justify many, for he shall bear their iniquities"

(Isaiah 53:11KJV). Isaiah also very aptly continues to give us a clearer picture of His suffering: "He hath no form nor comeliness; and when we shall see Him, there is no beauty that we should desire Him. He is despised and rejected of men; a Man of sorrows, and acquainted with grief; and we hid as it were our faces from Him, He was despised, and we esteemed Him not" (Isaiah 53:2-3 KJV).

Can you imagine that Jesus was actually forsaken by His heavenly Father? "My God, My God, why hast thou forsaken me?" (Matthew 27:46 KJV). "Yet it pleased the Lord to bruise him; he hath put him to grief . . ." (Isaiah 53:10 KJV). That was for you! That was for me! Heaven must have been silent; the angel's singing hushed, as God endured the pain of seeing His only Son suffer this dreadful and ghastly murder.

Be assured that Jesus knows and understands the feelings of our infirmities. He understands because He has experienced them. Thank you, Jesus, for Your healing power given to us so freely because of Your death upon Calvary!

But he was wounded for our transgressions,
he was bruised for our iniquities:
the chastisement of our peace was upon him;
and with his stripes we are healed.

ISAIAH 53:5 KJV

4) The Resurrection of Jesus speaks of power! And without the resurrection, Christianity would not exist. He arose with victory and mighty power over His foes. He left His woundedness, His pain, His humiliation, His grief, and ascended to His Father. The one thing He carried with Him was His feelings for our infirmities, so that He could identify with our humanity. He is able to divinely connect with our pain through the power of His resurrection and earthly suffering.

5) Jesus, in His love, did not leave us comfortless: "And I will pray the Father, and he shall give you another Comforter, that he may abide with you for ever" (John 14:16 NIV). That Comforter is the blessed Holy Spirit. Jesus knew our humanity would need the conviction and comfort of a greater power. He didn't send the Holy Spirit to tell us to "buck up," to "just keep a stiff upper lip." Or, "toughen up." I suppose those behaviors can be important at appropriate times in our lives, but Jesus' plan was to send a comforter, an encourager, someone who would embrace us as well as correct us. The Holy Spirit is a precious presence and friend:

> *I will talk to the Father,*
> *and he'll provide you another Friend*
> *so that you will always have someone with you.*
> *This Friend is the Spirit of Truth.*
> *The godless world can't take him in*
> *because it doesn't have eyes to see him,*
> *doesn't know what to look for.*
> *But you know him already*
> *because he has been staying with you,*
> *and will even be **in** you.*
>
> JOHN 14:16 MSG

INSIGHTS

1) **My healing was terribly costly!** Very often, when we ask God for healing, we so selfishly ask without considering what it cost. This bike ride, taken with Jesus, made me aware of my selfishness. As I began to consider the price that He paid, I was overwhelmed with such an awesome love that would sacrifice so willingly for all of us. It is an incomprehensible knowledge that He was wounded so severely for me. He so devotedly partnered with me through this ghastly disclosure and never once gave any inkling of wanting to "walk away" and leave me floundering. I'm sure I gave Him plenty of reason to. He so very faithfully

and lovingly took each fragmented piece of my heart and settled for nothing but healing and victory. What a God we serve!

"Lord, how is it that You so willingly paid such a terrible price for my healing?"

My Savior replied: *"It is because I was sent to do my Father's will and because my love for you is so far greater—greater than any other love you will ever know—that I was willing to suffer and pay this price for you."*

"I am so humbled that I am speechless and stand in awe of Your love," I answered.

He said: *"Just use the love and healing I give you to embrace and help others."*

"I will, Lord, with Your help and gifts of mercy and compassion. I love You!"

"And I love you, my daughter."

2) Forgiveness is one of the most difficult ventures I've ever taken. I surely did not want to forgive. I wanted to be angry. The corridor to forgiveness was a long and arduous pathway through pain. Ultimately, the Lord made it very explicit and unmistakable that to receive forgiveness, I must give forgiveness. This is His imperative and, to be accountable, I surrendered. I am so happy I did, for my soul has been set free.

3) His desire is for wholeness. From the beginning, in the womb, God sees a "complete" and finished product. It is not His desire for us to stand before Him one day behind schedule in the "under construction" division of our lives. So, He perseveres and aims for a "completed package." A lot of that, of course, depends on us, but He never tires in His task. Perfection, of course, will have to wait until we see Him face-to-face.

4) You and I are so very important to Him. God designed each of us and, after He made you, He threw away the mold. After He made me, He threw away the mold. Every characteristic about each one of us is matchless: our laugh, our smile, our mannerisms, our voice, our facial features, our viewpoints on life, our emotions, our intellect . . . anything that is special to you and to me. He planned our distinctiveness and each person is important to His kingdom. The following is David's perspective on our importance:

> *Oh yes, you shaped me first inside, then out;*
> *you formed me in my mother's womb.*
> *I thank you, High God—you're breathtaking!*
> *Body and soul, I am marvelously made!*
> *I worship in adoration—what a creation!*
> *You know me inside and out,*
> *you know every bone in my body;*
> *you know exactly how I was made, bit by bit,*
> *how I was sculpted from nothing into something.*
> *Like an open book,*
> *you watched me grow from conception to birth;*
> *all the stages of my life were spread out before you,*
> *the days of my life all prepared*
> *before I'd even lived one day.*
>
> PSALM 139:13-16 MSG

EMOTIONAL WHOLENESS
AS A STRONG STEM OF HIS GRACE

In the process of developing a strong stem of emotional wholeness out of which will blossom the fruit of the Spirit, we must find those areas in our lives that need pruning and healing. Giving to God those undesirable areas of our lives, and allowing Him to cut those areas away, provides opportunity for growth. Each one of us is diverse . . . diverse in personality, parental upbringing, environmental influences, Christian influences, education and academic influence. Whatever you "bring to the table" is a composite of you, who you are, what you believe, what affects you and what you are capable of. Ask the Lord to reveal to you those areas that need a "makeover." I can assure you that the Lord is more than willing and capable of healing and restoring those problem areas to wholeness. Emotional wholeness is key to our spiritual progress and development. It is definitely key to how He can and will use our lives.

An Addendum:
CHASING THE PHANTOMS OF THE PAST

While writing this chapter, I thought I was going to die—literally. Reliving past hurts can open old wounds, and I became so emotionally entrenched that I found myself on a dreadful physical and psychological journey of relentless pain. This journey started nearly a year or so ago as I was writing this chapter. I'm not one to blame everything on Satan, but just between you and me, he knew this chapter was about to be written and that was not a "go" for him. I'm sure that in the enemy's mind, there was a possibility that others may receive encouragement from my story. Also, and most importantly to his demons, this was an attempt to destroy me . . . and I do mean destroy. This became an opportunity to attack!

In December of '07, I had the "mother" of all colds. I had gotten a flu shot and directly after that I was the sickest, I think, in my lifetime. My family counted 20-some cold sores on my lips. I had bronchitis so severe that the pulmonary doctor put me on Prednisone (a steroid), the nebulizer every four hours, along with a cortisone atomizer. Previous to this sickness, I had contracted a bronchial problem in November and I was given a Zpack . . . a strong 3-4 day antibiotic. The problem subsided until the serious sickness in December. From December '07 to April '08, I had difficulty breathing. The cold had subsided, so the pulmonary doctor concluded that my problem was stress-related. I didn't feel stressed, but apparently I was, because while driving, I would often have to stop the car, get out and walk before I could take a deep breath.

I had a stress test, an oxygen level test, a chest x-ray, and the entire gamut of yearly exams and tests that doctors require. In every test, I was happily normal.

In May, it was suggested that my problem was "adrenal fatigue." That being said, one of the main responsibilities of the adrenal glands is to produce cortisol. However, when we ask our adrenal glands to chronically sustain high cortisol levels, they eventually become fatigued. Evidently, I was overwhelming my cortisol and adrenaline production with emotional distress, and all the remaining hormones that the adrenal glands produce were not happily coexisting together. I was put on a regimen of vitamins including rhodiola force (an adaptogen for stress) to counteract the effects of stress-related symptoms. Unfortunately, since I am so highly allergic to most interventions, my intake was reduced to Vitamin C and a multivitamin that I was able to tolerate. For around a month, I felt rather well.

That month was too good to be true. I knew that what I was experiencing was not life-threatening, but nevertheless, to me, it was traumatic. Anxiety became a familiar foe, and then the anxiety began to escalate to panic attacks. I had never had a panic attack and didn't have a clue what I was dealing with. If you have never had a panic attack, then you are unable to relate. Some of the symptoms are rapid heart rate, sweating, trembling, hyperventilation, chills, nausea, abdominal cramping, headache, faintness and a sense of impending death. I experienced just about all of those symptoms (sometimes some and sometimes all). I felt as though the spiritual forces of darkness were descending upon my very soul and I have never known such fear. Fear enveloped me to such a degree that I felt "frozen" . . . I couldn't move. Never do I want to know such terror again, or the need to cry out in anguish for help. Jesus told us in I John 4:18 KJV: "There is no fear in love; but perfect love drives out fear." Therefore, it's not hard to deduce where the fear was coming from.

Panic attacks can last for only 10 minutes or for as long as 30 minutes to a day (off and on). They can happen almost any time without warning. I pray you never encounter one! I am praying for deliverance. By the time this book is finished, I pray I will never again have known nor ever will know another panic attack. As I said, I am not one to blame everything on Satan. But, for certain, he uses every area of our lives, every event, every happening, every sickness, every thought, every attempt to serve the Lord, every door left ajar, every world catastrophe, every unforgiveness, every disobedience, and every sin to "bring us down." Satan's one desire is to destroy by deceiving and placing fear in our hearts. But . . . then, there is Jesus! "The Lord is my rock and my fortress and my deliverer; My God, my strength, in whom I will trust; my shield and the horn of my salvation, my stronghold" (Psalm 18:2 KJV). I stand on the "Rock" of my salvation!

As for Satan, the following aptly applies—his day is coming:

> *And the devil that deceived them,*
> *was cast into the lake of fire and brimstone,*
> *where the beast and the false prophet are,*
> *and shall be tormented day and night for ever and ever.*

REVELATION 20:10 KJV

I spent most of 2008-2009 trying to recover from stress, anxiety, panic attacks, adrenal fatigue and fear. Then, I was hit with another condition called IBS (translated means "Irritable Bowel Syndrome"). The panic attacks and anxiety had so irritated my digestive system that it no longer functioned normally. On any given day, I might experience anxiety, pain in my stomach, stomach spasms, diarrhea, chills, trembling, nausea and hyperventilation or all of the mentioned. I lost 43 lbs. in a short period of time due to the medication (which in the end I was unable to take due to the side effects). I have a drugstore in my house from the many medications doctors gave me to ease my discomfort. The bottom line: I was unable to use any of them. The various side effects from the medications were almost worse than the symptoms from the IBS. Due to trying all of the medications, I completely lost my appetite (even the smell of food made me sick). Thus, the weight loss! From December '08 through June '09, IBS had controlled my life. I have had every test imaginable and thankfully every test has come back negative.

In late June, we happened upon a prescription that calmed my stomach spasms so that I could, once again, enjoy food. In fact, it was such a quick recovery, that I gained back 15 lbs. in a month and a half. God is good!

TRUTHS OBSERVED

. . . That in any given situation in our lives, Satan desires to capitalize on our weaknesses. The panic attacks brought fear—"dark" fear, overwhelming fear—and I had to resist Satan's attempts to control me with that fear. I overcame by quoting scripture, rebuking Satan, singing, and learning breathing techniques to control hyperventilation and anxiety. I stood my ground! Even though physical weakness became overpowering at times, I stood my ground with the help of my husband, my daughter and the intercessors in my church. God has blessed me through their lives. I am stronger today (August of '09) and God is still holding my hand through the remainder of my recovery.

. . . That God desired to perform a little pruning in my thought life. My negative thinking had to undergo some serious surgery. I was given the assignment to "trash" every negative thought into the garbage and immediately replace that thought with a positive one. Easier said than done, but I think I can say, "I'm getting there." He chose to perform this pruning during my sickest moments of the first six months of 2009. Only His grace kept me on course. At the time it seemed unfair, but God always knows how to get our attention. The next chapter reveals more on this topic of negativity.

. . . Thirdly, that word *trust* imposed itself on me again. Did I trust God to see me through this, or was I going to fear and worry? At my lowest moments, I knew I had to say: "I trust you, Lord." Confessing and willing myself to believe His Word helped me climb over this mountain of sickness.

"Bless the Lord, O my soul: and all that is within me, bless his holy name.

"Bless the Lord, O my soul, and forget not all his benefits.

"Who *forgiveth* all thine iniquities; who *healeth* all thy diseases.

"Who *redeemeth* thy life from destruction; who *crowneth* thee with lovingkindness and tender mercies.

"Who *satisfieth* thy mouth with good things; so that thy youth is renewed like the eagle's" (Psalm 103:1-5 KJV).

THAT is something to trust in!!

I end this chapter not embarrassed, but humbled. Writing is a soul-searching process and I have tried to be as honest as possible. I remind myself that at the end of every storm there is a rainbow somewhere. That weeping may endure for a night, but joy comes in the morning. That He creates beauty out of ashes. That there is always a light at the end of the tunnel. That it is always darkest just before the dawn. That the Lord is my shepherd; I shall not want. That goodness and mercy shall follow me all the days of my life. That my expectation is from Him. That He will direct my paths. That He will never leave me nor forsake me. That we shall go out with joy and be led forth with peace. That we are rooted and built up in Him . . . and umpteen other promises and a few quips that have helped me to "look up." Occasionally, I paste them on my mirror where I am forced to read each and every one, every morning.

You may find yourself today encircled by darkness due to your past. Or, your present! Darkness knows no bounds. It is like a slithering snake looking for an opportunity to strike. Be brave. Grasp His hand and hold on for dear life. Close all those doors that give Satan entry, work through those strongholds, give your pain to Him and then . . . rejoice in your salvation!

Be strong and of good courage,
do not fear nor be afraid of them;
for the Lord your God,
He is the One who goes with you.
He will not leave you
nor forsake you.

DEUTERONOMY 31:6 KJV

Fear not . . . for all things work together for good. He has promised! **Yes, this chapter was all a test for me.** Waiting, submitting, trusting and abiding were all travels the Lord and I had gone through together. I refused to have those roots questioned or uprooted. I would not fear! It was a battle, but amidst the "panic" the Lord refused to allow me to "give in" or to "give up," even though I wanted to die, so great was the spiritual warfare. "The Lord is my light and my salvation; whom shall I fear? The Lord is the strength of my life; of whom shall I be afraid?" (Psalm 27:1 NIV).

He is so gracious to:

Heal the brokenhearted,
To proclaim liberty to the captives,
And the opening of the prison to those who are bound,
To comfort all who mourn,
To console those who mourn in Zion.

ISAIAH 61:1-3 KJV

In my next adventure, I deal with the battlefield of the mind . . .

CHAPTER V
Application & Review

The pathway to emotional health can often become a thorny corridor into pain. How exciting and reassuring to know that Jesus not only travels through that corridor with us, but, as we break through darkness into His light, He is waiting with open arms to bring healing—to bring wholeness.

1. Has your heart been shattered? How? Are you able to name those shattered pieces that are preventing you from experiencing wholeness? If so, list them.

2. Has betrayal been a part of your life? In what way has this taken place?

3. What does Zephaniah 3:17 say about you? For clarity, read the NIV translation.

4. In Matthew 18:21-22 (NIV), how many times does Jesus say we are to forgive? What does forgiveness mean to you?

5. Has someone sinned against you? Have you forgiven them? Read Matthew 6:14-15.

6. How are we to use the comfort given to us by the Lord, as stated in II Corinthians 1:3-4? Give an example from your own life.

CHAPTER VI

The Pathway to Mental Health

Developing a Renewed Mind

And be transformed
by the renewing of your mind . . .

ROMANS 12:2 KJV

CHAPTER VI

The Pathway to Mental Health
Developing a strong stem of a disciplined mind

Thou wilt keep him in perfect peace
whose mind is stayed on thee:
because he trusteth in thee.

ISAIAH 26:3 KJV

e stopped the tandem bike. We needed to rest. We needed to talk. It's hard to converse while avoiding potholes and winding around pitfalls. We found a sidewalk café where we could chain up our bike. I ordered a tea. He ordered water. What next? I knew, really, but didn't want to mention it. The fellowship was so sweet, the rest so relaxing. We talked about the past journeys; the roots established, the healing, and the spiritual insight I had gained. I thanked Him for His continued grace and strength. And then, it was time. I glanced at the bike and then I glanced at my best Friend. He spoke first and said it was time to go. I hesitantly stood and slowly walked to our bike. One consolation . . . this excursion would (hopefully) be the last bike ride for a while. We had come through some hard travels; however, the one ahead was going to be a "toughie." How would He help me transform my mind . . . to discipline my thinking? The road lies ahead and the answers are known only to Him. We, once again, strap on our bike helmets and ride into the sunset. Where would it lead?

THE BATTLE OF THE MIND

Having our minds renewed is not a one-time event. It is a process that often requires considerable time to conquer. The pruning process is immediate but the growth process into fruitfulness is sometimes slow. For me, it had taken a lifetime of negative thinking to necessitate this bike ride of (almost) reprimand. If I were to ask you, "where does Satan attack first," what would your answer be? If you said "the mind," you are so right. Your mind is the doorway to your heart, and it is here that those seeds of negativity must be stopped before they enter and gravely affect our hearts. We must intuitively keep the door to our heart closed and protected from evil. The enemy knows we belong to God forever, but that does not stop him from attacking our minds through negative thinking, discouragement, lies, and deceitfulness. Satan wants to remind you of your failures, your sinfulness and even any forgiven ungodliness in your past or in your present. He wants to remind you of past hurts and abuses. His plan is to condemn and set up strongholds or fortresses in our minds that he can use against us again and again.

> A stronghold starts with a thought;
> A thought becomes an idea;
> An idea becomes an attitude;
> An attitude becomes an action;
> Action, if repeated, becomes a habit, and
> A habit becomes a STRONGHOLD.[1]
>
> MARILEE HORTON / WALTER BYRD, M.D.

A Thought → Idea → Attitude → Action → Habit → Stronghold
. . . that's the progression for negative thinking. I needed a scolding as to my negativity and I knew that it was in the forecast. But, from past experiences, I also knew He would tenderly reprimand and not strip away my self-confidence. Understanding that He would never leave me nor forsake me, I gained the strength to stay on the bike, and to emotionally and mentally struggle through tunnels, up mountains and across rivers to master this impediment in my thinking. We need to leave past habits behind and strive for a renewed mind as the following scripture states:

> *But one thing I do:*
> *Forgetting what is behind*
> *and straining toward what is ahead,*
> *I press on toward the goal*
> *to win the prize for which God has called*
> *me heavenward in Christ Jesus.*
>
> PHILIPPIANS 3:13-14 NIV

SPEAKING AND CONFESSING

First and foremost, He would teach me the importance of "speaking the Word of God and confessing His truth."

To have our minds renewed, to change learned behaviors and wrong thinking patterns, we must know the Word of God and use it to counter-attack the darts that Satan so freely throws at us. We must speak and confess with our mouth the truth of God's Word if we are to defeat the enemy of our soul. This is God's reprimand to me, and one of the lessons I will be learning on this uphill journey of renewing the mind. I say "will be" because, upon reflection, I have observed that there is a preponderance of anecdotal evidence regarding my progress. I'm still "under construction," and definitely a "work in progress" in this battle of the mind. Old habits die hard! The following verse is the first truth He presented to me to use in this speaking and confessing program.

> *Submit therefore to God.*
> *Resist the devil*
> *and he will flee from you.*
>
> JAMES 4:7 KJV

Satan's strategy is to besiege and barrage our thoughts to the point of wearing down our resistance. He will just keep hammering away at our defenses in this most difficult area of spiritual warfare. The Word tells us to resist the enemy by ". . . bringing into captivity every thought to

❦

the obedience of Christ" (II Corinthians 10:5 KJV). We are to take each thought and evaluate it against the Word of God as to its truth or as to its misrepresentation of truth. If our thoughts are misrepresentations, then those thoughts are to be refused, resisted and rejected. Satan stalks us, looking for ways to corrupt our minds, increase negativity and encourage a stronghold in our lives. Therefore, "Be vigilant; because your adversary the devil, as a roaring lion, walketh about, seeking whom he may devour" (I Peter 5:8 KJV). Guard your mind with His Word.

JESUS VS. SATAN

The most practical outworking of resisting the devil and using God's Word as a rebuttal is recorded and modeled in Matthew 4:1-11 NIV.

1) Then Jesus was led up by the Spirit into the desert to be tempted by the devil.
2) After fasting forty days and forty nights, He was hungry.
3) The tempter came to Him and said: "If You are the Son of God, tell these stones to become bread."
4) Jesus answered, "It is written, 'MAN DOES NOT LIVE ON BREAD ALONE, BUT ON EVERY WORD THAT COMES FROM THE MOUTH OF GOD.'"
5) Then the devil took Him into the holy city; and he had Him stand on the highest point of the temple. "If you are the Son of God," he said, "throw yourself down, for it is written: 'He will command His angels concerning you, and they will lift you up in their hands, so that you will not strike your foot against a stone.'"
6) Jesus answered him, "It is also written: 'DO NOT PUT THE LORD YOUR GOD TO THE TEST.'"
7) Again, the devil took Him to a very high mountain, and showed Him all the kingdoms of the world, and their splendor; "All this I will give you," he said, "if you will bow down and worship me."

🌿

8) Jesus said to him, "Away from me Satan! For it is written: 'WOR-SHIP THE LORD YOUR GOD, AND SERVE HIM ONLY.' "

9) Then the devil left Him; and the angels came and attended him.

The following account of Matthew 4:1-11 is taken from *The Message*, which I found to have more of a modern presentation of this ancient event in Christ's life.

"Next, Jesus was taken into the wild by the Spirit for the Test. The Devil was ready to give it. Jesus prepared for the Test by fasting forty days and forty nights. That left Him, of course, in a state of extreme hunger, which the Devil took advantage of in the first test: "Since you are God's Son, speak the word that will turn these stones into loaves of bread."

Jesus answered by quoting Deuteronomy: *"It takes more than bread to stay alive. It takes a steady stream of words from God's mouth."* (Deuteronomy 8:3 MSG)

For the second test the Devil took Him to the Holy City. He sat Him on top of the Temple and said, "Since you are God's Son, jump." The Devil goaded Him by quoting Psalm 91: "He has placed you in the care of angels. They will catch you so that you won't so much as stub your toe on a stone."

Jesus countered with another citation from Deuteronomy: *"Don't you dare test the Lord your God."* (Deuteronomy 6:16 MSG)

For the third test, the Devil took Him on the peak of a huge mountain. He gestured expansively, pointing out all the earth's kingdoms, how glorious they all were. Then he said, "They're yours—lock, stock, and barrel. Just go down on your knees and worship me, and they're yours."

Jesus' refusal was curt: *"Beat it, Satan!"* He backed His rebuke with a third quotation from Deuteronomy: *"Worship the Lord your God, and only him. Serve him with absolute single-heartedness."*

❧

(Deuteronomy 6:13 MSG)

The Test was over. The Devil left. And in his place, angels! Angels came and ministered to Jesus' needs.

Satan persisted in his attempt to lure Jesus into sin. He was relentless in his endeavor to wear Jesus down. Jesus never gave in to the enemy. Is that a lesson for us, or what? His Word tells us to resist the Devil over and over and over again, especially when it comes to rejecting thoughts that are displeasing to God and detrimental to our emotional and mental health. He gave us that authority in His Word: "Greater is He who is in us than He who is in the world" (I John 4:4 KJV). The enemy must depart from us when we speak the name of Jesus. That doesn't mean he won't try a second, a third or a fourth time. But eventually, he'll get the message as we also say "Beat it, Satan." Enough is enough! Don't be afraid to address Satan; Jesus did. Also, don't hesitate to assert and declare the blood of Jesus over your mind: "And they overcame him because of the blood of the lamb and because of the word of their testimony . . ." (Revelation 12:11 KJV).

God cannot be tempted by evil,
nor does He Himself tempt anyone.
But each one is tempted when he is drawn away
by his own desires and enticed.
Then, when desire has conceived, it gives birth to sin;
and sin, when it is full-grown, brings forth death.
Do not be deceived, *my beloved brethren.*
Every good gift and every perfect gift is from above,
and comes down from the Father of lights,
with whom there is no variation or shadow of turning.

JAMES 1:13-17 KJV

May peace remain in our hearts as we keep our minds stayed on Him!

THINK ON THESE THINGS

Renewing the mind is particularly thorny if verbal, physical or emotional abuse has taken place. A person who has suffered in these areas has a fertile mind for Satan to grow contemptuous thoughts about themselves and others. And as you remember reading previously, a stronghold begins with a thought. It would be very easy for Satan to harass us throughout our lives if a stronghold has taken place. How do we slam that door shut and allow God to grow healthy thoughts? My abuse caused my thought processes to turn into negative thinking and I have needed to cultivate positive thoughts (but not without much anxiety and pain). But, how can God help us? By continuing to speak and confess His Word (not our contemptuous, unhealthy negative words). Paul gave us a chart to follow in Philippians.

Finally, brethren, whatsoever things are true,
whatsoever things are honest,
whatsoever things are just,
whatsoever things are pure,
whatsoever things are lovely,
whatsoever things are of good report;
if there be any virtue
and if there be any praise,
think on these things.
PHILIPPIANS 4:8 KJV

Vernon McGee depicts this portion of scripture as a concise biography of the life of Christ. In all aspects of this exacting scripture, the Lord embodies each and every attribute described.[2] We are changed into His image as we accept and behold the above characteristics. "But we all, with open face beholding as in a glass the glory of the Lord, are changed into the same image from glory to glory, even as by the spirit of the

Lord" (II Corinthians 3:18 KJV). I know of no other greater assistance in renewing the mind than observing and practicing these six traits of our Savior. I pray they will forever be embedded in our hearts and minds, creating in us acceptable qualities of servanthood and enabling us to become a little more like His image. I want so much to be positive in my thought life! Do you?

1) Whatsoever things are true: think on these things! The Lord is our truth:

    a) "Jesus saith unto him, I am the way, the truth, and the life: no man cometh unto the Father but by me" (John 14:6 KJV).

    b) "And the Word was made flesh, and dwelt among us (and we beheld his glory, the glory as of the only begotten of the Father), full of grace and truth" (John 1:14 KJV).

    c) "I am the true vine, and my Father is the husbandman" (John 15:1 KJV).

    d) "He shall cover thee with his feathers, and under His wings shalt thou trust: his truth shall be thy shield and buckler" (Psalm 91:4 KJV).

2) Whatsoever things are honest: think on these things! Jesus is honest, noble, trustworthy and praiseworthy:

    a) "God is not a man that He should lie" (Numbers 23:19 KJV).

    b) "Showing to the generation to come the praises of the Lord, and his strength, and his wonderful works that he hath done" (Psalm 78:4 KJV).

    c) "Thou art worthy, O Lord, to receive the glory and honor and power; for thou has created all things, and for thy pleasure they are and were created" (Revelation 4:11 KJV).

    d) "I will praise the Lord according to his righteousness: and will sing praise to the name of the Lord most high" (Psalm 7:17 KJV).

3) Whatsoever things are just: think on these things! Jesus is a just and fair-minded Savior:

    a)   "Justice and judgment are the habitation of thy throne . . ." (Psalm 89:14 KJV).

    b)   "And they sing the song of Moses, the servant of God, and the song of the Lamb, saying, great and marvelous are thy works, Lord God Almighty; just and true are thy ways, thou King of Saints" (Revelation 15:3 KJV).

    c)   "For Christ also hath once suffered for sins, the just for the unjust, that he might bring us to God . . ." (I Peter 3:18 KJV).

    d)   "He is the Rock, his work is perfect: for all his ways are judgment: a God of truth and without iniquity, just and right is he" Deuteronomy 32:4 KJV).

4) Whatsoever things are pure: think on these things! There is not one more pure, holy or righteous than Jesus:

    a)   "Thou art of purer eyes than to behold evil, and canst not look on iniquity" (Habakkuk 1:13 KJV).

    b)   "Beloved, now are we the sons of God, and it doth not yet appear what we shall be: but we know that, when He shall appear, we shall be like him; for we shall see him as he is. And every man that hath this hope in him purifieth himself, even as he is pure" (I John 3:2,3 KJV).

    c)   "But the wisdom that is from above is first pure, then peaceable, gentle and easy to be entreated, full of mercy and good fruits, without partiality, and without hypocrisy" (James 3:17 KJV).

    d)   "The statutes of the Lord are right, rejoicing the heart: the commandment of the Lord is pure enlightening the eyes" (Psalm 19:8 KJV).

5) Whatsoever things are lovely: think on these things! Jesus is kind, full of mercy and full of love:

    a)   "How lovely is your dwelling place, O Lord Almighty!" (Psalm 84:1 NIV).

❧❧

b) "... I have loved you with an everlasting love; I have drawn you with loving-kindness" (Jeremiah 31:3 NIV).

c) "... for you are a gracious and merciful God" (Nehemiah 9:31 NIV).

d) "All the ways of the Lord are loving and faithful . . ." (Psalm 25:10 NIV).

6) Whatsoever things are of good report: think on these things!
Jesus is full of goodness and full of good report:

a) "... they gathered the church together and reported all that God had done through them and how he had opened the door of faith to the Gentiles" (Acts 14:27 NIV).

b) "Jethro was delighted to hear about all the good things the Lord had done for Israel in rescuing them from the hand of the Egyptians" (Exodus 18:9 NIV).

c) "If you, then, though you are evil, know how to give good gifts to your children, how much more will your Father in heaven give good gifts to those who ask him!" (Matthew 7:11 NIV).

d) "Dear friend, do not imitate what is evil but what is good. Anyone who does what is good is from God. Anyone who does what is evil has not seen God" (III John 1:11 NIV).

As we were traveling along on our tandem bike, I told the Lord that I was catching a better glimpse of how He wanted me to discipline my mind. I told Him it wasn't easy to retrain one's thinking. He said: "that's why I'm traveling with you, showing you the 'ropes.'" He also said that nothing worth having in life comes easy. That I already knew, but I never thought transforming my thought life would require such constant vigilance. It stands to reason though . . . if I have thought whatever I wanted all these years, it must then take steady oversight to bring each thought under control. I'm seeing progress, though; thank you, Jesus!

We stopped the bike once again to catch our breath, while He explained the next valuable piece of information that would enable me to "stand" and not fall under the wiles of the devil as I grappled with this mind transformation ordeal. The air was crisp, clean and refreshing. We took in some deep breaths and geared ourselves for the next encounter. He, once again, graciously held my hand and assisted me as we mounted our bike. He had previously checked the tires and both were in good condition. He also checked our helmet straps, oiled the gears and adjusted our seats. It was time for another lesson. The journey continued . . . .

THE FULL ARMOR OF GOD

How many times have I read Ephesians 6? I have no idea, but there is a word—"application"—that the Lord wanted me to more fully comprehend. Apparently, I had read but not applied the verses containing the full armor of God. How many times do we read something and not fully absorb its full import? When I was in elementary school and just learning to read, comprehension was a word of great importance. We were never given an "A+" in reading class unless we comprehended (understood) what we were reading. Well, I quickly learned to comprehend . . . I wanted that "A+." But there is a vast difference between comprehending what is read and applying what is read to our lives. **Applying takes an act of the will in order for information to seep into our beings and become a part of the fabric that creates action.** To put on the full armor of God requires action. We need to apply each part of the armor in order to "stand." Protection is there, but you and I have to act upon it. The lesson was becoming clear as we traveled along on our bike.

Therefore put on the complete armor of God, so that you may be able to stand your ground in the evil day, and, having fought to the end, to remain victors on the field. Stand therefore, first fastening round you the girdle of truth and putting on the breastplate of

uprightness as well as the shoes of the gospel of peace . . . a firm foun-
dation for your feet. And besides all these, take the great shield of
faith, on which you will be able to quench all the flaming darts of
the Wicked One; and receive the helmet of salvation, and the sword
of the Spirit which is the word of God. Pray with unceasing prayer
and entreaty at all times in the Spirit, and be always on the alert to
seize opportunities for doing so. EPHESIANS 6:13-18, WEYMOUTH

Dressing in our spiritual wardrobe of truth, righteousness, peace, faith, salvation and the Word of God, we are well-equipped to stand against Satan's attempts to control our minds. In our most difficult moments, how easy it is to stand down, to relinquish our stance of readiness, to ease up on our vigilance and forget that the wardrobe given us can energize, invigorate, equip and, above all, stand the test of time. The only prerequisite to our wardrobes' usefulness is application. We can read about it, understand it, be thankful for it—but unless we wear it and apply its defensive mechanisms, it is useless to us.

LET'S GET DRESSED

A) The Girdle of Truth: Our girdle of truth is actually described as a belt, which was worn by soldiers to hold all their armor in place. The truth of this girdle is simply the story of the gospel . . . His death, burial and resurrection. It is "the truth that is in Jesus" (Ephesians 4:21 KJV) that will protect us from Satan's lies and deception. Such truths as His sovereignty, His wisdom and knowledge, His unchangeableness and His power will keep us strong while in the midst of battle. Jesus is the truth and Satan runs when he hears this declaration. Jesus said, "Then you will know the truth, and the truth will set you free" (John 8:32 KJV). "Gird up your loins" was a biblical reference to prepare for action. We should always be prepared for the attacks of Satan on our minds with the truth of His "Life."

❧

B) A Breastplate of Righteousness: I suppose a common everyday equivalent to the breastplate is the bulletproof vest worn by law enforcement officials. Its purpose was to protect the heart and vital organs. As Christians, our hearts need to be protected as well. After all, this is a warfare we are in. Righteousness is the key . . . it is our bulletproof vest. Satan wants nothing more than a chance to steal our righteousness. It is not a word that Satan wants to hear, and he can reach our hearts through our minds unless we "Keep our hearts with all vigilance . . . for out of it are the issues of life" (Proverbs 4:23 KJV).

C) Our Marching Boots: In biblical times, soldiers were very fussy about their boots. They were generally made of leather and the soles were layered with nails, or what we call today, cleats. This provided the soldier sure footing in battle. As Christians, our feet are to be shod with the gospel of peace for sure footing. Our hearts and our minds are to abide by the gospel, which includes peace with God, peace with ourselves and peace with others. "And the peace of God, which transcends all understanding, will guard your hearts and your minds in Christ Jesus" (Philippians 4:7 KJV). A peaceful heart and mind are almost impossible for Satan to penetrate.

D) The Shield of Faith: "Without faith it is impossible to please God, because anyone who comes to him must believe that he exists and that he rewards those who earnestly seek him" (Hebrews 11:6 KJV). Faith is our shield . . . it is to protect our entire body. Faith becomes a shield when applied and acted upon, and will quench those fiery darts Satan assails us with. In simple terms, faith is the belief that God is who He says He is: "For the Lord is our defense, and the Holy one of Israel is our King" (Psalm 89:18 KJV). Satan has no power to equal a Holy King.

E) The Helmet of Salvation: Our minds are protected and guarded by the gracious salvation of our Lord. Salvation is our helmet. "Putting on the

🌿

hope of salvation as a helmet" (I Thessalonians 5:8 KJV). As an active partner in this protection, we, as Christians, need to position a sentinel at the very gate to our minds ready to evict the onslaught of Satan's spiel and chatter. The devil's words are very recognizable . . . words of condemnation, lies, deceit, accusation, fear and discord. Our salvation provides a helmet of protection against such a barrage of evil. Our hope of salvation will comfort the soul and keep it from being tormented by Satan.

F) The Sword of the Spirit: The Word of God is the sword of the Spirit. Christ Himself resisted Satan's temptations with: "It is written" (Matthew 4:4-10 KJV). The Word of God is powerful and sharper than any two-edged sword. Satan cannot stand against the Word of God. Use it in prayer. Use it in battle. It is a tool that the Spirit gives us in time of need. We must act upon it. Use it to stand against Satan's darts. Satan has no authority over God's Word!

> *And that about wraps it up. God is strong, and he wants you strong. So take everything the Master has set out for you, well-made weapons of the best materials. And put them to use so you will be able to stand up to everything the Devil throws your way. This is no afternoon athletic contest that we'll walk away from and forget about in a couple of hours. This is for keeps, a life-or-death fight to the finish against the Devil and all his angels.*
>
> EPHESIANS 6:10-13 MSG

> *In the same way, prayer is essential in this ongoing warfare. Pray hard and long. Pray for your brothers and sisters. Keep your eyes open. Keep each other's spirits up so that no one falls behind or drops out.*
>
> EPHESIANS 6:18 MSG

Did you dress in your spiritual wardrobe of a soldier? Are you ready for battle? The Lord took me on this journey to point out that I was not appropriately wardrobed and that Satan's darts were finding entry rather than bouncing off. Our protection, our armor, is not complete unless we are clothed with a belt, a breastplate, shoes, a shield, a helmet and a sword. The battle for our minds can only be fought with His truth, righteousness, peace, faith, salvation, and His Word. We need to actively clothe ourselves and apply the protection He so graciously has provided. We will, most likely, have to redress and reapply many times in the future until we fully "get it." Jesus paid everything that we may employ this free gift of the Armor of God. Christians who encounter this relentless (at times) battle of the mind, especially appreciate His concern for our protection.

The Lord is a warrior,
The Lord is his name.
EXODUS 15:3 NIV

PRAISE AND WORSHIP AS A POWERFUL WEAPON

As we bicycled through the various possibilities for renewing my mind, the Lord had one more solution up His sleeve . . . praise and worship. As we praise the God of our salvation several important results take place:

1) Negative thoughts take flight. Negativity and praise cannot occupy the same space in our minds.
2) There is nothing that terrifies the Devil and his minions like praise. He will turn tail and run because praise brings the presence of our Lord. God gives us a ". . . garment of praise instead of a spirit of despair" (Isaiah 61:3 NIV).
3) Praise cleanses the soul and our faith is brought to a new level.
4) Above all, God is glorified through our praise.

Praise *the Lord*
Praise God in his sanctuary, praise him in his mighty heavens.
Praise him for his acts of power,

❧

praise him for his surpassing greatness,
Praise him with the sounding of the trumpet,
  praise him with the harp and lyre,
  praise him with tambourine and dancing,
  praise him with the clash of cymbals,
  praise him with resounding cymbals.
Let everything that has breath praise the Lord.

PSALM 150 NIV

Blessed be the Lord God, the God of Israel, who only doeth won-
drous things. And blessed be His glorious name forever: and let the
whole earth be filled with his glory; Amen, and Amen.

PSALM 72:18-19 KJV

Then sang Moses and the children of Israel this song unto the Lord,
and spake, saying, I will sing unto the Lord, for he hath triumphed
gloriously: the horse and rider hath he thrown in the sea. The Lord
is my strength and song, and he is become my salvation: he is my
God, and I will prepare him an habitation and I will exalt him.

EXODUS 15:1-2 KJV

And I beheld, and I heard the voice of many angels round about the
throne and the beasts and the elders: and the number of them was
ten thousand times ten thousand, and thousands of thousands;
Saying with a loud voice, "Worthy is the Lamb that was slain to re-
ceive power, and riches, and wisdom, and strength, and honor, and
glory, and blessing."

REV. 5:11-12 KJV

O Praise the Lord, all ye nations: praise him, all ye people. For his
merciful kindness is great toward us: and the truth of the Lord en-
dures forever. Praise ye the Lord.

PSALM 117:1-2 KJV

O come let us worship and bow down: let us kneel before the Lord
our maker.

PSALM 95:6 KJV

Exalt the Lord our God, and worship at his holy hill; for the Lord our God is holy. PSALM 99:9 KJV

A RENEWED MIND AS A STRONG STEM OF GRACE

Renewing the mind is so essential for spiritual development and spiritual health. Your mind, my mind, is a battlefield. It is especially a battlefield if our past was riddled with negativity, a critical spirit, abuse, a cloud of spiritual darkness, hurt caused by others, or any number of circumstances that Satan can use against us. One of the most powerful weapons in our arsenal is prayer:

> *"Father, I thank you that we can always overcome by the blood of the Lamb . . . especially in the area of transforming our minds. If there are areas in our lives that have been affected by our pasts, we ask you to reveal them to us so that Satan will not have access to our minds and thus his plans to destroy us will be thwarted. We ask you to protect our minds by your holy power each and every day. Help us to think on those things that are pleasing to you. When Satan comes to attack, give us your battle plan and may we always be dressed in your armor. I pray that praise will constantly be on our lips. Thank you for the precious Holy Spirit that empowers us to 'stand,' and thank you for the cross that bought our salvation at such a tremendous price. Thank you for the victory that is ours through your Son's shed blood. Amen."*

CONCLUSION TO PART TWO

As I close Part Two, I rejoice that the Lord has pressed upon me the need to use the tools He has provided for battle. I am anticipating a more transformed mind as I apply and utilize His solutions for negative thinking.

❧

This will be my last bike ride (in this book, that is). There will be more, I am sure! He will not be finished with me until the day I meet Him face to face. I am so grateful for His many lessons over the years . . . He is a superb partner and kept me topside many times. *"Thank you, Jesus, for loving me so unconditionally and making me into something that you can consider using."*

(Whew! Can I rest now?)

AND NOW . . . at this point in my travels, I am beginning to blossom into that flower that will reveal the fragrance of His grace in my life! It is the fragrance that comes from the Holy Spirit and His changing power. It does not come from me . . . I am powerless! Whatever fruit I possess . . . is His grace. It is His power and His fragrance that you are aware of. I take no credit. None!

CHAPTER VI
Application & Review

If I were to ask you, "where does Satan attack first," what would your answer be? If you said "the mind," you are so right. Your mind is the doorway to your heart; thus, it becomes a battlefield between good and evil. We must intuitively and deliberately protect our hearts by guarding our minds.

1. According to this chapter, what is the progression for negative thinking?

2. Explain the four areas for a positive, healthy thought-life as presented in this chapter.

3. Philippians 4:8 tells us to think on what things?

4. What are the four results of praise and worship explained in this chapter?

5. Name the six components of the Armor of God, as presented in Ephesians 6. What is the function of each?

PART THREE

The Blossom of His Grace
Fruitfulness

❧

*But the fruit of the Spirit is love, joy, peace,
patience, kindness, goodness, faithfulness,
gentleness and self-control.*
GALATIANS 5:22 NIV

CHAPTER VII

The Holy Spirit

Our Comforter and Guide

The Spirit itself beareth witness with our spirit, that we are the children of God. And if children, then heirs; heirs of God, and joint-heirs with Christ.

ROMANS 8:16,17 KJV

CHAPTER VII

The Holy Spirit

But ye shall receive power,
after that the Holy Spirit is come upon you,
and you will be my witnesses in Jerusalem,
and in all Judea and Samaria, and to the ends of the earth.

ACTS 1:8 KJV

The "fruit of the Spirit" is a glorious by-product of the Spirit's power and grace. The Spirit's continual process of developing and changing us into His workmanship creates channels through which God can use us. It is, as I stated in chapter I, no longer "I" but "we" together:

I have been crucified and I no longer live,
but Christ lives in me.
The life I live in the body,
I live by faith in the Son of God;
Who loved me, and gave Himself for me.

GALATIANS 2:20 NIV

It is not we who are expected to produce fruit. Thank God, for that is the job of the Holy Spirit as Christ lives through us. We simply "bear" His fruit. However, that word "abiding" is so very significant regarding the fruit of the Spirit, as stated by Rev. Charles Stanley: "The vine is Christ, I am the branch. The Holy Spirit is the sap that runs from the vine into the branches. The branch lives, grows, and bears fruit not by struggles and effort, but simply by abiding."[1] Simply by abiding!! Fruit is God's reward and the overflow of His rich investment in each of our lives:

❧❧❧

Fruit is the investment of His death on the cross for our salvation.
Fruit is the investment of His Grace in our lives.
Fruit is the investment of His pursuit of fellowship with us.
Fruit is the investment of His unconditional love.
Fruit is the investment of His workmanship in us.

Fruit, then, is any good work that glorifies God (Titus 3:14 NIV). Fruit is the outward manifestation of the inward work of the Holy Spirit in our characters that makes us more like Christ (Galatians 5:22,23 NIV).

Every tree, vine, branch and fruit-bearing object has a blossom! As you've traveled along with me on my journey, I'm curious to know how your blossom is. Are you only a small bud? Fret not—buds, when nurtured, grow rapidly; in God's time, that small bud will blossom into the fruit of His Spirit (not by struggling, but with nurturing that comes through abiding). Or, perhaps your blossom is only partly open and something seems to be holding you back. Is it possible that Satan has filled your heart with fear or is using an unsurrendered stronghold to keep you from flowering and flourishing for Him? Begin to trace your steps through your established roots, your emotional health and the renewed mind He has given you. Rebuke the enemy and cast that fear, stronghold or roadblock onto the Lord: "Casting all your care upon him; for he careth for you" (I Peter 5:7 KJV). His life, death and resurrection is meant to give us an abundant life:

> *The thief cometh not, but for to steal, and to kill, and to destroy:*
> *I am come that they might have life,*
> *and that they might have it more abundantly.*
> JOHN 10:10 KJV

Don't allow Satan to trample on your flower and thus destroy God's fruit. Believe instead in Romans 16:20, where Paul speaks of God crushing Satan under the heel of we who rely on the power of God for our hope. Stand strong; if there is a blossom, fruit is inevitable.

If, however, your blossom is flowering, then praise God! Just always bear in mind that it is the fruit of the Spirit from that blossom we are blessed with, not fruit that you or I produced. Humbleness is synonymous with meekness. If you have become proud because you possess certain fruit, then perhaps meekness is not a fruit you yet possess. Remember, the "fruit of the Spirit" is a gift, not something we can take credit for. Not in the least!!!

> *There is an orchard whose fruit is lush:*
> *Love is the definition of God.*
> *Joy is the response of those who brush the sleeve of love.*
> *Peace is the result of having all our conflicts washed in love.*
> *Patience is the art that never hurries love.*
> *Kindness is love's application.*
> *Goodness is the life grown moral by seeking love's pleasure.*
> *Faithfulness is love's servant.*
> *Gentleness is love's method.*
> *Self-control is love's submission to integrity.*[2]

As you read on, you will notice that I have chosen to use the *New International Version* of the fruit of the Spirit.

CHAPTER VII
Application & Review

The Holy Spirit is the conduit through which the Fruit of the Spirit flows. Fruit is God's gift to us, enabling us to become more productive and useful Christians. The precious Holy Spirit is our Comforter and Guide, whose work is to create acceptable channels through which Christ's life can be exemplified to the world.

1. Explain the meaning of Galatians 2:20 as it relates to producing fruit.

2. Are we expected to produce fruit? Read page 168 and fill in the following: We are simply to _____ His fruit.
   This is only possible by _____ in Christ.

3. How has God invested in our lives? Read page 169.

4. What kind of life does Jesus want to give us? Read John 10:10.

5. Name the nine fruit, and the function of each as it relates to love.

CHAPTER VIII

The Fruit of the Spirit is Love

Love is the definition of God

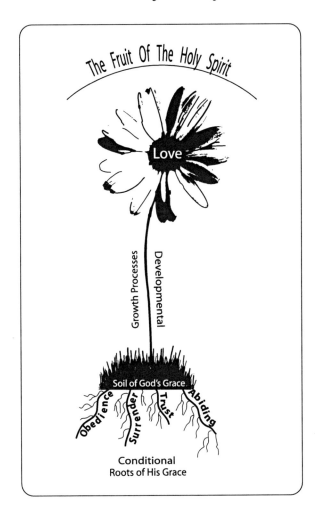

*But the greatest of these
is love.*

I CORINTHIANS 13:13B KJV

CHAPTER VIII

The Fruit of the Spirit is Love

The earth is filled with His tender love.

PSALM 33:5 TLB

I t is so absolutely and incontestably factual that LOVE is the very mo- tivation behind everything that God does and has ever done for us.

His love is immeasurable:

> *That Christ may dwell in your hearts by faith; that ye, being root- ed and grounded in love, may be able to comprehend with all saints what is the breadth, and length, and depth, and height; and to know the love of Christ, which passeth knowledge.*
>
> EPHESIANS 3:17-19 KJV

How does one measure such love?

We cannot be separated from His love:

> *For I am persuaded, that neither death, nor life, nor angels, nor principalities, nor power, nor things present, nor thing to come, nor height, nor depth, nor any other creature, shall be able to separate us from the love of God, which is in Christ Jesus our Lord.*
>
> ROMANS 8:38,39 KJV

His love protects us:

> *. . . Fear not: for I have redeemed thee, I have called thee by thy name; thou art mine. When thou passest through the waters, I will be with thee; and through the rivers, they shall not overflow thee: when thou walkest through the fire, thou shalt not be burned: nei- ther shall the flame kindle upon thee.* ISAIAH 43:1,2 KJV

❦

His love is unconditional:

> *Fear thou not: for I am with thee: be not dismayed: for I am thy God: I will strengthen thee: yea, I will help thee; yea, I will uphold thee with the right hand of my righteousness.* ISAIAH 41:10 KJV

True love gives everything:

> *For God so loved the world, that He gave His only begotten Son, that whosoever believeth in Him should not perish but have everlasting life.* JOHN 3:16 KJV

The following captures the essence of His love far more eloquently than I ever could:

> *Put together all the tenderest love you know,*
> *The deepest you have ever felt,*
> *And the strongest that has ever been poured out upon you,*
> *And heap upon it all the love of*
>   *all the loving human hearts in the world,*
> *And then multiply it by infinity,*
> *And you will begin, perhaps,*
> *To have some faint glimpse of the love God has for you.*[1]
>   —HANNAH WHITALL SMITH

AN EARTHLY EXPRESSION OF LOVE

I found the following article in a book by Barbara Johnson titled *We Brake For Joy!* and thought you might enjoy the humanness and earthiness of the heart.

CALLING LONG DISTANCE

I read about one man who called his wife from an airport pay phone. When he had used up all his coins, the operator interrupted to say he had one minute left. The man hurriedly tried to finish his conversation with his wife, but before they could tell each other good-bye, the line went dead. With a sigh the man hung up the phone and started to leave the little telephone cubicle. Just then the phone rang. Thinking it was the operator wanting more money, the man almost didn't answer. But something told him to pick up the phone. And sure enough, it was the operator. But she didn't want more money. Instead she had a message for him.

"After you hung up, your wife said she loves you" the operator said. "I thought you'd want to know." [2]

— BARBARA JOHNSON

"I thought you'd want to know?" Yes, for certain, *I* would want to know! Of course in today's technology the above scenario would most likely not occur. With cell phones, emails, text messages, etc., all so readily available, somehow that message of love would get passed along. But I have to tell you, whatever the technology used, we, in our family, never end a conversation without saying: "I love you." Whenever my husband travels or any one of my children, we all wait to hear the other's expressions of love before hanging up or signing off. Whatever the language, culture, country, belief system, or color of skin, saying "I love you" is a manifestation of the heart's condition and its longing for expression.

A HEAVENLY EXPRESSION OF LOVE:
1 CORINTHIANS 13 (PARAPHRASED)

If I have the language ever so perfectly and speak like a pundit, and have not the love that grips the heart, I am nothing. If I have decorations and diplomas and am proficient in up-to-date methods and have not the touch of understanding love, I am nothing. If I am able to worst my opponents in argument so as to make fools of them, and have not the wooing note, I am nothing. If I have all faith and great ideals and magnificent plans and wonderful visions, and have not the love that sweats and bleeds and weeps and prays and pleads, I am nothing.

*If I surrender all prospects, and leaving home and friends and comforts, give myself to the showy sacrifice of a missionary career, and turn sour and selfish amid the daily annoyances and personal slights of a missionary life, and though I give my body to be consumed in the heat and sweat and mildew of India, and have not the love that yields its rights, its coveted leisure, its pet plans, I am nothing, **nothing.** Virtue has ceased to go out of me.*

If I can heal all manner of sickness and disease, but wound hearts and hurt feelings for want of love that is kind, I am nothing. If I write books and publish articles that set the world agape and fail to transcribe the word of the cross in the language of love, I am nothing. Worse, I may be competent, busy, fussy, punctilious (scrupulous), and well-equipped, but like the church at Laodicea . . . nauseating to Christ (Emphasis added).[3]

— ANONYMOUS

This paraphrased copy of I Corinthians 13 was found in the wallet of a 30-year-veteran-missionary to the Sudan. The author and the name of the missionary are quite anonymous, but this composition remains, in my estimation, one of the most profound ever written on love. No wonder she carried it with her for over 30 years. What a reminder of what true love should be.

I CORINTHIANS 13 MSG

If I speak with human eloquence and angelic ecstasy but don't love, I'm nothing but the creaking of a rusty gate.

If I speak God's Word with power, revealing all his mysteries and making everything plain as day, and if I have faith that says to a mountain, "Jump," and it jumps, but I don't love, I'm nothing.

If I give everything I own to the poor and even go to the stake to be burned as a martyr; but I don't love, I've gotten nowhere. So, no matter what I say, what I believe, and what I do, I'm bankrupt without love.

> Love never gives up.
> Love cares more for others than for self.
> Love doesn't want what it doesn't have.
> Love doesn't strut,
> Doesn't have a swelled head,
> Doesn't force itself on others,
> Isn't always "me first,"
> Doesn't fly off the handle,
> Doesn't keep score of the sins of others,
> Doesn't revel when others grovel,
> Takes pleasure in the flowering of truth,
> Puts up with anything,
> Trusts God always,
> Always looks for the best,
> Never looks back,
> But keeps going to the end.
> LOVE NEVER FAILS!![4]

Out of LOVE will flow the blessing of the remaining fruit of the Spirit. They all intermingle in one fruit but find their source in love. Dare to love others richly! Love is never quite so rewarding as when we make a choice to give it away.

LOVE IS THE BRIGHTEST AND MOST BEAUTIFUL FRUIT IN LIFE'S GARDEN! IT IS THE VERY DEFINITION OF GOD!! THE TREASURE OUR HEART SEARCHES FOR IS FOUND IN THE RICHES OF GOD'S LOVE. GIVE SOME LOVE AWAY TODAY TO OTHERS FOR JESUS' SAKE.

MAKE "OTHERS" YOUR PURPOSE IN LIFE.

❧❦❧

CHAPTER VIII
Application & Review

It is absolutely and incontestably factual that LOVE is the very motivation behind everything that God does, and has ever done, for us.

1. Name the five areas of God's love presented at the beginning of this chapter

2. Give your own explanation of God's love.

3. How has God shown His love to you? Explain.

4. Name at least six elements of God's love, according to I Corinthians 13.

5. Give an example of how you have expressed love (beyond measure) to another.

6. Love is the _____ of God. (See page 173.)

CHAPTER IX

The Fruit of the Spirit is Joy

Joy is the response of those who brush the sleeve of love

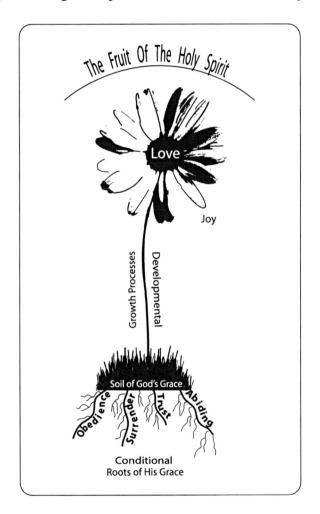

. . . yet I will rejoice in the Lord,
I will joy in the Lord of my salvation.

HABAKKUK 3:18 KJV

CHAPTER IX

The Fruit of the Spirit is Joy

. . . for the joy of the Lord is your strength.

NEHEMIAH 8:10

Happiness and joy have the same connotation but come from completely different sources. Happiness is quite conditional. It depends on circumstances, situations, relationships, the weather, our prosperity, our health, our contentment, work site conditions, our past and its influence on our present, human errors, our desires and needs, our purposes and beliefs, etc., etc. It is so human!!

In contrast, joy is an effervescent spring of rejoicing that is attainable only as a gift from the Holy Spirit, and does not depend on human circumstances. It is true that many human situations bring joy, but the spirit of joy does not rely on such occasions. Rather, joy rejoices in spite of pain and sings in spite of hurts, and this again and again brings glory to God. Even when circumstances are not good and "such is life," joy prompts us to glorify God by offering up a sacrifice of praise.

Happiness is more clearly seen as a false sense of joy, since it fills our lives only when the "good times roll." Therefore happiness can be rather intangible and conditional. Joy, on the contrary, is a source of strength that we can draw upon regardless of dark clouds, sadness, pain, tribulation, testings, and many other unfavorable conditions. Joy lives within us, and the Holy Spirit uses that gift to make us stronger Christians and to exalt the Lord who died to give us a joyful existence. The following story is a very touching expression of joy.

❧

AN EARTHLY EXPRESSION OF JOY:
IN PRAISE OF TEACHERS

In 1972, I returned to Miami Beach High School to speak to the drama class. Afterward I asked the drama teacher if any of my English teachers are still there. Irene Roberts, he tells me, is in class just down the hall.

I was no one special in Miss Roberts' class . . . just another jock who did okay work. I don't recall any one special bit of wisdom she passed on. Yet I cannot forget her respect for language, for ideas and for her students. I realize now, many years later, that she is the quintessential selfless teacher. I'd like to say something to her, I say, but I don't want to pull her from a class. Nonsense, he says, she'll be delighted to see you.

The drama teacher brings Miss Roberts into the hallway where stands this 32-year-old man she last saw at 18. "I'm Mark Medoff," I tell her. "You were my 12th-grade English teacher in 1958." She cocks her head at me, as if this angle might conjure me in her memory. And then, though armed with a message I want to deliver in some perfect torrent of words, I can't think up anything more memorable than this: "I want you to know," I say, "you were important to me."

And there in the hallway, this slight and lovely woman, now nearing retirement age, this teacher who doesn't remember me, begins to weep; and she encircles me in her arms.

Remembering this moment, I begin to sense that everything I will ever know, everything I will ever pass to my students, to my children, is an inseparable part of an ongoing legacy of our shared wonder and eternal hope that we can, must, make ourselves better.

Irene Roberts holds me briefly in her arms and through her tears whispers against my cheek, "Thank you." And then, with the briefest of looks into my forgotten face, she disappears back into her

classroom, returns to what she has done thousands of days through
all the years of my absence.

On reflection, maybe those were, after all, just the right words
to say to Irene Roberts. Maybe they are the very words I would like
to speak to all those teachers I carry through my life as part of me,
the very words I would like spoken to me one day by some return-
ing student. "I want you to know you were important to me."[1]

— MARK MEDOFF

Teaching can be, sometimes, a thankless job. Teaching is hard work . . .
I've seen it first-hand in our private school that we started in 1985. Very
few students appreciate a teacher's skills until years later. Can you imagine the "joy" Irene Roberts experienced when she realized the importance of her influence on one of her students? Teaching, at times, can
be discouraging as the desired results from their efforts are not always
directly or openly visible. This was the case with Mark Medoff. What
joy to know he had attended her class and returned later as a successful
playwright, screenwriter, film and theatre director, actor and professor.
She may not have recognized him at first, but I am sure she was quickly told of his success; one being his famous play: *Children of a Lesser
God.* Mr. Medoff had become a famous literary scholar, and Irene
Roberts played a significant role in that success. She left a lasting
impression that would later reap rewards for Mr. Medoff and the recipients of his works. Teachers are enablers! Teachers are those who inspire
us to climb higher mountains, to reach for the stars. The legacy of their
impact on students is far-reaching, and only eternity will reveal the selflessness of such a magnanimous gift to others. I say "gift," because not
everyone is blessed with the ability to teach. Teaching may not be your
gift, but use the gift God has given you, and pass along some JOY today.
It will make your heart sing. Your gift is important!

A BIBLICAL EXPRESSION OF JOY:
THE PRODIGAL

Likewise, I say unto you, there is more Joy in the presence of
the angels of God over one sinner that repenteth.

LUKE 15:10 KJV

There was a man who had two sons. In his greed and selfishness, the younger son said: *"I want my share of your estate now, instead of waiting until you die!"* (Luke 15:12 TLB). Whereupon, his father agreed to take his wealth and divide it between his sons, giving the younger son his share.

Soon after, the younger son found all his belongings . . . put everything he owned together and began his long journey to a far away land. *". . . and there he wasted his substance on riotous living"* (Luke 15:13 KJV). About the same time his inheritance was gone, a great famine swept over the land, and he began to starve. He must have thought he had certainly gotten himself into a "pickle." He had no money, no friends, no job and he had no food . . . he was literally starving. He talked a farmer into hiring him to feed his pigs. *"The boy became so hungry that even the pods feeding the swine looked good to him. And no one gave him anything"* (Luke 15:16 TLB).

Eventually, this younger son started to come to his senses and said to himself: *"All those farmhands working for my father sit down to three meals a day, and here I am starving to death. I'm going back to my father. I'll say to him, 'Father, I've sinned against God, I've sinned before you; I don't deserve to be called your son. Take me on as a hired hand'"* (Luke 15:17-18 MSG).

So he pulled himself together and returned home to his father. *"When he was still a long way off, his father saw him. His heart pounding, he ran out, embraced him, and kissed him"* (Luke 15:19 MSG).

The son started his prepared speech: *"Father, I have sinned against heaven and you, and am not worthy of being called your son . . ."* (Luke15:21 TLB).

But his father wasn't listening and said: *"Quick! Bring the finest robe in the house and put it on him. And a jeweled ring for his finger; and shoes! And kill the calf we have in the fattening pen. We must celebrate with a feast, for this son of mine was dead and has returned to life. He was lost and is found"* (Luke 15:22-23 TLB). So, they began to have a wonderful feast and the party began.

Meanwhile, the older son was laboring in the fields and upon his return home, he began to hear dance music coming from the house. He was confused. What was going on? He then asked one of the servants what the festivities were for. What was the occasion?

"Your brother is back," he was told, *"and your father has killed the calf we were fattening and has prepared a great feast to celebrate his coming home again unharmed"* (Luke 15:27 TLB).

The older brother became so angry he refused go in and join the celebration. His father came out and begged him, but he replied, *"All these years I've worked hard for you and never once refused to do a single thing you told me to; and in all that time you never gave me even one young goat for a feast with my friends.*

"Yet when this son of yours comes back after spending your money on prostitutes, you celebrate by killing the finest calf we have in the place."

"Look, dear son," his father said to him, *"you and I are very close, and everything I have is yours. But it is right to celebrate. For he is your brother, and he was dead and has come back to life!* **He was lost and is found!"** (Luke 15:29-31 TLB).

While reading this portion of scripture, I noticed several themes appearing:

❧

1) SELFISHNESS: The first and most obvious theme is the selfishness and greed of the younger son. With no regard for his father or the extra work the older brother would have to assume, he was determined to leave. I suppose he wanted to see what the world offered. He soon found out! Even his so-called friends and partygoers left when he had nothing to offer. He was left alone, starving! He defected from his home in search of happiness, but found none. He left for the wrong reasons . . . self-serving reasons!

2) ANGER: It does seem that the older son had every reason under the sun to be angry. After all, he was the one who stayed, who worked, was faithful to his father, etc. But there is one ingredient in this theme that muddies the waters, and that is jealousy. He was very jealous that his younger brother was receiving everything that he had not worked for . . . unlike him. Doesn't seem fair, does it? I had that happen to me once. I had a very wayward brother and when he was released from prison, my mother lavished him with new clothes, special meals (the robe, the ring, the feast); the whole smear. And I have to say, I was jealous. I was the one who stayed, was a decent person, and took care of my mother. But I began to look at the picture from her viewpoint. Her son had come home . . . this brought her much joy and that brings me to my third point.

3) JOY: The theme of Joy is the main reason I included this biblical account for us to review. Is there any greater joy for a parent than to greet an unruly son (or daughter) upon returning home? It so aptly portrays the unconditional love the parent has for the child. This father did not stand still and wait for his son, he didn't slowly walk to meet him; he ran. He ran as fast as his legs could take him. The father's love for his son gave wings to his feet. He so desperately wanted to express his JOY at, once again, seeing him . . . knowing he was safe . . . knowing he was unharmed. Isn't God like that with us? We are His children and, often, we are sinful children. But if we make the slightest response to his overtures, He doesn't stand or walk—He reacts by running to us. Even at this very moment, at our least whimper or request, your Father and my Father is running to embrace us . . . to enfold us in His arms . . . and He is filled with JOY!!

BANDITS

Marauders, robbers, and thieves are all Satan's minions who try to steal away our joy. Two of their tools are "Fear" and "Worry." They use these tools to discourage, dishearten and depress us. Our counter tool is the Word of God.

WORRY

We, who worry, have to put on our combat boots and go to battle. Worry is contrary to peace! It's interesting that we can believe God for redemption, for eternal life, and for making us a part of His family, but we stumble when we have to trust God for today, tomorrow, the next week, month and year. Why are we like that? It's the unknown!! We know we have eternal life, but we don't know about life here tomorrow. It certainly does reveal our lack of faith and trust. I'm a worrier. I admit it! And the truth of it is, when we worry, we are allowing circumstances to rule our lives. We have to decide to not go along with Satan's ploy to rob us of peace through worry. Somewhere along my journey I copied the following: "Worry is a conscious choosing of an ineffective method of coping with life." How true is that? It definitely implies the absence of trust and a willful decision that only escalates and spirals into more worry. Worry begets more worry.

God has given us the magnificent gift of life today . . . let's live in the joy of this moment. Each day He gives us a promise of peace, and included in that promise of peace is the strength for one day at a time.

❧

Take a look at your past. Has He sustained you? Then He will sustain you in the future. Distrust equals worry. Trust equals peace. Let's trust the character of God and allow His Word to help us:

"Then Jesus said to his disciples: "Therefore I tell you, do not worry about your life, what you will eat; or about your body, what you will wear. Life is more than food, and the body more than clothes. Consider the ravens: They do not sow or reap; they have no storeroom or barn; yet God feeds them. And how much more valuable you are than birds! Who of you by worrying can add a single hour to his life?" (Luke 12:22-26 NIV).

"And my God will meet all your needs according to his glorious riches in Christ Jesus" (Philippians 4:19 NIV).

"I bless you, Lord, for caring so deeply about each human You created. We're ashamed that we worry and ask for Your forgiveness—especially, Lord, when You have given so many of us less than what others may have to worry about. Your blessings are innumerable, and renewed every morning. What an awesome God You are! Bless those who have good reason to worry and help us to encourage and assist those that need us in the days ahead. Give to those that are weary, Your strength; to those that are in financial difficulty, Your heavenly supply; to those that are depressed, Your peace; to those who are sick, Your healing power. Help us to turn our "cares" over to You and accept Your grace for each moment. May we always spread Your joy to others, especially to those who need You more than we do. Amen."

FEAR

We've all heard the following quote: Fear is "**F**alse **E**vidence **A**ppearing **R**eal." What an excellent explanation of one of Satan's counterfeit scams. I experienced fear first-hand while in the midst of a panic attack. There was no evidence in my life that I should have been fearful; yet the fear, at the time, appeared real to me. It wasn't! And when I told myself it was not real, the panic subsided.

Fear is fear!! To write about the trillion fears we may all need to confront in a lifetime, is like trying to gather a trillion feathers blowing in the wind. They are hard to gather, assemble and rein in. There are, many times, no explanations for a fear, and yet other times there may be a reasonable clarification. Fear can be indefinable, hard to pin down, subtle, intangible, or indescribable. I'm not talking about the fear of God, which is a healthy, spiritual respect and awe for our Creator. Rather, I'm talking about a human response to an earthly encounter. It could be anything. It is, many times, an ambiguous emotion to explain. Therefore, I have chosen instead to include in this section of the book the antonym (the opposite) of fear, which is courage. Charles Swindoll explains it well:

COURAGE. It has several names: bravery, valor, fearlessness, audacity, chivalry, heroism, confidence, nerve . . . and a few nicknames: guts, grit, gristle, backbone, spunk. But whatever the name, it's never met its match. The heights of the Himalayas only encourage it. The depths of the Caribbean merely excite it. The sounds of war stimulate it. The difficulty of a job motivates it. The demands of competition inspire it. Criticism challenges it . . . adventure arouses it . . . danger incites it . . . threats quicken it.

COURAGE. That's another word for inner strength, presence of mind against odds, determination to hang in there, to venture, persevere, withstand hardship. It's got keeping power. It's what kept the pioneers rolling forward in those covered wagons in spite of the elements and mountains and flaming arrows. It's what makes the amputee reject pity and continue to take life by the throat. It's what forces every married couple having trouble never to say, "Let's terminate." It's what encourages the divorcee to face tomorrow. It's what keeps the young mother with the kids in spite of a personal energy crisis. It's what keeps a nation free in spite of attacks.

COURAGE. David had it when he grabbed his sling in the Valley of Elah. Daniel demonstrated it when he refused to worship Nebuchadnezzar's statue in Babylon. Elijah evidenced it when he faced the prophets of Baal on Carmel. Job showed it when he was covered with boils and surrounded by misunderstanding. Moses used it when he stood against Pharaoh and refused to be intimidated. The fact is, it's impossible to live victoriously for Christ without courage. That's why God's thrice spoken command to Joshua is as timeless as it is true:

> *Have not I commanded thee?*
> ***Be strong and of a good courage;***
> *Be not afraid, neither be thou dismayed:*
> *For the Lord thy God is with thee whithersoever thou goest.*
> JOSHUA 1:6,7,9 KJV

*Let it be remembered that real courage is not limited to the battle-field or the Indianapolis 500 or bravely catching a thief in your house. The **real** tests of courage are much broader . . . much deeper . . . much quieter. They are the **inner** tests, like remaining faithful when nobody's looking . . . like enduring pain when the room is empty . . . like standing alone when you're misunderstood.[2]*

— CHARLES SWINDOLL

Recently my daughter, son-in-law and grandson went whitewater rafting in Colorado. As they donned their wet suits, life jackets, and helmets (attire worn in case one should fall out of the raft), my family members prepared for their journey. They had gone rafting in the morning and I was not aware that they intended to try a more serious, rigorous and difficult whitewater path in the afternoon. Meanwhile, at home, I had this troublesome feeling and urgency to pray for them. Each member in the raft is given an oar to help propel the boat through the rapids and away from rocks. Thank goodness, their boat had mostly strong rowers. Nevertheless, they were still thrown about in the raft and the guide was thrown from the back to the front of the raft (called "guide ejection") which usually means the guide in thrown out of the raft—but in this case, he was spared and just thrown to the front. I guess that's why they call them "guide ejection rapids." I'm glad I prayed! While other rafts were actually turning over and people were bobbing along in the rapids, the raft my family was in remained topside and was pulling any "floaters" into their raft as they came close to them.

Now for me to get into that raft, it would not take that **inner** courage spoken of earlier. It would take one of those nicknames called plain "guts" and, after the first inundation of the raft and water was spraying everywhere, I would begin to question my sanity. *Why on earth did I decide to do such a thing?*

This is why: because courage is like that . . . it spurs us on . . . it emboldens us . . . it frees us from fear . . . it calls upon our determination . . . it makes us reach deep inside for that fortitude that all of us possess . . . it creates a desire to persevere . . . it challenges bravery and our nerve and it makes us better people.

Fear can be conquered even if we're just deciding to go whitewater rafting for recreation. Of course, realistically speaking, life deals many blows and Satan is always lurking around the corner waiting for an opportunity to fill our beings with fear. Many have serious and somber reasons to fear: lack of finances, a terminal disease, a sick child, and a good deal of just "life stuff." Sometimes merely existing can be a challenge! Take courage, God is still on the Throne and heeds the cries of those who seek to be brave. He will lift your heavy hearts with His "keeping power" . . . for He is a fearless King of His Universe. Be fearless!!

I sought the Lord, and he heard me, and delivered me from all my fears.   PSALM 34:4 KJV

Strengthen the feeble hands, steady the knees that give way; say to

those with fearful hearts, be strong, do not fear; your God will come, he will come with vengeance, with divine retribution he will come to save you. ISAIAH 35:3,4 NIV

There is no fear in love; but perfect love casteth out fear: because fear hath torment. He that feareth is not made perfect in love.

I JOHN 4:18 KJV

God is our refuge and strength, an ever-present help in trouble. Therefore we will not fear, though the earth give way and the mountains fall into the heart of the sea, though its waters roar and foam and the mountains quake with their surging. PSALM 46:1 NIV

Take your fears and slide them into a locked box of unwanted memories. Throw them into the deepest ocean. Toss them to the wind, where they will travel as far as the east is from the west. Replace those fears with the Joy of the Lord Who will never fail you. Rejoice and again I say rejoice!

"If you obey my commands, you will remain in my love, just as I have obeyed my Father's commands and remain in his love. I have told you this so that my **JOY** may be in you and that your **JOY** may be complete" (John 15:10,11 NIV).

JOY TO YOU! EACH AND EVERY DAY!

CHAPTER IX
Application & Review

Take a walk on the lighter side of life and be filled with His joy—joy that will last, in spite of the "curve balls" life throws your way; joy that says: "Life is worth living." Find His joy, and you will never want to let go of it. Joy to you each day!

1. Is happiness the same as joy? Explain.

2. What are the three themes found in Luke 15:11-32?

3. What are two of Satan's bandits that rob us of joy?
   Give the definition for each, found on pages 188 and 189.

4. Are you a worrier? In what way(s)?

5. Name some of the fears you face. How do they keep you from experiencing His joy?

6. What is God's thrice-spoken command in Joshua 1:6,7,9?

7. What does John 15:10-11 say about a life filled with joy?

CHAPTER X

The Fruit of the Spirit is Peace

Peace is the result of having all our conflicts washed in love.

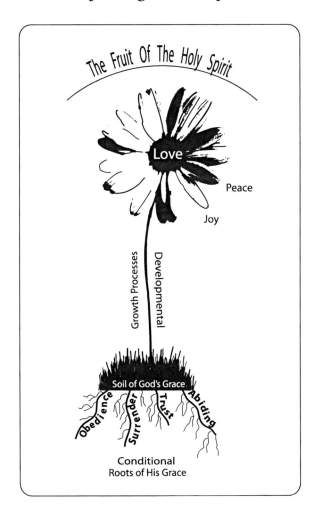

The Lord will give strength unto his people;
the Lord will bless his people with peace.

PSALM 29:11 KJV

CHAPTER X

The Fruit of the Spirit is Peace

These things I have spoken unto you,
that in me ye might have peace.

JOHN 16:33 KJV

Years ago, my husband's father used to tell a story he knew, and he would tell this story and make it his conception of what he thought peace was. While researching, I happened upon the exact story recently, and it surely does just that . . . it illustrates a perfect picture of peace:

AN EARTHLY PICTURE OF PEACE:

There once was a king who offered a prize to the artist who would paint the best picture of peace. Many artists tried. The king looked at all the pictures. But there were only two he really liked, and he had to choose between them.

One picture was of a calm lake. The lake was a perfect mirror for peaceful towering mountains all around it. Overhead was a blue sky with fluffy white clouds. All who saw this picture thought that it was a perfect picture of peace.

The other picture had mountains, too. But these were rugged and bare. Above was an angry sky, from which rain fell and in which lightning played. Down the side of the mountain tumbled a foaming waterfall. This did not look peaceful at all.

But when the king looked closely, he saw behind the waterfall a tiny bush growing in a crack in the rock. In the bush a mother bird had built her nest. There, in the midst of the rush of angry water, sat the mother bird on her nest . . . in perfect peace.

❧

Which picture do you think won the prize? The king chose the second picture. Do you know why?

"Because," explained the king, "peace does not mean to be in a place where there is no noise, trouble, or hard work. Peace means to be in the midst of all those things and still be calm in your heart. That is the real meaning of peace."[1]

— CATHERINE MARSHALL

Rest assured that when tempests roll and life is difficult, His peace that dwells within us is available for the asking. If that mother bird found it, surely we can—especially when we know the price He paid to make that fruit of peace available. When you are being tested and tried, remind yourself of the following points I discovered several years ago and confiscated from one of my notebooks. Andrew Murray, in a church tract, wrote the following points:

- **By God's Appointment:** I am here by God's will, exactly where He planned I should be. I may not like the distressing situation, I may not even understand, but my *submission* to His will, at this moment, is key to knowing peace.

- **In His Keeping:** Since God brought me into this difficult situation, He will surely give me the *grace* to act as an adult Christian. He arranged this state of affairs, and it is my responsibility to honor His reasons. He said His grace would be sufficient!

- **Under His Training:** The Lord will *teach* me why He brought me into this trial. Not only do I have to submit and then receive His grace, but I must have a teachable heart also. He will make the trial a blessing, teaching me the lesson He intended I learn.

- **For His Time:** If it is God's will that brought me here, then He surely can also bring me out of this problem, at His own time and in His own way. I am responsible to remain *peaceful* until He feels satisfied that His plan has been completed.

Years ago, when I first came upon Andrew Murray's recommendations for peace, my first thought was, "Yeah, right!" Then I said: "Do I submit, have a teachable heart and thus eventually become on familiar terms with peace, or do I just 'can' this part of the fruit of the Spirit?" Must we always be teachable? Yes, unfortunately, we must; we are only carnal beings learning how to be spiritual.

I decided to give the four points a try on a small situation that arose. It worked!! I have since tried the above on very difficult situations. It worked!! Peace can become addictive!! Becoming teachable is a good thing. It is so much better than turmoil. Once you get the hang of the process and are willing to accept the terms presented, it becomes a somewhat enjoyable spiritual habit . . . to the degree, that is, that you know the end plan is for your good. The testing, tribulation, trial, etc. etc., is definitely the unenjoyable part . . . but it's bearable when peace comes rolling in, either in the midst or at the finale. He surely does know exactly when to filter in that needed peace.

There is peace *with* God and there is the peace *of* God. The peace *with* God means you have a right relationship with God, you have the knowledge and assurance that you will live in eternity, and you know that you belong to the kingdom of God. The peace *of* God is a gift of the fruit of the Spirit. This fruit gives every Christian a fresh understanding that God is always with us. He is an omnipresent God and is aware of our every move and need. That is an awesome God indeed! The peace of His presence is an overwhelming and remarkable promise, especially amidst the turmoil, chaos and mayhem we face in a world full of evil. You can find the peace of His presence everywhere:

> *You know when I leave and when I get back;*
> *I'm never out of your sight.*
> *You know everything I'm going to say*
> *before I start the first sentence.*

❦

I look behind me and you're there,
then up ahead and you're there, too—
your reassuring presence, coming and going.
This is too much, too wonderful—
I can't take it all in!

Is there anyplace I can go to avoid your Spirit?
to be out of your sight?
If I climb to the sky, you're there!
If I go underground, you're there!
If I flew on morning's wings
to the far western horizon,
You'd find me in a minute—
you're already there waiting!
Then I said to myself, "Oh, he even sees me in the dark!
At night I'm immersed in the light!"
It's a fact: darkness isn't dark to you;
night and day, darkness and light, they're all the same to you.

PSALM 139:2-12 MSG

A BIBLICAL VERSION OF PEACE: THE STORM

One day about that time, as he and his disciples were out in a boat, he suggested that they cross to the other side of the lake.

On the way across he lay down for a nap, and while he was sleeping the wind began to rise. A fierce storm developed that threatened to swamp them, and they were in real danger.

They rushed over and woke him up. "Master, Master, we are sinking." They screamed.

So he spoke to the storm: "Quiet down," he said, and the wind and waves subsided and all was calm! Then he asked them, "Where is your faith?"

🌿

*And they were filled with awe and fear of him and said to one
another, "Who is this man, that even the winds and waves obey him?"*

LUKE 8:22-25 TLB

Isaiah 26:3 says the following: "Thou wilt keep him in perfect peace
whose **mind** is stayed on thee: because he trusteth in thee." What Jesus
was saying, and the disciples were having difficulty understanding, is
this: "If I am with you, why are you afraid?" **Unfortunately, they took
their minds off the One who was with them in the boat.** Instead, the
disciples allowed their circumstances to overwhelm them and fill them
with fear. We all have to remember that the key to our peace is not the
absence of trouble, danger, fear or conflict, but the presence of God.

Where is your faith; where is my faith? To trust Him and be blessed
by His presence is a choice and a matter of the will. Be encouraged by
the following:

*And the peace of God, which passeth all understanding,
shall keep your hearts and minds through Christ Jesus.*

PHILIPPIANS 4:7 KJV

SWEET PEACE, THE GIFT OF GOD'S LOVE

There comes to my heart one sweet strain,
A glad and a joyous refrain,
I sing it again and again,
Sweet peace, the gift of God's love.

Through Christ on the cross peace was made,
My debt by His death was all paid,
No other foundation is laid.
For peace, the gift of God's love.

When Jesus as Lord I had crowned,
My heart with this peace did abound,

In Him the rich blessing I found,
Sweet peace, the gift of God's love.

In Jesus for peace I abide,
And as I keep close to His side,
There's nothing but peace doth betide.
Sweet peace, the gift of God's love.

CHORUS

Peace, peace, sweet peace,
Wonderful gift from above,
Oh, wonderful, wonderful peace,
Sweet peace, the gift of God's love.

LYRICS AND MUSIC BY PETER P. BILHORN (1863-1936)

Years ago, Philip Bilhorn was the song leader for Billy Sunday and several other leading evangelists. One night he sang one of his most popular songs, "I Will Sing the Wondrous Story," at a camp meeting. A friend jokingly remarked, "I wish you would write a song to suit my voice as well as that song suits yours."

Bilhorn responded, "What shall it be?"

"Oh, any sweet piece."

That evening, Bilhorn composed the music for the new hymn. It was not until the following winter, however, that he wrote the lyrics under very dire circumstances.

While traveling on a train, that cold winter, Mr. Bilhorn observed a tragic accident. He saw one poor individual left lying in a pool of blood. It seems a rather gruesome thought, but the event reminded him of Christ's blood atoning for our sins, and this quickly prompted him to write the lyrics (above) right there on the train. Life is fleeting, but we have the peace and assurance of eternal life. "Sweet Peace, The Gift of God's Love." Amidst the anguish that is presented to us while on this earth, only His peace is able to sustain us as we stay close to His side.

And, only God's peace was able to uphold Mr. Bilhorn amidst the present suffering which he observed and which seemed to envelope him.

Love is available to us as we completely rest our entire being on our heavenly Father's chest.

Joy makes its arrival when we quietly listen to the heartbeat of our Father.

Peace follows along as we live harmoniously and sweetly with His heartbeat.

There is constant comfort in the closeness of our relationship with our Father, and there is a peace that settles over our souls when possessing the knowledge that we are resting in His complete will.

> *Peace I leave with you, my peace I give unto you:*
> *not as the world giveth, give I unto you.*
> *Let not your heart be troubled, neither let it be afraid.*
>
> JOHN 14:27 KJV

Jesus said He would keep our thoughts and our hearts quiet and at rest as we trust in Him. He is, after all, the Prince of Peace. Love, Joy, Peace —all present themselves as nouns or "attitudes."

Next, we'll meet up with a few verbs or action fruit. Patience is calling our names . . . let's see what this fruit requires.

LOVE, JOY AND PEACE IN OUR BLOSSOM PREPARE THE WAY FOR PATIENCE.

CHAPTER X
Application & Review

Peace is God's precious gift of a safe haven and sanctuary amidst the chaotic world of mayhem and turmoil that life often brings. Regardless of those intrusions in our lives, God's gift of peace provides a calmness of Spirit and a refuge in times of storms. Take His peace . . . He offers it freely.

1. Give your definition of God's peace.

2. Name the four points Andrew Murray suggests for obtaining peace. (See page 197.)

3. How do you respond to the chaotic moments in your life? How can you change your responses, if negative?

4. Explain the presence of God according to Psalm 139:2-12 (Delightful from *The Message Translation*).

5. Give an explanation of the disciple's reaction to the storm described in Luke 8:22-25. How does Jesus reprimand them? Explain.

CHAPTER XI

The Fruit of the Spirit is Patience

Patience is the art that never hurries love

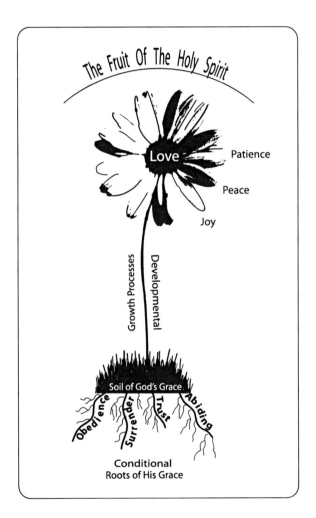

Be still before the Lord
and wait patiently for Him . . .

PSALM 37:7 NIV

CHAPTER XI

The Fruit of the Spirit is Patience

. . . let us run with patience the race that is set before us.

HEBREWS 12:1 KJV

swald Chambers once stated that remaining patient and waiting upon God is the perfection of activity[1] (paraphrased). Now that's a dichotomy if I've ever heard one. Waiting and activity are not related. Rather, they are miles apart in meaning. However, Mr. Chambers obviously felt that waiting was activity, in the sense that more will be accomplished by the act of waiting than aggressively running ahead of God. So, when you observe the statement from that perspective, it is more logical. Very often we become impatient and, in our hurried bustle, miss the message God intended, and even miss the will of God. God can perfect more in us when we wait than when we "take things into our own hands." We sometimes, instead, miss out on a blessing.

Unfortunately, blessings don't always come easy. There are times when Jesus asks us to be longsuffering. To be longsuffering is to possess *the quality of endurance without complaint,* and the Word of God invariable intertwines the two words . . . patience and suffering (together). Another word used occasionally in reference to patience is joy. Thus, there becomes a trilogy that includes patience, suffering, and joy, all mingling in one cluster of fruit

Strengthened with all might,
according to his glorious power,
unto all patience and longsuffering with joyfulness.

COLOSSIANS 1:11 KJV

There are several other words the Bible uses in relation to patience: words like virtue, temperance, godliness, knowledge, hope and tribulation. They all seem to be interrelated and intermingle together, with each dependent on the other.

And besides this, giving all diligence,
add to your faith virtue; and to virtue knowledge;
And to knowledge temperance; and to temperance patience;
And to patience godliness; and to godliness brotherly kindness.

II PETER 1:5-7 KJV

We glory in tribulations also;
knowing that tribulation worketh patience;
and patience experience; and experience, hope:
and hope maketh not ashamed; because the love of God
is shed abroad in our hearts by the Holy Ghost which is given unto us.

ROMANS 5:3-5 KJV

In another section, the Bible likens patience to a race. And again we have a dichotomy because the words "run" and "patience" invariably are extreme opposites. However, God *can* teach us to run, with a peaceful and quiet heart, the race that is set before us and wait patiently for the finish line. Perhaps that was the meaning in a broad sense.

"Wherefore seeing we also are compassed about with so great a cloud of witnesses, let us lay aside every weight, and the sin which doth so easily beset us, and let us *run with patience* the race that is set before us. Looking unto Jesus the author and finisher of our faith; who for the joy that was set before him endured the cross, despising the shame, and is set down at the right hand of the throne of God" (Hebrews 12:1,2 KJV).

The well-known poem "The Race" depicts the meaning the author of Hebrews intended to portray:

THE RACE

The race is often run in obscure places.
The runners seldom appear as ones able to compete for the Prize.
Many come ill-prepared,
thinking the race to be no more than a brief sprint.
Some start with fear and apprehension,
certain that if they survive the course,
they will come in last.
Others enter, encumbered with weights
that must soon be stripped away.
A few begin, confident of crossing the finish line
with breath to spare,
only to find themselves weak and breathless
after the first steep incline.
Even those who checked out the course with great care
discover unforeseen obstacles that threaten to undo them.

But all the runners have one thing in common:
each has come in response to the
Divine Summons.
In this race there are no volunteers,
only those who have heard the call, and
entered in; and, having begun,
soon discover there is only one requirement for
staying in the race—
Each must keep his eyes fixed with steadfast persistence on the Prize.
In this, all runners have equal status.
To those whose progress is painfully slow and awkward,
to those who gain
ground with swift confident strides,
there is the same assurance of gaining the
Prize.

❧❧

For together they have come to the knowledge
that the One who calls them is the
One who enables them to run the race and finish the course.
And they have known all along, He is also the Prize.[2]

— CHARLENE LEACH

What a God! His road stretches straight and smooth,
Every God-direction is road-tested.
Everyone who runs toward him makes it.

PSALM 18:30 MSG

"May each one of us run this race with patience and with integrity! May we run for one reason and one reason only . . . for that prize of seeing our Savior and bowing before Him. Knowing that we all have equal status in this race, encourage us to help each other; for it is He who enables us . . . the weak, the strong, the confident, the ill-prepared, the apprehensive and those who carry heavy weights. We all come to the race with different perspectives and diverse abilities, but thank you, Lord, for empowering us no matter who we are or what talents we possess. Just see us all as Your children, running to expectantly hear You say: 'Well done, thou good and faithful servant.' Amen."

AN EARTHLY PORTRAYAL OF PATIENCE

The following story gives us an enlightened insight to the word "patience" in that His patience gives us the strength to endure:

OUR EYES ON THE GOAL

The other night Jack and I watched a television drama called, "See How She Runs." The story concerned a 40-year-old divorced teacher from Boston who decided to become a jogger and eventually entered the 26-mile Boston Marathon. To finish the race became her goal, and in spite of being harassed, jeered at and assaulted, she did not lose sight of it. The day of the race came and she faced her ultimate test. As she ran, huge blisters developed on her feet. She was also hit and injured by a bicycle. And several miles short of the finish line found her utterly exhausted. Yet she kept going. Then, within a few hundred yards of the finish line, late at night, when most other runners had either finished or dropped out, she fell and lay flat on her face, too tired to raise her head. But her friends had put a crude tape across the finish line and began to cheer her on. She lifted her head with great effort, saw the tape, and realized her goal was within sight. With a supreme effort she got up on her bruised and bleeding feet, and in a burst of energy dredged up from deep inside her courageous heart, she ran the last few yards.

She had kept her eyes on the goal and for the joy of finishing, she endured. *We are to do what our example, Christ, did on earth. He kept looking at the goal, not the going. He was seeing the prize, not the process; the treasure, not the trial; the joy, not the journey. And we must do the same.*[3]   CAROLE MAYHAL

Several other translations place patience in the same category as endurance, perseverance and suffering:

1) "We *patiently endure* suffering and hardship and trouble of every kind" (II Corinthians 6:4 TLB).

2) ". . . let us run with *perseverance* the race marked out for us" (Hebrews 12:1 NIV).

3) "But you, man of God . . . pursue righteousness, godliness, faith, love, *endurance* and gentleness" (I Timothy 6:11 NIV).

4) "Of course, you get no credit for being patient if you are beaten for doing wrong; but if you do right and *suffer* for it, and are *patient* beneath the blows, God is well pleased" (I Peter 2:20 TLB).

❧

A BIBLICAL PORTRAYAL OF PATIENCE: JOB

It seems that the word "suffering" is linked to patience throughout the Bible. In Romans, Paul states: "We rejoice, too, when we run into problems and trials, for we know that they are good for us . . . they help us learn to be patient" (Romans 5:3 TLB). James presents a similar account: "Dear brothers, is your life full of difficulties and temptations? Then be happy, for when the way is rough, your patience has a chance to grow. So let it grow, and don't try to squirm out of your problems. For when your patience is finally in full bloom, then you will be ready for anything, strong in character, full and complete" (James 1:3 TLB). In another instance, Moses lost his patience while suffering at the hands of the rebellious Israelites: "By the waters of Meribah they angered the Lord, and trouble came to Moses because of them; for they rebelled against the Spirit of God and rash words came from Moses' lips" (Psalm 106: 32,33 NIV). James also gives another account: "For examples of patience in suffering, look at the Lord's prophets. We know how happy they are now because they stayed true to him then, even though they suffered greatly for it. Job is an example of a man who continued to trust the Lord in sorrow. From his experiences, we can see how the Lord's plan finally ended in good, for he is full of tenderness and mercy" (James 5:10,11 TLB).

Speaking of Job! He is a striking example of patience working its way through a life. The suffering was supreme and I can think of no other example that illustrates the connection between suffering and patience other than our Lord's sufferings on our behalf.

Job was an upright man: *"In the land of Uz there lived a man whose name was Job. This man was blameless and upright; he feared God and shunned evil."* He was a man who cared for others and prayed for his family (he had seven sons and three daughters). The Bible says, *"He was the greatest man among all the people of the East"* (Job 1:1-3 NIV). Job was a very wealthy man and the people of those times thought that God had surely honored him for his godliness.

Then comes the question: "Why do the righteous suffer?" There appears to be no clear answer in Job's case. It seems as though there was a spiritual battle that was taking place between Satan and the Lord. It was a contest of sorts to see if Job would turn from his faith, and God was confident that Job's love and trust were unimpeachable. I have read somewhere that patience is the ability to suffer and not sin against God. Job proved that statement true! And secondly, as Christians, we must assume the posture that God surely does know what is best for us and, even if He remains silent for a season, we are to patiently trust and praise Him. Job proved that statement true also! Not too comforting, but nevertheless, truth we must heed. No one desires suffering. Regardless, it was God who allowed Satan to touch Job's life. Otherwise, Satan would have been powerless! Ultimately, God rewarded Job's faithfulness by giving him twice as much as he had lost.

I want to tell you straight up, I pray I am never called upon to suffer as Job did. After his first test, he was no longer wealthy. As quick as lightening, he was stripped of his children and their families, and most of his wealth was destroyed: his 7,000 sheep were burned up, his 500 yoke of oxen and 500 donkeys were confiscated by the Sabeans, his 3,000 camels were stolen by the Chaldeans, and his sons and daughters were killed when a strong wind destroyed the home where they were feasting. The house fell upon them and no one escaped. The response from Job follows:

> *"Naked I came from my mother's womb,*
> *and naked I will depart.*
> *The Lord gave and the Lord has taken away;*
> *may the name of the Lord be praised."*
> *In all of this Job did not sin by charging God with wrongdoing.*
>
> JOB 1:21,22 NIV

In His second test, God allowed Satan to cover Job's entire body with

❧

sores: *"So Satan went out from the presence of the Lord and afflicted Job with painful sores from the soles of his feet to the top of his head"* (Job 2:7 NIV). *His own wife said to him: "Are you still trying to be godly when God has done all this to you? Curse him and die"* (Job 2:8 TLB). That's a helpful wife, I must say!! But I'm sure she was full of grief also. After all, she had lost everything along with Job. His second response:

> *"You are talking like a foolish woman.*
> *Shall we accept good from God and not trouble?"*
> *In all this Job did not sin in what he said.*
> JOB 2:10 NIV

However, after this, Job, in his discouragement, cursed the day he was born: *"Let the day of my birth be cursed," he said, "and the night when I was conceived"* (Job 3,3 TLB). Whereupon, his so-called faithful friends enter the scene: Eliphaz, Bildad and Zophar are all basically accusers, not comforters. The conversations between his friends and Job continue from chapters 4 to 16, and finally Job has heard and argued enough: *"I have heard all this before. What miserable comforters all of you are. Won't you ever stop your flow of foolish words? What have I said that makes you speak so endlessly? But perhaps I'd sermonize the same as you . . . if you were I and I were you. I would spout off my criticisms against you and shake my head at you. But no! I would speak in such a way that it would help you. I would try to take away your grief"* (Job 16: 2-5 TLB).

The discourse continues between Job and his friends and then suddenly within his reach is a more positive outlook and he states: *"But he knoweth the way that I take: when he hath tried me, I shall come forth as gold. My foot hath held his steps, his way have I kept, and not declined"* (Job 23:10,11 KJV). From this point on, the Lord condemned his three friends and spoke to Eliphaz: *"I am angry with you and with your two friends, for you have not been right in what you have said about me, as my servant Job was. Now take seven young bulls and seven rams and go to my servant Job and offer a burnt offering for yourselves; and my servant Job will pray for you, and I will accept his prayer on your behalf, and won't destroy you as I should because of your sin, your failure to speak rightly concerning my servant Job"* (Job 42:7,8 TLB).

Job had patiently struggled through his physical and mental pain, and he came out victorious. He struggled with his contentious, pious friends and patiently prayed for them. After he had prayed for them, the Lord graciously restored his wealth and happiness. In fact, as I said, the Lord gave him twice as much as before!

"Then all of his brothers, sisters, and former friends arrived and feasted with him in his home, consoling him for all his sorrow, and comforting him because of all the trials the Lord had brought upon him. And each of them brought him a gift of money and a gold ring. So the Lord blessed Job at the end of his life more than at the beginning. For now he had 14,000 sheep, 6,000 camels, 1,000 teams of oxen, and 1,000 female donkeys. God also gave him seven more sons and three more daughters" (Job 42:11-14 TLB).

Job was tried, tested, suffered tremendous loss, suffered unbearable physical pain and endured unbelievable mental anguish, but arose from his bed, dusted himself off, and God honored him. You've heard people use the term: "That person has the patience of Job." Well, we should all be so fortunate! But, would we want to suffer as Job? His most precious reward: he did come forth as pure gold. God is truly a merciful King. Patience is a virtue and a fruit that only God can offer us. It is definitely not a fruit that we can conjure up and use at will. Only the Holy Spirit can empower us!

My favorite verses in Job come from *The Living Bible,* chapter 19 and verses 25-27: "But as for me, I know that my Redeemer lives, and that he will stand upon the earth at last. And I know that after this body has decayed, this body shall see God! Then he will be on *my* side! Yes, I shall see him, not as a stranger, but as a friend! What a glorious hope!"

AND SO, WE PATIENTLY WAIT FOR THAT DAY
WHEN WE SHALL SEE HIM FACE TO FACE!

CHAPTER XI
Application & Review

Patience is a virtue. We all long for it; we all strive for it; but only the Holy Spirit can empower us. Patience often eludes us—especially in a world that seems to be turned upside down—and our spiritual graces are challenged at every hand.

1. Name some words from this chapter that are often coupled with patience.

2. How should we run our race (or journey) according to Hebrews 12:1-2? By what are we so easily beset?

3. From Chapter XI, name verses that intermingle and combine suffering with patience.

4. How did Job's friends treat him, according to Job 16:2-5?

5. How did Job respond to his suffering? Give examples.

6. Name areas where your patience level needs improvement.

7. What steps can you take when you feel impatient?

CHAPTER XII

The Fruit of the Spirit is Kindness

Kindness is love's application

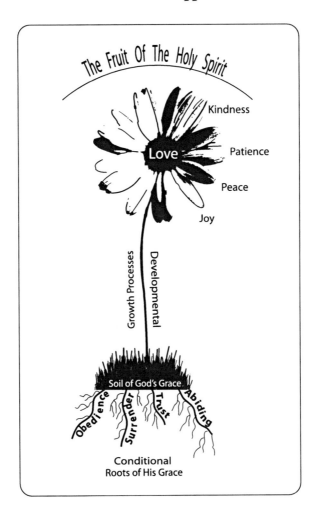

. . . but with everlasting kindness
will I have mercy on thee.

ISAIAH 54:8B KJV

CHAPTER XII

The Fruit of the Spirit
is Kindness

. . . for he is gracious and merciful,
slow to anger and of great kindness.

JOEL 2:13B KJV

Words that correlate and interrelate with kindness are as follows: compassion, consideration, benevolence, sympathy, giving, caring, generosity and forgiving. These are all action words requiring a selfless frame of mind.

> *Be kind and compassionate to one another, forgiving each other,*
> *just as in Christ God forgave you.*
>
> EPHESIANS 4:32 NIV

God can more readily use the fruit of the Spirit in our lives if they have been observed in others. There is somewhat of an osmosis process that takes place. For example, if you received love, you are automatically more able to pass that love to others It is the same with joy. If your home, while growing up, was joyous, you are more likely to have a joyful spirit. When you observe peace and patience in others, it often rubs off on you. The process is the same with the remaining fruit. We become what we have absorbed as children and what we have received regarding the fruit of the Spirit, but the power to use them lies within the Holy Spirit. It is the Holy Spirit's gift; we are simply the recipients and channels through which that power and expression of kindness is passed on to others.

My children, thank God, are kind people and have observed kindness first hand from the ministry of their father. My husband worked his fingers to the bone while remodeling the church on 41st Street in Astoria and, just when he thought he was finished for the day, invariably someone would stop by the church with a problem that needed a quick solution. My husband would never say: "Can you come back tomorrow?" That thought would never occur to him. He would run upstairs to our apartment that was attached to the church, wash up, change his clothes and while flying back downstairs, yell up to me: "Keep my supper warm, I'll eat it later." To my knowledge, he has never said "No" to anyone. He was and is always compassionate, kind and caring. If someone needed money, he would take money from our struggling church account (that was in the early days) and either loan or outright give a person the exact amount of money they needed. God never failed us though . . . He always gave the money back to the church tenfold. There are hundreds of stories of kindness by my pastor husband that have accumulated over the past 48 years, and only heaven will reveal them all. My children observed my husband's kind servant heart and it rubbed off on them in various ways.

Years ago our oldest son, Brian, was contemplating his future. What would it hold for him? What would his career be? Where would God use him? These inquiries came after he was married and working for UPS (United Parcel Service), later as Evangel's Nehemiah Project Director, and finally as Physical Education director for Evangel School. He had taken courses at King's College in Briarcliff Manor and, later, Physical Education courses at Nyack College.

However, after a short experience at teaching Phys. Ed., Brian came to grips with the knowledge that teaching was not a career where he could best use his abilities. He then began to research other careers and filled out an application for Christian Herald, an organization that includes the renowned Bowery Mission where hundreds of homeless are fed every day. The Herald also has a women's ministry, children's program, a summer camp located in Pennsylvania for inner city kids, and a transitional center for men. His application was accepted, but he had to start at the bottom. Where was the bottom? Security! Brian had also made out an application for the New York City Police Force and passed all the tests with flying colors. It's interesting to note that his acceptance to the Police Force and his acceptance to the Christian Herald came on the same day. He chose the Christian Herald and in the meantime, while working his way up the ladder, obtained an MPA (Masters in Public Administration).

Today, Brian is the Vice President of Christian Herald. In retrospect, Brian always had a heart for people who were hurting. When he was a teenager and into his early 20s, he would load the church van with a big pot of soup and sandwiches he had prepared, head for the homeless in New York City, and minister to them. God gave him a passion for the down-and-out in the gutters of the city. He has spent many hours ministering to people less fortunate than himself. He heeded that call to pass along the kindness he saw while growing up. The legacy lives on!

Our daughter, Carolyn, became passionate about children and teenagers. I think she knew from a young age that being a part of education was her calling. She taught for several years at our school (Evangel) and then tried the administrative area of education. Then, our school needed a 5th grade teacher, and she went back to teaching again. However, it was the administrative part that drew out her many talents. Although she enjoyed teaching and related so well to the students, she found that being a part of the larger picture was her calling. After teaching 5th grade, she became the principal for our middle school. At that time our school contained classes from PK3 to 8th grades. She flourished in this position and became a great asset to the school. One day, as she was signing applications for the 8th grade students to attend high school, she said: "We have to start a high school. I feel like I'm sending my students out to the wolves" (which, in general terms, would mean public school). Some students, however, did attend Catholic high schools. The remaining students would have to attend public schools and be influenced by the drugs, illicit sex, the cursing and disrespect for authority that many of our graduating students found difficult to endure. She knew how impressionable middle school-age students are and, in light of this, Carolyn began a high school in 2000. Our first graduating class, in 2004, consisted of only 7 students. This year, 2009, we graduated 62. Today we have over 250 in the high school alone. Total attendance is 560.

Carolyn has also worked tirelessly with the state to acquire state certification for Evangel. We now have a full charter. She also spent hours talking with Albany (our state capital) to have our high school become Regents certified. We now offer our students the academic equivalent of any public school diploma. A few years ago, Carolyn worked with Nyack College and we are now able to offer 23 college credits to our students. She also instituted an international section in our school and, today, we have 45 international students enrolled. During the writing of this book, the school also became certified through CITA and Middle States. We are proud to have her as the Principal of Evangel Christian School.

She is known for her kindness to her teachers, parents and students. She gives students many chances to improve academically and behaviorally. She spends many hours counseling both parents and students. The legacy of kindness lives on!

Our second son, Stephen, works for a Christian company and has a prominent position in the computer department. The company re-manufactures automobile parts and was founded by Mr. Cardone, who wanted his employees to enjoy working in a Christian atmosphere. Thus, he built a special auditorium dedicated to chapel services held on every Friday. Stephen has a degree in music, so he offered his abilities to play the piano for the Friday chapels. Stephen is a very kind person and has reached out to many in his company. He has also played the piano in church services for many years.

This particular company was also kind to Stephen. When his wife was carrying their fourth child, she had to remain in the hospital for over 70-some days. As you remember from the chapter on trust, she had lost two children due to the inability to carry them once she conceived. The first pregnancy was successful, the next two were lost and finally, the fourth time she became pregnant, the doctors said she must remain in the hospital where emergency care was readily available. I said all that to say this: the Cardone Company picked up the entire cost of the hospital stay and that bill must have been in the thousands.

One day, Stephen said: "I'd like to give something back to my small community . . . help out in some way." His decision was to become a volunteer fire fighter. Now, this is not as easy as it sounds. His training was strenuous, difficult, arduous and complex. The training was equal to a paid fire fighter. He has to wear a beeper and can be called anytime . . . evenings, the middle of the night, and weekends. Anytime except, of course, his work hours at Cardone. The volunteer fire fighter course also required training in EMT emergency medical care. He is regarded as a vital part of the volunteer unit in the small community where he lives. And, the legacy lives on . . .

The legacy of kindness! But kindness, as a fruit of the Spirit, requires more. Do you remember what I stated in the introduction? A learned behavior that represents our spiritual background is good. However, to be effective, it necessitates a spiritual resource—strength—a well to draw from and a power that is greater than we. That's where the Holy Spirit comes into the picture. Since kindness is a fruit of the Holy Spirit, we can call upon the Spirit's ability to enable us—that is, if we have come to a position in our spiritual walk where the asking is viable. Kindness is a by-product of the workings of the Holy Spirit in our lives and is available to those who possess obedient, surrendered, abiding and trusting lives. It is available to those who have conquered emotional difficulties and have worked on renewing their minds. The fruit of the Spirit is a gift, but that gift, many times, has to be pruned and disciplined before it becomes usable. Work through those blockades that are keeping you from extending kindness. Being kind is a selfless act. May we all learn to be selfless!

❧❧

AN EARTHLY DEPICTION OF KINDNESS:
A BRAND-NEW PAIR OF SHOES

The teacher was young and enthusiastic, in her first year of teaching. The school she was assigned to was in one of the poorest towns in the province of Havana. Water was scarce. Most of it came from wells located on one side of town. She saw people around the school carrying buckets of water every day for use in their houses. The children were always clean no matter how old, tattered or patched their clothing was.

The teacher's favorite pupil was a nine-year-old girl with brown hair and expressive eyes. She smiled all the time. She was always tidy and her hair well combed. Her dress was washed and ironed but her shoes were almost gone. The teacher didn't believe much more could be done for them. By the beginning of the second semester, the little girl's shoes were nothing more than rags wrapped around her feet. That weekend the teacher bought a brand-new pair of shoes for the little girl. They were made of genuine leather and had a bow on top. They looked lovely on the girl's feet.

At the end of the school year, the teacher was successful in her bid to transfer to the city of Havana to a school where most children came from a better background. She taught there for over 30 years until she retired and began devoting her time to reading and writing.

One day she was taken to a small private clinic with double pneumonia. She had been paying her membership quota at the clinic for years but had never used it. She was surprised at the good services and attention she received from the clinic's personnel. It seemed as if the doctors and nurses were going out of their way to please her. One day, she told another patient how satisfied she was with the care she was receiving at the place.

"You can certainly say so," the other lady said. *"I will say since you've been coming, the rest of us have been treated more kindly, also."*

"What are you trying to imply?" the teacher asked. *"I'm nobody important, and I don't know anyone here. Why would they give me more attention?"*

"Well, ask if you don't believe me."

That evening, when her favorite nurse came to see her, the teacher asked, "Is it true that I have been given special attention here?"

"Yes, it is," the nurse answered. *"The director, Dr. Mendez, asked us to take good care of you."*

Mendez was a very common name, and the teacher didn't remember anyone in particular with that name. Upon dismissal, she decided to thank Dr. Mendez personally. She knocked at her door.

"Come in," a voice said.

Upon entering, the teacher saw an attractive lady in her forties, who smiled at her.

"Dr. Mendez, I came to thank you for ordering your staff to take care of me in such a wonderful way. How can I repay you?"

"You repay me?" the director said. *"I'm the one trying to repay you."*

"I don't understand. I don't remember having met you before."

"Oh, but you have, my dear. You were my inspiration, my role model. You were the motor which propelled me to strive for a better future. You gave me the desire to improve myself and my lot. I owe you everything I am and have achieved in life."

"But I don't see how . . ."

"You don't remember me, do you? I'm that poor girl for whom, one day, you bought a brand-new pair of shoes, the most precious leather shoes in the whole wide world."[1]

— GRACIELA BEECHER

The above story is dedicated to the memory of Ms. Graciela Beecher, whose literary contributions have appeared in such publications as

Today's Catholic Newspaper, The Holy Rosary and *Notable Hispanic American Women.* I am grateful to the Catholic Diocese of Fort Wayne, Indiana, for their permission to use this beautiful story.

A BIBLICAL DEPICTION OF KINDNESS: RUTH

The story of Ruth is full of kindness. The proceedings in the book of Ruth are set in the time of the Judges. The story of Ruth is a haven of tenderness and compassion placed in the Bible amidst the harshness of the Judges. Two themes run through the book of Ruth: one is the account of a Gentile woman from Moab, and her close companionship with Naomi, who was a Hebrew woman from Bethlehem. The second theme is the rising romance between Ruth and Boaz, who is a relative of Naomi.

Because of a famine that ravaged Bethlehem, Naomi, her husband Elimelech and their two sons migrated to the country of Moab. Moab was located on the east side of the Dead Sea. The Bible does not reveal their mode of transportation but it had to have been either by foot, camel, donkey or perhaps partly by boat. *"During the time of their residence there, Elimelech died and Naomi was left with her two sons"* (Ruth 1:3 TLB). As time and love would have it, these young men, Mahlom and Chilion, married girls of Moab—Orpah and Ruth.

They lived in Moab for around 10 years, and then Mahlon and Chilion died and the three women were left alone. What to do? Naomi decided to return to her people because she had heard that God had helped them to prosper. She encouraged her two daughters-in-law to return to their parent's homes but their response was as follows: *"No,"* *they said. "We want to go with you to your people"* (Ruth 1:10 TLB). Orpha finally surrendered and returned to her home. But Ruth's love was shown to Naomi in her **kindness** to remain with her mother-in-law. Her second response to Naomi's entreaty was: *"Don't make me leave you, for I want to go wherever you go, and live wherever you live; your peo-*

ple shall be my people, and your God shall be my God; I want to die where you die, and be buried there. May the Lord do terrible things to me if I allow anything but death to separate us" (Ruth 1:16 TLB).

So began their journey back to Bethlehem. When they arrived it was just the beginning of harvest-time. *"Now Naomi had an in-law there in Bethlehem who was a very wealthy man. His name was Boaz"* (Ruth 2:1 TLB). Ruth suggested that perhaps she could go to the fields and glean the free grain that was left behind by the reapers. *"All right, dear daughter. Go ahead"* (Ruth 2:2b TLB). She providentially happened upon the fields of Boaz. Upon inquiring who the Moabite woman was, Boaz learned she had returned from Moab with Naomi.

According to the Bible, he owned several fields of grain and was desirous of sharing his wealth with Ruth and Naomi, her mother-in-law. Boaz, after learning who Ruth was, said: *"Listen, my child . . . Stay right here with us to glean; don't think of going to any other fields. Stay right behind my women workers; I have warned the young men not to bother you; when you are thirsty, go and help yourself to the water"* (Ruth 2:8,9 TLB). Ruth was surprised that he was being so **kind** to her because, by then, Boaz must have known that she was a foreigner. She said as much. His reply: *"Yes, I know, and I also know about all the love and **kindness** you have shown your mother-in-law since the death of your husband, how you left your father and mother in your own land and have come here to live among strangers. May the Lord God of Israel, under whose wings you have come to take refuge, bless you for it"* (Ruth 2:11,12 TLB).

When Naomi learned where Ruth had gleaned, she exclaimed: *"Why that man is one of our closest relatives"* (Ruth 2:20 NIV). The wheels in Naomi's head began to turn. Boaz would be a good husband for Ruth! You know how it is, when others begin to scheme on your behalf. But, in this case, God had a plan as well.

Naomi decided to sell her husband Elimelech's property. Boaz was interested but, as is the custom in Israel, the closest relative receives the first bid on a property in this sort of situation. However, when queried,

⚘⚘⚘

the closest relatives were not interested because the property would also come with Ruth as well as Naomi. And again, as is the custom, the closest relative is to marry Ruth so that she can bear children to carry on her previous husband's name. If that should happen, the son of Ruth would become an heir to the same property. No one was interested.

This placed Boaz in a good position. He was next in line as the closest relative, and he bought from Naomi all the property that had previously belonged to Elimelech, Chilion and Mahlon.

Those who had spoken to Boaz replied: *"We are witnesses. May the Lord make this woman, who has now come into your home, as fertile as Rachel and Leah, from whom all the nation of Israel descended! May you be a great and successful man in Bethlehem and may the descendants the Lord will give you from this young woman be as numerous and honorable as those of our ancestor Perez, the son of Tamar and Judah"* (Ruth 4:11,12 TLB).

As divine intervention would have it, Boaz married Ruth and she gave him a son. They named him Obed. The women in the city were extremely happy for Naomi and said: *"Bless the Lord who has given you this little grandson; may he be famous in Israel. May he restore your youth and take care of you in your old age; for he is the son of your daughter-in-law who loves you so much, and **who has been kinder to you than seven sons!"*** (Ruth 4:14-15 TLB).

> *And they named him Obed.*
> *He was the father of Jesse*
> *and grandfather of King David.*
>
> RUTH 4:17 TLB

And again, as God would have it, Christ came from the lineage of King David. I have often wondered what the story would be if Ruth had not returned to Bethlehem with Naomi. As it turned out, everyone won. Naomi had a grandson and the love of her daughter-in-law. Ruth had the love of Boaz, and Boaz was presented with a son who would be in the lineage of Christ. God's plans are always so perfect. But, I still wonder: *What if Ruth had not been so kind to Naomi and returned to Beth-lehem?* It's something to ponder. But if the truth is known, Ruth would-n't have refused, because God was guiding her, whether she knew it or not. The choice was really not hers to decide.

I end kindness with these two short accounts:

CHOSEN

Whenever I'm disappointed with my lot in life, I stop and think about little Jamie Scott. Jamie was trying out for a part in his school play. His mother told me that he's set his heart on being in it, though she feared he would not be chosen. On the day the parts were awarded, I went with her to collect him after school. Jamie rushed up to her, eyes shining with pride and excitement. "Guess what, Mum," he shouted, and then said those words that remain a lesson to me: "I've been chosen to clap and cheer." [2]

— MARIE CURLING

True kindness is clapping and cheering others on, and expecting noth-ing at all in return. There may be times when your kindness seems empty to you; that you are not making a difference, especially when someone doesn't return your smile, or when you've tried to help and you've been rebuffed. Never mind! You've been chosen nevertheless to clap and cheer. Always count that a privilege . . . you may never know the blessing you have brought to another, but heaven knows.

LOOK-ALIKES

While working at a medical center, I noticed a distinguished gentle-man and his young son on their daily visits to the chemotherapy cen-ter. Impeccably tailored suit and a head of lush salt-and-pepper hair made the man stand out. As I admired him and his smiling five-

year-old, I found it impossible to tell who was receiving treatment.

One day, as they walked past, my attention was drawn to the boy. The cap he usually wore was missing, and I could now see a shiny bald head. I turned toward the father. To my surprise, he was as bald as his son.

"Look at my dad." the boy said cheerfully. "He shaved his head so we'd look the same. We're going to grow our hair back together!"

His father simply smiled, looking more distinguished than ever.[3]

— LINDA MANGO

Does that father have a kind, compassionate heart or what?

LIFE IS SHORT:
BE SWIFT TO LOVE,
AND MAKE HASTE TO BE KIND!

CHAPTER XII

Application & Review

Kindness is an "action" fruit and is expressed through compassion, consideration for others, sympathy, giving, caring and generosity. It is a fruit that is very often learned through osmosis in our homes. However, only the Holy Spirit can give us the insight, wisdom and power necessary to help express God's care for all people.

1. Is kindness a part of your life? In what ways have you shown kindness to others?

2. Will you be able to pass on a legacy of kindness to your children? In what way?

3. Read Ephesians 4:32 and name the words mingling together with kindness. Give a primary reason why we should forgive.

4. How was Ruth kind to Naomi in Ruth 1:10 and 4:14-15? How was Naomi rewarded?

5. How was Boaz kind to Ruth? (Ruth 2:8-9)

CHAPTER XIII

The Fruit of the Spirit is Goodness

Goodness is the life grown moral by seeking love's pleasure

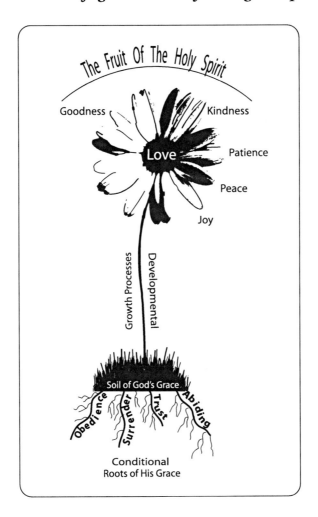

*. . . for the fruit of the Spirit is in all goodness
and righteousness and truth . . .*

EPHESIANS 5:9 KJV

CHAPTER XIII

The Fruit of the Spirit is Goodness

Surely goodness and mercy shall follow me all the days of my life . . .
PSALM 23:6 KJV

When God measures a man,
He puts the tape around the heart
Instead of the head.
AUTHOR UNKNOWN

oodness is expressed as righteousness, excellence, being virtuous, honest, pleasant and kind. It falls in the same category as kindness in that, as Christ's examples, we are to treat others out of the goodness of our hearts, no matter who that person should be. The following story gives us a clear glimpse into the goodness of a man's heart:

AN EARTHLY ACCOUNT OF GOODNESS: THE SANDWICH MAN

What would you do if you wanted to make a difference in the world, leave a mark or put a deposit on a ticket into heaven? Would you think big and pick the flashiest or most grandiose of acts? Or would you quietly persevere every day, doing one personal deed at a time?

Michael Christiano, a New York City court officer, rises every morning at 4 A.M., in good and bad weather, workday or holiday, and walks into his sandwich shop. No, he doesn't own a deli; it's really his personal kitchen. In it are the fixings of his famous sand-

wiches, famous only to those who desperately need them to stave off hunger for the day. By 5:50 A.M., he's making the rounds of the makeshift homeless shelters on Centre and Lafayette Streets, near New York's City Hall. In a short time, he gives out 200 sandwiches to as many homeless people as he can, before beginning his workday in the courthouse.

It started 20 years ago with a cup of coffee and a roll for a homeless man named John. Day after day, Michael brought John sandwiches, tea, clothes, and when it was really cold, a resting place in his car while he worked. In the beginning, Michael just wanted to do a good deed.

But one day a voice in his head compelled him to do more. On this cold, winter morning, he asked John if he would like to get cleaned up. It was an empty offer, because Michael was sure John would refuse. Unexpectedly, John said, "Are you gonna wash me?"

Michael heard an inner voice say, **put your money where your mouth is.** Looking at this poor man, covered in ragged and smelly clothes, unkempt, hairy and wild-looking, Michael was afraid. But he also knew that he was looking at a big test of his commitment. So he helped John upstairs to the locker room of the courthouse to begin the work.

John's body was a mass of cuts and sores, the result of years of pain and neglect. His right hand had been amputated, and Michael pushed through his own fears and revulsion. He helped John wash, cut his hair, shaved him and shared breakfast with him. "It was at that moment," Michael remembers, "that I **knew** I had a calling, and I believed that I had it within me to do anything."

With the idea for his sandwiches born, Michael began his calling. He receives no corporate sponsorship, saying, "I'm not looking for an act of charity that goes in the record books or gets media attention. I just want to do good day by day, in my small way. Sometimes it comes out of my pocket; sometimes I get help. But this is really something that *I* can do, one day and one person at a time.

"There are days when it's snowing," he says, "and I have a hard time leaving my warm bed and the comfort of my family to go downtown with sandwiches. But then that voice in me starts chattering, and I get to it."

And get to it he does. Michael has made 200 sandwiches every day for the past 20 years. "When I give out sandwiches," Michael explains, "I don't simply lay them on a table for folks to pick up. I look everyone in the eye, shake their hands, and I offer them my wishes for a good and hopeful day. Each person is important to me. I don't see them as 'the homeless,' but as people who need food, an encouraging smile and some positive human contact."

"Once Mayor Koch turned up to make the rounds with me. He didn't invite the media; it was just us," says Michael. But of all Michael's memories, working side by side with the Mayor was not as important as working next to someone else . . .

A man had disappeared from the ranks of the sandwich takers, and Michael thought about him from time to time. He hoped the man had moved on to more comfortable conditions. One day, the man showed up, transformed, greeting Michael clean, warmly clothed, shaven and carrying sandwiches of his own to hand out. Michael's daily dose of fresh food, warm handshakes, eye contact and well wishes had given this man the hope and encouragement he so desperately needed. Being seen every day as a person, not as a category, had turned this man's life around.

The moment needed no dialogue. The two men worked silently, side by side, handing out their sandwiches. It was another day on the streets of New York, but a day with just a little more hope.[1]

— MELADEE McCARTY (EMPHASIS ADDED)

Now that is a good person. Would you do that? Would I do that? These are questions we have to ask ourselves. The homeless, the disadvantaged, the diseased, the drunks, the ravaged, the unfortunates, the revolting and repulsive in this world are considered highly significant to the kingdom of God—more so, I would suggest, than you or I. These are the people Christ ministered to while on earth. And so should we.

> *Then the King will say to those on his right. "Come you who are blessed by my Father; take your inheritance, the kingdom prepared for you since the creation of the world. For I was hungry and you gave me something to eat. I was thirsty and you gave me something to drink, I was a stranger and you invited me in. I needed clothes and you clothed me, I was sick and you looked after me, I was in prison and you came to visit me."* MATTHEW 25:34,35 NIV

His disciples were in a quandary as to how they had ministered to the Lord in such a way and His reply was: *"I tell you the truth, whatever you did for one of the least of these brothers of mine, you did it for me"* (Matthew 25:40 NIV). From the King James version the same scripture reads: *"Verily I say unto you, inasmuch as ye have done it unto one of the least of these my brethren, ye have done it unto me."*

I've heard my husband say numerous times when visiting a patient in the hospital: "I'm on my way to visit with Jesus." "I'm on my way to see Jesus and minister to Him." It was a truth made clear on a very snowy, bitter cold day while living in Rochester. He was tired, not feeling up to par, the winter wind was biting, it was getting late and darkness was creeping into the city. He had been traveling from hospital to hospital all day and this was supposed to be his last stop. He stopped his car beside the road and said to himself: "Maybe I'll save this next stop for tomorrow." His old Volkswagen had a temperamental heater and sometimes never gave any heat until you neared your destination, and he shivered most of the day while traveling. To top everything off, this last hospital was located on the other side of Rochester, and traffic was horrendous due to the weather. He wanted to go home, have a good meal and relax. But that was not to be. While sitting by the road,

God made it real to him that he wasn't just visiting congregants, but would be going to visit Jesus as well. It was one of those profound revelations that gripped his heart. He turned his car in the direction of the hospital and, as fate would have it, the man he was to visit needed prayer "now" and not tomorrow morning. While driving along, he kept saying to himself: "I'm on my way to see Jesus. I'm going to minister to Jesus as well as minister to Mr. Carini." It surely does bring a new perspective when others need us so desperately. It especially adds a new dimension to our purpose. And if the truth is known, my husband was actually becoming excited about the whole concept and that experience left him rather in awe. The truth of seeing and ministering to Jesus was profound. His Word is truth!

Goodness, as a fruit of the Spirit, has a way of tenderly unfolding into the very fiber of our beings once we start to reach out. Today, locate someone to encourage, to lift from the miry clay, to empower, to express goodness to—and then, sit back and watch their lives change. Being good to people changes lives! Watch it happen. I have! We have! "Heaviness in the heart of man maketh it stoop: but a good word maketh it glad" (Proverbs 12:25 KJV).

"It is more blessed to give than to receive" (Act 20:38b NIV). Even though the Bible clearly states that giving is more important than receiving, Jesus does reward those who extend themselves to others in an unmistakable fashion. Check our the following verses:

"Try to show as much compassion as your Father does. Never criticize or condemn . . . or it will all come back on you. Go easy on others; then they will do the same for you. For if you give, you will get! Your gift will return to you in full and overflowing measure, pressed down, shaken together to make room for more, and running over. Whatever measure you use to give . . . large or small . . . will be used to measure what is given back to you" (Luke 6:37,38 TLB). Let's be good to each other . . . givers, not takers.

❧

A HEAVENLY ACCOUNT OF GOODNESS: MOSES

Have you ever felt trapped? It is not a pleasant experience to know you are backed into a corner and your escape eludes you. What to do! Where to go! How do I survive? Panic attacks are like that. Panic brings fear and, rather than escaping, the fear envelopes your entire being. A person becomes a victim of his/her own emotional responses. One feels trapped.

However, panic attacks are nothing compared to what the Israelites had to endure when faced with the Red Sea in front of them and the Egyptians closing in from behind. Now, that is a reason to panic! They were literally trapped between the desert and the sea. Their story follows:

"Leaving Succoth, they camped in Etham at the edge of the wilderness. The Lord guided them by a pillar of cloud during the daytime, and by a pillar of fire at night" (Exodus 13:20 TLB). This provided Israel the opportunity to travel either during the day or during the night and they could adjust their pace. They were instructed by the Lord to travel on to Migdol, which was actually nearer the shores of the Red Sea. They were really trapped now. But God had a purpose. He hardened the heart of Pharaoh yet again, and the Egyptians became irate that the slaves they depended on were released. This encouraged a pursuit! *"And once again I will harden Pharaoh's heart and he will chase after you. **I have planned this to gain great honor and glory over Pharaoh and all his armies, and the Egyptians shall know that I am the Lord**"* (Exodus 14:4 TLB).

Pharaoh's heart was hardened and he became bold again. As any leader in pursuit, Pharaoh gathered his cavalry, which consisted of horses and 600 chariots plus his horsemen and his army. The Egyptians began their chase and were delighted that the Israelites were now in a trapped position. *"And when Pharaoh drew nigh, the children of Israel lifted up their eyes, and behold, the Egyptians marched after them: and they were sore afraid; and the children of Israel cried out unto the Lord"* (Exodus 14:10 KJV).

The Israelites began to turn against Moses for allowing them to be trapped like caged animals. The whining and crying continued and this reminded Moses of their contentious spirits before leaving Egypt: *"Isn't this what we told you, while we were slaves, to leave us alone? We said it would be better to be slaves to the Egyptians than dead in the wilderness"* (Exodus 14:12 TLB).

Moses kept his "cool," and put his trust in the Lord. He was familiar with their many previous complaints and was not moved by them. Instead He said: *"Don't be afraid. Just stand where you are and watch, and you will see the wonderful way the Lord will rescue you today"* (Exodus 14:13 TLB). I like the King James version of these verses also: *"Fear ye not, stand still, and see the salvation of the Lord."*

The situation is getting serious now: The Red Sea, the desert, the Egyptians charging—the Israelites must have thought Moses had completely lost his mind. Can't you hear them saying: "What does Moses mean, 'stand still?'" "We have to do something to fight back, but what?" "Why is Moses so calm?" "What can God possibly do?" "How can God rescue us?" "We're just trapped." "Oh, God!"

Their leader, Moses, however, was still in tune with God's voice, and God said: *"Quit praying and get the people moving! Forward! March! Use your rod . . . hold it out over the water, and the sea will open up a path before you, and all the people of Israel shall walk through on dry ground"* (Exodus 14:15,16 TLB). I wonder what went through Moses' mind when God gave him this instruction? If they marched forward, they would be heading toward the water, but God said He would open a path through that water. I'm assuming that Moses was not worried; yet, he must have been excited also, to once again witness God's intervention. He surely had seen God perform many miracles while in Egypt, why not now? Moses must have held that rod out and waited in anticipation, and this is what he saw: *"Moses stretched his rod over the sea, and the Lord opened up a path through the sea, with a wall of water on each side; and a strong east wind blew all that night, drying the sea bottom. So the people of Israel walked through the sea on dry ground"* (Exodus 14:21, 22 TLB). Moses, I'm sure, would have expected anything from God; but when the Israelites were trapped, the sea opening up was not an option they would have entertained.

In the interim, God had held Pharaoh and his 600 chariots at bay by moving the cloud used to guide the Israelites to a position where the Egyptians were unable to see where the Israelites were. So, the Egyptians were in the dark, but the Israelites were in the light from the pillar of fire. When Pharaoh found the Israelites, he and his huge army followed . . . straight through the wall of water. As soon as the Israelites were on the opposite shore, God spoke to Moses again: *"Stretch out your hand again over the sea, so that the waters will come back over the Egyptians and their chariots and horsemen"* (Exodus 14:26 TLB).

Not one Egyptian was able to escape the wrath of God that day. His people rejoiced at the mighty miracle they witnessed and they were in awe as they revered the Lord. He wanted the Egyptians to know: **"I am the Lord."** He displayed His Lordship in a mighty presentation of power. It is possible that God said: **"Now they know that I am the Lord for they have had to 'let my people go.'"**

Why did I tell this story? I wanted to portray the **goodness** of God. He is an awesome God of compassion and goodness. He forgets not His own. Never!! Never!! Today, keep a vigilant watch for a person that needs the goodness of God in their life, and minister to their need. Then, stand back and see a life transformed before your eyes. Allow the Lord to show forth the fruit of His goodness through you!

IT IS SUCH A COMFORT TO DROP THE TANGLES OF LIFE INTO GOD'S HANDS . . . INTO HIS GOODNESS AND LEAVE THEM THERE. GOD IS GOOD!!

Trust in the Lord and do good.

PSALM 37:3 NIV

—an entire recipe for life with only two ingredients!!

CHAPTER XIII
Application & Review

Goodness falls into the same category as kindness in that, as Christ's examples, we are to treat others out of the goodness of our hearts. Goodness, as a fruit of the Spirit, has a way of tenderly unfolding into the very fiber of our beings once we start to reach out. It is God reaching out to others through us—His life in us!

1. Name the last time you did a good deed for someone. How can you improve?

2. How does Jesus explain kindness in Matthew 25:34-35?

3. How could you "go the second mile" to help someone, as illustrated in Matthew 5:41-44?

4. How did God portray His goodness to Moses and the Israelites? See Exodus 13-14.

5. What is the reward for showing goodness to others? (See Luke 6:38.) To what measure?

6. What was God's initial purpose in helping the Israelites? See Exodus 6:5-7 and 14:4.

CHAPTER XIV

The Fruit of the Spirit is Faithfulness

Faithfulness is love's servant

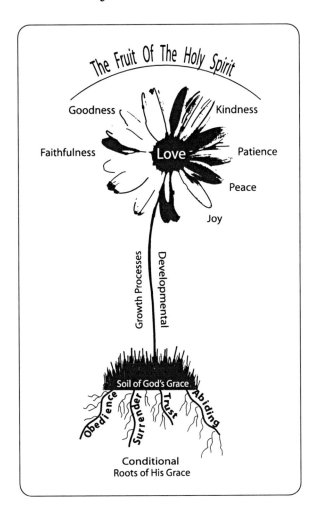

I will sing of the mercies of the Lord forever:
with my mouth will I make known thy faithfulness to all generations.

PSALM 89:1 KJV

CHAPTER XIV

The Fruit of the Spirit is Faithfulness

. . . for we walk by faith, not by sight.

II CORINTHIANS 5:7 KJV

What happened to honesty? To where did the faithfulness of our past Presidents disappear? Remember George Washington and his statement: "I can never tell a lie?" Today, lies shroud our government. Presidents, senators and representatives have made promises that are not feasible, yet they lie just the same. Remember "honest Abe" Lincoln? He walked several miles to return an incorrect amount of money that was given him. America has lost its way and has no conscience. Today, the first priority of Congress is not to be faithful to their constituents. Their first priority is to control, and control they do by spending taxpayers' money.

How have we arrived at such a condition and state of immorality? I can give you a simple answer. God has been allocated to the far corners of the world. America has abandoned our faithful forefathers who founded this country, and placed ideologues in their place. We, as a government and a country, have abandoned God. The apostle Paul states: ". . . the wisdom of this world is foolishness in God's sight. As it is written: 'He catches the wise in their craftiness.' The Lord knows that the thoughts of the wise are futile" (I Corinthians 3:19,20 NIV).

Therefore, the youth of our nation are lost; they have no compass, no models to follow and no moral integrity to duplicate or look up to. Children in our public schools are becoming rebellious, disrespectful, immoral and without direction. Very few students have goals and most

❧❦❧

will simply "float" along through life empty in soul and spirit. This is such a sad commentary. Parents have lost hope and many marriages end in divorce. Many are unable to control their children and most have no moral compass to guide them and pass along to their children. Our youth, instead, have been lost to a corrupt society that neither reveres God nor respects authority. Faith in our country, in our schools, in parental responsibilities is dissipating fast. Faith, belief, trust and loyalty are being creatively challenged in our culture today by ideologues and by the forces of evil. We must, therefore, walk by faith and not sight. If we walked by sight only, our hearts would fail, for fear would overwhelm us. Faith brings hope!!

EXERCISES IN FAITH: AN UNEXPECTED GIFT

During that physically-spent period in my life which I wrote of in Chapters I and II, my husband and I found ourselves in a position where exercising our faith was a matter of necessity. It seemed prudent to relocate further from the church, where He could "lead me beside still waters" and I could "lie down in green pastures." At the time, that visual picture was very comforting. I longed for green grass, flowers, a garden and quietness where my soul could be restored. We had lived in the apartment attached to the church for 10 years, with a great deal of commotion, and the thought of solitude warmed my soul. We began to pray and believe that God would provide. Of course, in God's scheme, He had already made a plan . . . a solution was in place. However, we were not privy to that resolution until almost a year later.

A Mr. Taylor attended our church off and on for several years. He was somewhat of a peculiar man. He came to church in rather tattered clothing and, on occasion, we would tell him to gather a few pieces for himself from our missionary boxes. He never did. He was quiet, reserved and seemed reticent to establish relationships. He loved my husband, though, and could converse on a very intellectual level on various subjects. Many people thought of him as odd. I found him fascinating and charming as the years went by. He was a frugal man and was even found groping in the corner street garbage can for the "today's" newspaper. Why pay if you can find it left behind in the garbage, right? He also had a beautiful collection of crystal that I thought was odd considering the rags he wore.

To make a long story short, one day Mr. Taylor died of old age. I missed him. He had endeared himself to me. He had previously asked that my husband perform his funeral service. My husband had quickly said "of course," and this seemed to bring him peace. We later learned that all his funeral expenses had been paid beforehand. We wondered where the money had come from.

Several months after Mr. Taylor's funeral, his niece approached my husband and said his presence was required at the reading of the will. We were astonished! It was made known that Mr. Taylor had left my husband an inheritance of $15,000. I said, "What?" It was true! Mr. Taylor was not poor. He had, instead, hoarded his fortune and quite lived as a pauper. "Things" were just not important to him. With that money, we were able to make a down payment on a house where I began to restore physically. There was even a grassy park one street over from us. I also grew flowers . . . what a treat. To top the story off, in his will he also included several gorgeous pieces of crystal for me. If you knew how much I love crystal, you would then understand how precious this gift was to me. His niece explained that the crystal had belonged to his wife but he wanted me to have it. God is so faithful to meet our need and He even threw in a little extra blessing . . . crystal! *As you look down from heaven, my dear Mr. Taylor, please gaze into my grateful heart and do take time to view the crystal I have placed in a prominent space for all to see. I shall always remember you with great fondness.*

THE GOLD COINS

"More to be desired are they than gold, yea, than much fine gold . . ." (Psalm 19:10 KJV). In this particular Psalm, David was explaining that God's laws, statutes, precepts and commandments were to be desired more than gold and even more than fine gold. Gold was precious, but God's law was more precious. And yet, it was gold that God used to assist, support and give wings to a fledgling church spoken of in chapter two. Let me tell you the story:

In the late '60s and early '70s an elderly lady by the name of Martha Reichle attended our small congregation. She was of German descent and had escaped her homeland during WWI and made America her home. However, before she left Germany, she attempted to take her money out of the bank. She was not the only one. Many were removing their money in fear of a financial collapse of the country. When she arrived at the bank, the line extended around the block. Unfortunately, when she presented her documents to draw her money out, there was no more money to be had.

Upon her arrival in America, she found work cleaning homes or offices . . . the same employment as in Germany. She saved her money. But, this time, she bought gold and stashed her treasure in a locked box at a Chemical Bank on the corner of Steinway Street and Broadway in Long Island City. She told no one of the gold coins she had purchased; not even her husband. As the years went by, she continued to add to the locked box supply.

One day, she approached my husband and asked him to drive her to the Chemical Bank. He complied, of course, and picked her up the next morning at 10:00. When they arrived at the bank, she turned to my husband and asked him if he would please accompany her inside. My husband parked the car and as they entered the bank, Mrs. Reichle asked to be admitted into the vault area. By this time, my husband was curious beyond words. The bank attendee opened her safe-deposit box with the bank key and then she continued the opening process with her key. (As you know, as a precautionary measure, a safe-deposit box can only be opened by two keys . . . never by just one.)

Before my husband's eyes were gold coins . . . many, many gold coins! Mrs. Reichle handed the box to my husband and they made their way to the manager of the bank. She wanted to redeem the coins for cash. After the counting process, the bank manager said the face value of the coins was $6,000. They left the bank with the $6,000! As my husband drove her home, Mrs. Reichle said: "Come to my place to-morrow; I want to give a large amount of this cash to the church."

However, the story doesn't end there. After arriving home with this hefty sum of money, the bank called Mrs. Reichle. The manager said that after further review of the coins, it was their opinion that the coins were antique. If the coins were antique, this knowledge would change the value, placing the remuneration to a much larger amount. Did she want to consult with a coin dealer? Of course she did! That meant going back to the bank where the money was exchanged for the coins and, once again, the coins were placed in the vault. Mrs. Reichele said to my husband: "You find the coin dealer and then we'll negotiate." My husband saw three coin dealers. One offered $9,000. The second offered $9,500. The third offered $10,000. Bingo!! My husband knew, after researching coins and their value, that $10,000 was a generous offer. He then spoke with Mrs. Reichle, and it was a done deal.

This money, minus a couple thousand that Mrs. Reichle kept for herself, was seed money that catapulted our church into the renovation projects mentioned in Chapter II. Faith! God has a storehouse full of treasure that is ours for the asking. *Mrs. Reichle: I know that God has replaced your gift to us tenfold, for you are now in the presence of Him whose wealth is untold. You now have access to all the treasures of heaven. Enjoy them! You deserve them! As you look down upon us, you can see that your seed money of $10,000 was blessed and has grown to a newly-completed*

❧❦∴

*$10,000,000 project. We shall always be grateful for your gift of encourage-
ment in those early, struggling years of the late '60s.*

AN EARTHLY INTERPRETATION OF FAITHFULNESS:
FANNY CROSBY

I am abundantly thankful for the faithfulness of those in years gone by,
who still remain with us through tradition, books and songs. Whenever
I thought of music, Fanny Crosby came to my mind. Her faithfulness
to her Lord was unwavering in spite of her blindness, and she remains
a superlative example to all Christians. Fanny Crosby wrote over 8,000
Christian hymns despite her handicap. Her blindness was the result of
an inept doctor and a botched procedure. When questioned regarding
this unfortunate incident, her reply was: "If perfect earthly sight were
offered me tomorrow, I would not accept it. I might not have sung
hymns to the praise of God if I had been distracted by the beautiful and
interesting things about me." One of her most precious hymns is "All
The Way My Savior Leads Me," and it has been a blessing to me more
than once when dark trials shut out the light. We can become spiritually blind, as well as physically blind you know!!

Fanny wrote the lyrics to this beloved hymn as a result of a prayer.
She had been struggling financially and was in dire need of some money.
As was her usual custom, she began to pray. She related that only a few
minutes later, a man tapped her on the shoulder and offered her five
dollars—which, by the way, was the exact amount she needed. When
she later related this episode, she said, "I have no way of accounting for
this except to believe that God put it into the heart of this good man to
bring the money." The poem she wrote afterward is as follows:

ALL THE WAY MY SAVIOR LEADS ME

All the way my Savior leads me—what have I to ask beside?

Can I doubt His tender mercy,
Who through life has been my guide?
Heavenly peace, divinest comfort,
here by faith in Him to dwell!
For I know, whate'er befall me, Jesus doeth all things well;
For I know, whate'er befall me, Jesus doeth all things well.

All the way my Savior leads me—
cheers each winding path I tread,
Gives me grace for every trial, feeds me with the living bread.
Though my weary steps may falter
and my soul a-thirst may be,
Gushing from the Rock before me, Lo! A spring of joy I see;
Gushing from the Rock before me, Lo! A spring of joy I see.

All the way my Savior leads me—O the fullness of His love!
Perfect rest to me is promised in my Father's house above.
When my spirit, clothed immortal,
Wings its flight to realms of day,
This my song through endless ages: Jesus led me all the way;
This my song through endless ages: Jesus led me all the way.[1]

— FANNY CROSBY

God bless you, Fanny, for blessing me with your words . . . and not just any old words, but heartfelt words of encouragement from your heart to mine, and many others along their journeys.

The faith and faithfulness of Fanny Crosby is inspiring! Those of us who remain are also asked to carry burdens . . . some small, some large, some easier, and some more difficult. But, whatever those burdens are, may we be as faithful as Fanny. May we apply our spiritual sight and use it wisely. May we carry His name and fame to the ends of the earth according to each one's calling and inspiration! On Fanny Crosby's tombstone are the lyrics from one of her hymns: "Blessed Assurance,

Jesus is mine. Oh, what a foretaste of glory divine." What an assurance! Jesus will be yours, mine, ours and how divine that will be!

A HEAVENLY INTERPRETATION OF FAITHFULNESS

The following narrative portrays the faithfulness of our Lord. He said:

> *Let not your heart be troubled:*
> *ye believe in God, believe also in me.*
> *In my Father's house are many mansions:*
> *if it were not so, I would have told you.*
> *I go to prepare a place for you.*
> *And if I go and prepare a place for you,*
> *I will come again, and receive you unto myself;*
> *that where I am, there ye may be also.*
>
> JOHN 14:1-3 KJV

WHEN CHRIST RETURNS

You are in your car driving home. Thoughts wander to the game you want to see or the meal you want to eat, when suddenly a sound unlike any you've ever heard fills the air. The sound is high above you. A trumpet? A choir? A choir of trumpets? You don't know, but you want to know. So you pull over, get out of your car, and look up. As you do, you see you aren't the only curious one. The roadside has become a parking lot. Car doors are open, and people are staring at the sky. Shoppers are racing out of the grocery store. The Little League baseball game across the street has come to a halt. Players and parents are searching the clouds.

And what they see, and what you see, has never been seen.

As if the sky were a curtain, the drapes of the atmosphere part. A brilliant light spills onto the earth. There are no shadows. None. From whence came the light begins to tumble a river of color . . .

spiking crystals of every hue ever seen and a million more never seen. Riding on the flow is an endless fleet of angels. They pass through the curtains one myriad at a time, until they occupy every square inch of the sky. North. South. East. West. Thousands of silvery wings rise and fall in unison, and over the sound of the trumpets, you can hear the cherubim and the seraphim chanting "Holy, holy, holy."

The final flank of angels is followed by twenty-four silver-bearded elders and a multitude of souls who join the angels in worship. Presently the movement stops and the trumpets are silent, leaving only the triumphant triplet: "Holy, holy, holy." Between each word is a pause. With each word, a profound reverence. You hear your voice join in the chorus. You don't know why you say the words, but you know you must.

Suddenly, the heavens are quiet. All is quiet. The angels turn, you turn, the entire world turns . . . and there He is. Jesus. Through waves of light you see the silhouetted figure of Christ the King. He is atop a great stallion, and the stallion is atop a billowing cloud. He opens his mouth, and you are surrounded by his declaration: "I am the Alpha and the Omega."

The angels bow their heads. The elders remove their crowns. And before you, is a figure so consuming that you know, instantly you know. Nothing else matters. Forget stock markets and school reports. Sales meetings and football games. Nothing is newsworthy. All that mattered, matters no more, for Christ has come . . . [2]

— MAX LUCADO

When I first read the above, I just sat in my chair in awe with tears streaming down my cheeks. Nothing here really matters. We are only here for a "season." Jesus will one day return. **We will one day reach out our arms, and He will gently raise us up into eternity with His strong arm of *faithfulness.***

Shout for joy to the Lord all the earth,
Worship the Lord with gladness;
come before him with joyful songs.
Know that the Lord is God.
It is he who made us, and we are his;
we are his people, the sheep of his pasture.
Enter his gates with thanksgiving and his courts with praise,
give thanks to him and praise his name.
For the Lord is good and his love endures forever;
*His **faithfulness** continues through all generations.*

PSALM 100 NIV

FAITH

Faith, in plain terms, is just simply believing what God has promised. Faith is not a power; it is a gift of the Spirit. It can be powerful, though, when employed. You cannot see it. It is not something you can conjure up inside of yourself. Then what is it? Faith is trusting that whatever the Bible states regarding God is true. It is believing that God will always and forever honor His Word. It is trust in the character and nobleness of God Himself!

When we find ourselves in positions which seem impossible to solve; or when you become ill and the answer for your illness is not forthcoming; when you are in a financial bind and you have been laid off; when your child strays from God and God's ears seem deaf to your prayers; when a hurricane destroys your home and you've lost everything; when your small business is in the red and your only option is to sell; or simply put, when life itself, with all its ups and downs, creates an emptiness that just seems to go unfulfilled; then it's time to take hold of the hand of Faith. Oh Boy! (I think I've just backed myself into a corner.) Would I, could I, believe while in the midst of any of the above scenarios? (Me thinks I may be in trouble!!) All kidding aside, Faith is one of the precious fruit of the Spirit. In myself, I would do more than struggle. I may just want to throw in the towel. This is when we need to be strengthened, enabled and have our spiritual eyes opened. Jesus is coming again. I started this chapter so discouraged with our country and its "ills," but feel so refreshed and excited just realizing that the best is yet to come . . . we will soon see Him in all His glory.

"Help us, Lord, to believe. Open our spiritual eyes to your truth. Thank you for giving us this precious gift of faith from the Holy Spirit, and may we find strength in your Holy Word when we need to exercise this gift. We look forward to your return. We look forward to seeing you face to face! Amen."

Faith is being sure of what we hope for
and certain of what we do not see.
HEBREWS 11:1 NIV

SHARE YOUR FAITH TODAY!

CHAPTER XIV

Application & Review

God is faithful! His faithfulness continues throughout all generations. Let's place our hand in His, and confidently allow Him to lead us into the future, knowing that we can trust a faithful God who fills our hearts with hope.

1. Have you experienced His faithfulness in a specific way? Explain.

2. Explain God's faithfulness, as seen in John 14:1-3.

3. What is God's promise to those who faithfully serve Him? Read Matthew 25:21.

4. How have you been faithful in your endeavors to serve Him? Give details.

5. Give your interpretation of Hebrews 11:1.

CHAPTER XV

The Fruit of the Spirit is Gentleness

Gentleness is love's method

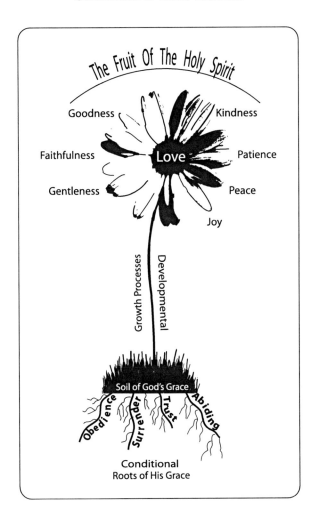

Be completely humble and gentle; be patient,
bearing with one another in love.

EPHESIANS 4:2 NIV

CHAPTER XV

The Fruit of the Spirit is Gentleness

. . . the unfading beauty of a gentle and quiet spirit.

I PETER 3:4B NIV

Gentleness is that quality of the Spirit that exemplifies the true meaning of tenderness, compassion and understanding.

I read somewhere, someplace in time, that what dew is to a flower, gentle words are to the soul. Words can either hinder or help. They can scar us for life or they can lift us to heights we never thought we could attain. Words are seeds that, when planted, can produce a flower of beauty or a flower whose growth is stunted from lack of nourishment and harsh conditions. Gentle words open a little bit of heaven to a soul; harsh words can cause a soul to venture into a living hell. Words can produce hope within our beings or words can bring despair to all our tomorrows. Gentle words can add fragrance to our souls or cruel words can cause souls to wither and die. Words can cause you to reach for the stars or they can cause stagnation and discouragement. Words of gentleness are a precious gift and we need to use them to brighten the lives of those who cross our paths.

While attending school, I distinctly recall several teachers who immensely impacted my life:

In second grade my teacher's name was Mrs. Overheiser. Unfortunately, some in the classroom used to call her Mrs. "Oversizer" because she was very, very, very humongous. However, I was told by my strict mother that if I ever called her Mrs. Oversizer, I would either get the switch to my legs or have my mouth washed out with soap. It was my choice. My choice was none of the above. So, I was especially careful to never say Oversizer, especially in my mother's presence . . . but I thought it! She was not my favorite teacher by any stretch of the imagination. I tried to like her but she was just about the meanest teacher in this entire world. This was second grade and my second grade mind just couldn't find room for liking someone so mean. To top everything off, I had to be in her classroom for an entire year.

One particular day, I was having difficulty with math. I mean, how hard can second grade math be? I guess for my seven-year-old mind, something just wasn't clicking and I remember asking for the teacher's help. Well, I remember Mrs. Oversizer . . . ooops, I mean Overheiser, saying: "Well, I just don't see why you don't understand this, it's not that difficult." That did it! I felt like the dumbest kid in the classroom. It's amazing what we remember, right?

Throughout my school years and even into college, I faced every math test with fear and trepidation. The reason? Mrs. Overheiser, in one grand swoop, had stripped away my confidence. Her negative words to my innocent question made me doubt myself. To this day, I have an aversion to thoughts of balancing a checkbook, comprehending the intricacies of the financial world, or just plain numbers anywhere or any place. Mrs. Oveheiser's words were far from gentle. They were, instead, destructive.

Secondly, I remember a Miss Miller. I was just learning how to spell. I said to her one day so proudly: "I know how to spell God." She was so attentive and said: "Please, let me hear." I said "God" (you always had to say the word before you spelled it). Then I spelled God: "D-O-G." As soon as I spelled "dog" for "God," I knew I had made a mistake; I had reversed the G and D. I was so horrified, I cried all the way back to my seat. Miss Miller left her desk, approached me, leaned down and whispered to me: "Honey, you almost got it right." She then proceeded to show me what I did wrong (but, of course, I already knew). She said: "Just practice and spell it later for me. I know you can do it!" I practiced and later spelled God correctly and Miss Miller gave me a huge gold star and said: "See, I knew you could do it. You're a great speller."

Why did I tell such a silly little story? Because Miss Miller's gentle words inspired me. In fact, she made me feel so confident that I won all the "spelling bees" in grade school. I received many awards! They're stashed away among all the memorabilia we often save but never look at. I know, I know, you're all going to be looking for misspelled words now, right? I do have "spell check" on my computer but that does not guarantee you won't find some errors. I have never forgotten Miss Miller's gentle words to my little unsure heart way back in the mid '40s. Her positive words not only gave me confidence, but I felt loved.

Thirdly, there was Mr. Fraizer. He was my English teacher in high school. He discovered I had an aptitude for writing. Well, "better than most," he said. He gave me extra writing assignments such as essays, short stories, etc. to encourage me. I was skeptical at first, but realized I enjoyed the process of learning writing skills. Mr. Fraizer was gentle; his words were always positive. He would give my papers back with his little notations and corrections but then add at the bottom: "Don't stop trying . . . you're a very thoughtful person and it comes through in your writing." I think I still have some of those old essays and stories with their many corrections. Today I love to write, I love to read and I love anything to do with English. I thank Mr. Fraizer for his gentle, kind and positive words to me as I discovered an aptitude I was unaware of, but he was perceptive enough to observe.

AN EARTHLY EXPRESSION OF GENTLENESS: DON'T QUIT

The following story, strongly speaks of a person who possesses such a gentle, compassionate, understanding and encouraging heart. You'll enjoy it!

Ignace Jan Paderewski, the famous composer-pianist, was scheduled to perform at a great concert hall in America. It was an evening to

❦

remember; black tuxedos and long evening dresses, a high-society extravaganza. Present in the audience that evening was a mother with her fidgety nine-year-old son. Weary of waiting, he squirmed constantly in his seat. His mother was in hopes that her son would be encouraged to practice the piano if he could just hear the immortal Paderewski at the keyboard. So, against his wishes, he had come.

As she turned to talk with friends, her son could stay seated no longer. He slipped away from her side, strangely drawn to the ebony concert grand Steinway and its leather tufted stool on the huge stage flooded with blinding lights. Without much notice from the sophisticated audience, the boy say down at the stool, staring wide-eyed at the black and white keys. He placed his small, trembling fingers in the right location and began to play "Chopsticks." The roar of the crowd was hushed as hundreds of frowning faces pointed in his direction. Irritated and embarrassed, they began to shout:

"Get that boy away from there!"

"Who'd bring a kid that young in here?"

"Where's his mother?"

"Somebody stop him!"

Backstage, the master overheard the sounds out front and quickly put together in his mind what was happening. Hurriedly, he grabbed his coat and rushed toward the stage. Without one word of announcement he stooped over behind the boy, reached around both sides, and began to improvise a countermelody to harmonize with and enhance "Chopsticks." As the two of them played together, Paderewski kept whispering in the boy's ear:

"Keep going. Don't quit. Keep on playing . . . don't stop . . . don't quit."

And so it is with us. We hammer away on our project, which seems about as significant as "Chopsticks" in a concert hall. And about the time we are ready to give up, along comes the Master who leans over and whispers:

🙡🙠

"Now keep going; don't quit. Keep on . . . don't stop; don't quit,
as He improvises on our behalf, providing just the right touch at just
the right moment."[1]
— CHARLES SWINDOLL

I read this story years ago and do you know the numerous times I have
said: "Keep going. Don't quit. Don't stop" to myself? The Master of my
soul was always there with just the right touch to gently encourage me,
exactly as Mr. Paderewski unselfishly had compassion on this innocent
9-year-old-boy. With his prominence, Mr. Paderewski surely could
have exhibited impatience or anger and allowed the situation to play
itself out in an ugly fashion. He could have been outraged that a parent
had allowed such behavior. Instead, he had compassion and whispered
gentle expressions of support. The message the pianist said, in other
words, was: "You didn't exactly do the right thing, but I'm here to support you anyway and make everything okay . . . we'll make it work for
good." How often does the Lord do that for us? Gentleness! The word
itself seems to connote a calm, peaceful, tender and caring spirit.

Let your speech always be with grace,
seasoned, as it were, with salt,
so that you may know how you should respond to each person.
COLOSSIANS 4:6 NIV

A HEAVENLY EXPRESSION OF GENTLENESS

Children are exceedingly important to me. They are my passion. Children are so vulnerable, so impressionable, and I want to protect each
and every one. I suppose psychologists would say that my passion is the
result of abuse in my own life. I was unable to protect myself. Therefore,
psychologists would explain that I'm transferring that inability into a
"grand stance" to protect all other children. I wish I could! Perhaps they
are right. All I can tell you is that my passion for children was there long
before I was cognizant of the fact that I had been abused.

❧❧❧

Eventually, my passion led me to school counseling. I was a school counselor for 20 years and, during those years, I've had to confront inept parents, call the CPS (Child Protective Services) to report parental child abuse, attend court sessions as a witness, require parents to attend "Parent Training Classes," and counsel parents, families as well as children. I've made sure the learning disabled were receiving that extra needed care also. Above all, our school never allowed a child to demean another child. Unkindness and bullying was (and is) absolutely not permitted. If you have ever worked with children, you know how devastating their remarks can be to one another. Once children begin to develop their own autonomy and personhood, and deal with their own insecurities, it becomes a standard method to lift themselves up by demeaning others. If their home life has provided the emotional, academic and spiritual building blocks needed for healthy development, than that child sails along through school without any glitches. Many, however, are not so fortunate.

Some children even abuse themselves instead of abusing other children. I am thinking of one child in particular who hated herself. She would cut herself, scratch her forehead until it bled, bite her arm leaving serious bite marks, and pinch herself until she left bruise marks. While in my office, she said: "I just hate myself and I want to commit suicide." Well, as a counselor, I was mandated to report the incident to the CPS. How sad I was! It was obvious, after reviewing her home environment, why she was in such a state of mind. The home was beyond dysfunctional; it was repugnant and revolting for any child to remain in.

Jesus had strong words for such behavior to children: "And who shall receive one such little child in my name receiveth me. But whoso shall offend one of these little ones which believe in me, it were better for him that a millstone were hanged about his neck, and that he were drowned in the depth of the sea" (Matthew 18:5,6 KJV).

Here is the same account from *The Message:*

"What's more, when you receive the childlike on my account, it's the same as receiving me. But if you give them a hard time, bullying or taking advantage of their simple trust, you'll soon wish you hadn't. You'd be better off dropped in the middle of the lake with a millstone around your neck. Doom to the world for giving these God-believing children a hard time! Hard times are inevitable, but you don't have to make it worse . . . and it's doomsday to you if you do."

GENTLE JESUS:
JESUS BLESSES THE LITTLE CHILDREN

Jesus had just left Capernaum and decided to go south toward the shores of the Jordan River. As usual, there were always crowds of people waiting for Him. The teaching became a discourse on marriage and divorce, but this topic was interrupted when some mothers brought their children to Jesus for a blessing.

"Once when some mothers were bringing their children to Jesus to bless them, the disciples shooed them away, telling them not to bother him" (Mark 10:13 TLB). It seems that in the disciple's eyes, children were really not that significant and Jesus had a more superior schedule pending. He surely should not waste His precious time on children! Jesus became aware of the ongoing scene that unfolded before Him and was quite unhappy, to say the least: *"But when Jesus saw what was happening he was very much displeased with his disciples and said to them, 'Let the children come to me, for the Kingdom of God belongs to such as they. Don't send them away! I tell you as seriously as I know how that anyone who refuses to come to God as a little child will never be allowed into his Kingdom."* (Mark 10:14,15 TLB).

The Message Bible expresses Jesus' love for children this way: *"The people brought children to Jesus, hoping he might touch them. The disciples shooed them off. But Jesus was irate and let them know it. 'Don't push these children away. Don't ever get between them and me. These children are at the very center of life in the kingdom'"* (Mark 10:14 MSG).

❧

The disciples must have dropped their heads in embarrassment at this reprimand. They most likely huddled together and said: "What did we do wrong; we were only trying to help." The disciples just didn't "get it." What's more vital in this world than blessing defenseless and powerless little children? *"Then he took the children into his arms and placed his hands on their heads and he blessed them"* (Mark 10:16 TLB).

WHAT A GENTLE, TENDER AND PRECIOUS SAVIOR WE HAVE!

CHAPTER XV
Application & Review

Gentleness is that attribute of the Spirit that exemplifies the true meaning of tenderness, compassion and understanding. It is love's method. It is Jesus personified!

1. According to the first paragraph in chapter XV, how is gentleness expressed? Explain how "words" (negative or positive) have affected your life.

2. What does Colossians 4:6 say regarding gentleness and speech?

3. What does Matthew 18:5-6 say about the mistreatment of children? What was Jesus' response?

4. How does Jesus regard children, as found in Mark 10:13-16? Explain.

5. Does your speech express gentleness and bring glory to God? How?

CHAPTER XVI

The Fruit of the Spirit is Self-Control

Self-control is love's submission to integrity

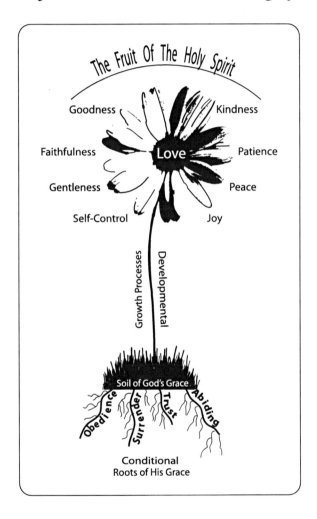

. . . let us be self-controlled,
putting on faith . . .
I THESSALONIANS 5:8B NIV

CHAPTER XVI

The Fruit of the Spirit is Self-Control

. . . live self-controlled, upright and godly lives.

TITUS 2:12B NIV

The fruit of self-control is the same as "temperance" in the King James version. The Holy Spirit has given us this gift as an internal strength to keep us strong against wrong attitudes, desires, or impulses and wrong thinking.

Some people never become disciplined enough to control their behaviors. It is especially difficult to see an adult lose control in front of a child. If the parent is to be the model, is it any wonder that a child lacks self-control as well? As the saying goes, "The apple doesn't fall far from the tree."

AN EARTHLY LACK OF SELF-CONTROL

The following story took place during a counseling session in my office in 2001. It relates how the lack of self-control in an adult parent can cause damage to a child.

Years ago, a man and his wife came to my counseling office and asked for help with their son. When I inquired what the problem was, the father said: "He's uncontrollable, he won't obey, he's obstinate and I'm at my wit's end." These negative adjectives used to describe his son were often spoken in front of the son, which only created more defiance. The boy, at the time, was in first grade and had already been referred to me for a case study.

After one counseling session, it was determined that this particular boy needed some professional psychological testing. While in my office,

I asked him to perform certain cognitive exercises to determine the basis for his behavior. When I tried to engage him in these exercises, he absolutely refused. He sat in a chair with his arms crossed, and exhibited much displeasure. He pouted, gave me mean looks and refused to cooperate. I even tried play therapy, where dolls or plastic figures are used to represent members of the family, but he just threw them across the room. I tried positive reinforcement as well, but he would receive none of it. He was extremely disruptive in the classroom, displayed an acute lack of self-control, and was a deeply disturbed and angry little boy. He had become exactly what his father often told him he was . . . Bad!

To see a child on a regular basis I need the permission of the parent, so I was pleased that they had sought me out. However, when I related the above story to the parents, the father became irate—especially when I said: "Before we can allow your child to remain at Evangel, he must be psychologically tested." He said: "Never, I will never allow such a thing to happen." He also said: "In my culture, a son is very highly valued. To have him tested would be such an embarrassment to us." The conversation continued, while he was pacing the floor, and I said: "How does your wife feel about the testing?" His quick response was: "I speak for my wife, she has nothing to do with this." O-k-a-a-ay!! At this point, he was yelling and pretty much "getting into my face." So, I stood up and said: "Sir, I appreciate your position, but you are now in America and in American culture, we respect women and we also respect their opinions. However, it remains your prerogative to treat your wife according to your culture while in your home, but not here in my office. In our school, both parent's opinions are crucial to a child's progress." I also stated: "Please don't let your pride interfere with your child's academic achievement. I have stated the criteria and terms for your son to remain in our school; the decision is yours." He then walked toward me and screamed in my face, "We take him out of this school." With that, he stormed out of my office with his meek and mild wife crying hysterically behind him.

❧

That type of behavior can only be summed up as a total lack of self-control. Unfortunately, the distressing component in this complete episode is the welfare of the son. Was he ever tested? Did he ever receive any type of behavior modification? Does he continue to exhibit the same lack of self-control as his father? Most likely! Especially if the father's domestic behavior is comparable to the behavior I witnessed in my office. My only option was to pray and give that little boy over to God's care and keeping. I continue to pray for him. May God watch over him!

Being a positive role model to your child is one of the greatest gifts a parent can bestow, especially one who models self-control. Many parents do not recognize how impressionable little ones are. Nine times out of ten, a child will become the same person that was modeled to them. If love was expressed, they will possess the ability to express love. It's the same for negative behavior. For example, an alcoholic parent will most likely have an alcoholic child. Children will also become what you tell them they are, negatively or positively. When praise is part of a child's experience, they will try to reach for success. If children are constantly told they are "bad," they will live up to that title and continue to exhibit bad behavior. If there is any encouragement I could give to parents, it is to understand and acknowledge that adult behaviors, and especially WORDS, speak volumes. Children are like sponges and will soak up every word you use and closely observe your behaviors. What is the legacy that you are presenting to your children? Is it faith, hope, love, positive words, and acceptable behaviors? It is a daunting thought that the hopeful future of your children's lives depends on whether they are given positive or negative influences while in your home.

A HEAVENLY PICTURE OF SELF-CONTROL:
THE STORY OF ESTHER

Upon the release of the Israelites from Persia, many Jews returned to their homeland, but a larger assembly stayed to enjoy the easy and lucrative lifestyle they had grown accustomed to living. Esther was one of those who remained behind. Many fruit of the Spirit could be chosen to describe her character, such as gentleness, goodness, patience and faithfulness. I have chosen self-control. Let's see how that plays out:

The book of Esther takes place during the reign of King Xerxes. He was an extremely wealthy man, so he invited all the leaders, princes and nobles from the entire Media-Persia area for a banquet. These provinces stretched from India to Ethiopia . . . 127 provinces in all. His intent was to flaunt his tremendous display of wealth with a celebration that was to last for six months.

During one evening of revelry, he sent for his wife Vashti. He wanted her to arrive wearing her royal crown and display her beauty to all the royalty present. She received the message but refused: *"But when the attendants delivered the king's command, Queen Vashti refused to come. Then the king became furious and burned with anger"* (Esther 1:12 NIV). He then consulted experts, lawyers and friends as to what his response should be. Their solution was the following: *"Women everywhere will begin to disobey their husbands when they learn what Queen Vashti has done. We suggest that you issue a royal edict that can never be changed, that Queen Vashti be forever banished from your presence and that you choose another queen more worthy than she"* (Esther 1:17-19 TLB). This edict was to guarantee that wives within all the provinces would respect their husbands.

The door has now been opened for the entrance of Esther. Because King Xerxes realized he would never see Queen Vashti again his aids suggested they find the most beautiful girls in the empire that he could choose from. Among those chosen to be presented to the king was Esther, whose real name was Hadassah because she was a Jew.

Mordecai, also a Jew, was a cousin of Esther. After Esther's parents had died, Mordecai took it upon himself to raise her. Now Esther was very beautiful and lovely. Because of the decree, she had no choice but to comply once she was chosen, among others, to be presented to the king. The long and short of the story is that King Xerxes chose Esther. She had never revealed that she was a Jewess because Mordecai had said not to: *"Well, the king loved Esther more than any of the other girls. He was so delighted with her that he set the royal crown on her head and declared her queen instead of Vashti"* (Esther 2:17 TLB). Esther constrained her emotions for she had not yet told anyone that she was a Jew. She used her self-control, because it certainly was not her wish to be the wife of Xerxes.

At this point in the story, Esther hears of a plot to assassinate the king. Mordecai worked at the palace and was on duty when he overheard the plot. He referred the information to Esther, who then relayed the message to the King. The two men were killed and this placed Mordecai in good standing with the king.

Following this, the king then appointed Haman as prime minister: *"He was the most powerful official in the empire next to the king himself. Now all of the king's officials bowed before him . . . but Mordecai refused to bow. Haman was furious, but decided not to lay a hand on Mordecai alone but to move against all of Mordecai's people, the Jews, and destroy all of them throughout the whole kingdom of Xerxes"* (Esther 3:2,5,6 TLB).

Haman was bad news! He was a proud, selfish, arrogant and hateful man who became enraged due to Mordecai's refusal to bow, and he approached the king about the matter: *"There is a certain race of people scattered through all the provinces of your kingdom,"* he began, *"and their laws are different from those of any other nation and they refuse to obey the king's laws; therefore, it is not in the king's interest to let them live"* (Esther 3:8 TLB).

ESTHER RISES TO THE OCCASION

When Mordecai learned that a decree had gone out that all Jews should be killed, he *"tore his clothes and put on sack cloth and ashes, and went out into the city, crying with a loud and bitter wail"* (Esther 4:1 TLB). When Esther heard of Mordecai's sorrow, she sent her maid to inquire as to why he was grieving. Word came back to Esther that an edict had been sent to the governors that all Jews should be killed. Mordecai also sent the following message: *"Tell Esther that she should go to the king to plead for her people"* (Esther 4:8 TLB). She immediately sent back her reply: *"All the world knows that anyone, whether man or woman, who goes into the king's inner court without his summons is doomed to die, unless the king holds out his scepter"* (Esther 4:11 TLB). The following is Mordecai's reply: *"Do you think you will escape there in the palace, when all other Jews are killed?* **What's more, who can say but that God has brought you into the palace for just such a time as this?"** (Esther 4:13,14 TLB).

Esther then sent word to Mordecai that he should gather every Jew to fast and pray for her. She also said to do this for three days, night and day . . . *"and I and my maids will do the same; and then, though it is strictly forbidden, I will go in to see the king: **and if I perish, I perish**"* (Esther 4:16 TLB).

NOW THAT IS STRENGTH AND SELF CONTROL. Can you imagine having that kind of determination? But, she dressed in her royal robes and entered where the king was sitting upon his royal throne. He welcomed her and held out his scepter. He then asked her to present her request to him: *"What do you wish, Queen Esther? What is your request? I will give it to you, even if it is half the kingdom!"* (Esther 5:3 TLB). She must have said to herself, *I didn't perish—not yet, anyway.* Esther then replied by inviting the king and Haman to two banquets. Haman, in the meantime, was still furious because Mordecai had not bowed down to him and, at the suggestion of his wife, proceeded to build a 75-foot-high gallows.

After the first banquet, King Xerxes was reviewing some of the historical records and realized that Mordecai had never been recompensed for saving his life against those who plotted to assassinate him. Thus, as it were, Haman happened to be in the palace and the King asked him how to honor a man who truly pleases him. Out of Haman's own mouth he said: *"Bring out some of the royal robes the king himself has worn, and the king's own horse, and the royal crown, and instruct one of the king's most noble princes to robe the man and to lead him through the streets on the king's own horse, shouting before him, 'This is the way the king honors those who truly please him'"* (Esther 6:7,8 TLB). And so it was that Haman was to be the chosen one to parade Mordecai through the streets. What humiliation, but total humiliation that he so deserved!

At the second banquet, Esther calmed her emotions and made her request to the King in complete self-control. The king once again asked what her wish was. And at last Queen Esther replied: *"If I have won your favor, O king, and if it please Your Majesty, save my life and the lives of my people. For my people and I have been sold to those who will destroy us. We are doomed to destruction and slaughter. If we were only to be sold as slaves perhaps I could remain quiet, though even then there would be incalculable damage to the king that no amount of money could begin to cover"* (Esther 7:3,4 TLB). Understandably, the king was more than upset and requested to know who would dare touch her. Esther's reply was: *"This wicked Haman is our enemy"* (Esther 7:6 TLB).

The conclusion of the story is that Haman grew pale with fright after Esther's revelation, and when one of the king's aides approached, he said: *"Sir, Haman has just ordered a 75-foot gallows constructed, to hang Mordecai, the man who saved the king from assassination! It stands in Haman's courtyard." "Hang Haman on it," the king ordered* (Esther 7:9 TLB).

To top off this incredible story, the king gave Haman's estate to Queen Esther (which she graciously turned over to Mordecai), and the king also made Mordecai the new Prime Minister.

I love that story. I love the revenge part. I know, I know, the Bible says "vengeance is mine saith the Lord." But isn't that what happened? God took vengeance upon the enemies of His people through the courageous **self-control** of Queen Esther. God "settled the score" through Esther's obedient heart. **She could have refused Mordecai's request, but self-control kept her calm and she cleverly maneuvered the drama completely around to her advantage and to the advantage of her people.**

CONSISTENCY

What will guard us against foolish extremes? What will help us as parents to model self-control? What brings security in relationships? What adds more weight to our witness for Christ than anything else? Consistency!! That's the answer to all those questions.

Steadiness. You can count on it. It'll be there tomorrow just like it was yesterday. Consistency is reliable and faithful. It is not opposed to change or reason, but trustworthy. Not stubborn, but solid. Consistency is a living model of patience, determination and strength. It's the stuff most mothers are made of when their little ones get sick. It knows little of ups or downs, highs or lows. It thrives on sacrifice and unselfishness. It's an obvious mark of maturity. **Diligence is its brother, dependability, its partner . . . discipline, its parent.**[1]

There is only one word I would stress to parents, and that is *consistency.* It will bring peace and order to your home, all your relationships, and your witness for Christ. Self-control and consistency are strongly connected . . . each depends on the other. Without consistency, one struggles with self-control. Without self-control, one will most likely be inconsistent. Make consistency a part of your life . . . especially if you have children.

This is a fruit that, if exercised and relied upon, could save many in this world a great deal of grief. I'm working on it; I hope you are.

BE A ROLE MODEL. THE WORLD NEEDS MODELS! OUR CHILDREN NEED MODELS! CHRISTIANITY NEEDS HONEST AND SURRENDERED EXAMPLES TO SHOW "THE WAY" TO OTHERS. BE CONSISTENT, AND SELF-CONTROL WILL BRING PEACE TO YOUR SOUL!

CHAPTER XVI
Application & Review

The Holy Spirit has given us the gift of self control as an internal strength to keep us strong against wrong attitudes, desires, impulses and unacceptable self-indulgent behaviors. By the grace of God, walk before Him in the Spirit of self-control, and present yourself as an exemplary Christian to God and others.

1. Do you struggle with self-control? Explain.

2. Show the areas where you have exemplified self-control.
   Give examples.

3. After reading this chapter, explain how Esther exhibited self-control.

4. In particular, what were God and Mordecai asking Esther to do?
   Read Esther 4:1-17.

5. Are you *consistent* in modeling self-control? Explain how, or why not.

Epilogue

Writing a book on one's spiritual journey is incredibly difficult—especially when the book contains developing roots, disciplines and ultimately possessing "the right of passage" to the fruit of the Spirit. When a person finishes reading this type of book, it intimates that the author has "arrived." It implies that the author has mastered the subject matter. Let me be the first to say that nothing could be further from the truth.

We are all on a journey, and how you perceive your progress is between you and the Lord. The same goes for me. The most I could do was share honestly the path that the Lord and I traveled together on. Have I become more gracious? I hope so. I surely do not want all those bike rides to have been for naught. Have I reached perfection? No, and never will! Not until I see Jesus. Have I learned and been able to grasp certain spiritual principles? Yes! It is now my responsibility to take advantage of those learned principles and continue to live in His abundant grace.

In my thoughtful estimation, the entire package-of-9-fruit come out of suffering as well as spiritual development. Love, joy, peace, patience, kindness, goodness, faithfulness, gentleness and self-control all are tested in God's refinery. The question is, do we exemplify purified gold? Our hearts, our souls, our spirits and physical beings all undergo reconstruction and testing while in the refiner's hands. The following poem is about the crucible of God's refining fire and it ultimately displays His grandeur, His grace.

The Refiner's Fire
He sat by a fire of sevenfold heat
As He watched by the precious ore
And closer He bent with a turning gaze
As He heated it more and more.

He knew He had ore that could stand the test
And He wanted the finest gold
To mold as a crown for the King to wear
Set with gems with price untold.
So, He laid out gold in the burning fire
Though we fey [to dispute or argue] would have said, "Nay,"
And He watched as the dross that we said
We had not seen was melted and passed it away.
And the gold grew brighter and yet more bright,
But our eyes were filled with tears.
We saw but the fire, not the Master's hand
And questioned with anxious fears.
Yet our gold shown out with a richer glow
As it mirrored a form above
That bent o'er the fire, though unseen by us
With the look of ineffable [wonderful, inexpressible] love.
Can we think that it pleases His loving heart
To cause us moments of pain?
No. But He saw through the present cross
The bliss of eternal gain.
So He waited there with a watchful eye
With a love that is strong and sure
And His goal did not suffer a bit more heat
Than was needed to make it pure.[1]

— AUTHOR UNKNOWN (EMPHASIS ADDED)

"So be truly glad! There is wonderful joy ahead, even though the going is rough for a while down here. These trials are only to test your faith, to see whether or not it is strong and pure. It is being tested as fire tests gold and purifies it . . . and your faith is far more precious to God than mere gold; so if your faith remains strong after being tried in the test tube of fiery trials, it will bring you much praise and glory and honor on the day of his return" (I Peter 1:6,7 TLB).

This day (but not always yesterday), I am thankful for the refiner's fire. I now realize that if I had not established roots, traveled through my emotional maze, renewed my thinking processes, I would not have access today to the fruit of the Spirit. I would have been too encumbered with baggage. Even though this marvelous fruit is a gift of the Holy Spirit, it is a learning process. God has to have an open, uncluttered channel to work through. As I said, I'm still a work in progress but thank God for His Grace. Let your life blossom and show forth His glory. Love, joy, peace, patience, kindness, goodness, faithfulness, gentleness, and self-control: to these I commit my future. If I succeed, I will give thanks.

A METAPHOR:
A FRAGRANT FLOWER OF HIS GRACE

Flower so fragrant, flower so fair,
From where did you come? God surely is aware!
Carefully planted, you were just a small seedling,
Waiting for nurture, for the gardener's preening.

Your first root "obedience" waited silently in His presence,
Patiently gathering courage . . . receiving of His essence.
Obedience then heard: "My yoke is easy, my burden is light,
Come unto me and new strength will be your delight."

Your second root "surrender" became entwined in full splendor,
As you submitted your will . . . to the greatest of tenders.
Knowing a heart full of "self," would only bring sorrow,
You submitted to His will for grace in your tomorrow.

Your root of trust began to struggle;
it had been crushed and lost its hope,

The darkness of horrible evil had made it difficult to cope.
Then Jesus said, "Arise my daughter, for you I will always fight,"
Your soul will heal, and then it will take flight.

Your root of abiding aided obedience, surrender and trust,
Allowing each to grow strong and know He is just.
Your taproot went deep into the "Living Water" of our Lord,
Providing a sense of belonging with Love as its central cord.

Then your stem grew strong by facing the past,
He said: "Emotional upheaval just cannot last."
Encumbered with darkness and strongholds untold,
Jesus broke fetters and gave peace to behold.

"Bringing into captivity the thoughts that beset you,"
Made your stem stronger because to self you were true!
Your mind was the battlefield where two kingdoms did feud,
But renewing all your thoughts is where His grace was renewed.

The precious Holy Spirit came with His generous power,
To encourage and uplift, at just the right hour.
Conviction and direction are also His great traits,
Freeing your conscience from evil that awaits.

And now, dear flower, so fragrant, dear flower so fair,
Now is your time to show the world you care.
Your roots are strong; your stem stands firm,
It's time to flourish and blossom; you've grown full term.

What fruit shall you bear? Will it stand the test of time?
Are you ready to share the fruit of the Spirit all combined?
Others need His Love, Joy, Peace, Patience and Kindness,
Followed by Goodness, Faithfulness, Gentleness, Self-control
and His likeness.

❦

Grace was the conduit, through which you carefully grew,
Are you now ready to spread His Love to more than a few?
Continue to blossom, and spread God's Grace liberally,
For many are dying and will never live eternally. — JJ/09

**AS YOU BEAR HIS FRUIT,
LAVISH HIS LOVE UPON A DYING WORLD
AND ALLOW THE _FRAGRANCE OF HIS GRACE_
IN YOUR LIFE TO DRAW OTHERS TO HIMSELF!!**

*THE GRACE OF OUR LORD
WAS POURED OUT ON ME ABUNDANTLY.*

I TIMOTHY 1:14 KJV

The Fragrance of His Grace

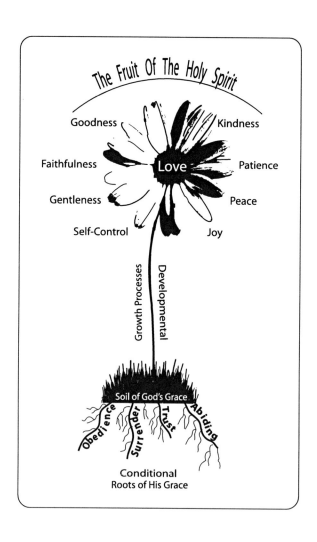

Appendix A

IN HONOR AND RECOGNITION OF REV. WILLIAMS

The original founder of Evangel Church was Rev. Evan Williams, who is my husband's grandfather. Rev. Williams pastored Evangel Church for 30-some years before we came, and the following is his account of the commencement of a ministry in Astoria, N.Y. Astoria today, however, has been renamed Long Island City, N.Y. Several titles have graced this church over the years, such as: "Gospel Tabernacle," "Community Gospel Church," and today it is widely known as "Evangel Church." In the history of this church, there have only been two pastors, Rev. Williams and my husband (Rev. Robert Johansson . . . we have been here for 44 years). I now present Rev. Williams in his own words:

My childhood years:

I was born in a town called Liverpool, near Wilkes-Barre, Pennsylvania. I was raised in a poor family as this world is concerned, but it was "rich toward God." My father lost his health before I was born and therefore they weren't looking forward to my arrival. I was the seventh child.

One of the most effective sermons I have ever heard was by my father, who was not a preacher. He had sold a baby goat to a boy, who was not very reputable, for fifty cents. After several months he came with the money. However, it was on a Sunday and my Dad said: "You must come another day, my boy, this is Sunday." Now the Lord had always supplied our needs, but fifty cents was a lot of money in those days. A laboring man received ten cents an hour, or one dollar for a days' work of ten hours. The next day a man came to visit my father. There was a reason for the visit . . . my Dad had boarded with him many years ago when work was scarce and loaned him money for his lodging. I shall never forget seeing my Dad receive five dollars when they parted. Five dollars was ten times the fifty cents he would have taken the day before if it had not been "the Lord's day." Five dollars was the equivalent of fifty dollars today. What an experimental sermon that I saw with my own eyes and heard with my own ears! It left a stamp upon my life. Sunday is no business day apart from the Lord's business. I have since then made a small fortune in carpentry and building, but never have I gone near my business on the Lord's Day.

Coal mining was the only industry around the vicinity where I lived. I wanted to be a "man" like the rest of the boys, and at the age of nine I worked ten hours a day for forty cents a day (a boy's wage). Later, when I was close to fourteen years of age, I was in the coal breaker when I had an accident. My job was to sort the slate from the coal. The oiler had been around oiling the machinery and to do this he had to open a floorboard. Its hinges were worn or broken and the floorboard did not fit back right. I came along in the black dust from the coal and stepped on this very board. It suddenly tipped, and my leg went down, just skipping the cogwheels that operated the coal crusher. My three largest toes were severed and about one quarter of my foot; plus, one side of the calf of my leg was torn off.

My Conversion:

Now, this story is the telling of the greatest miracle that can happen to anyone . . . conversion. While at the hospital I was meditating upon the Lord in the midnight hour. Suddenly hell appeared below me as a lake of fire. God, the Father, held me by the back of the neck over hell. He wanted me to know that all of my good "bringing up," all of my good deeds, all my works of self-righteousness were but "filthy rags" in His sight, and that I was a hell deserving sinner. As I was about to be dropped into hell, I lifted up my eyes and saw Jesus clothed in pure white standing with outstretched arms at the foot of the bed. I cried to Him and He saved me . . . from hell itself. My sins rolled away; they were put "as far as the east is from the west," and God "remembered them against me no more."

My Personal Testimony:

I thank God that He saved me many years ago. I first started to attend the Free Gospel Church of Corona, Long Island, and for 10 years I labored for the Master there. As I sat in the meetings and listened to the inspiring messages of my Pastor, Rev. W.K. Bouton, my heart burned within me and I felt a deeper love for God; a greater desire to serve Him came into my life. I realized that the Christ that was in my heart was a great power. I understood Paul when he said, "I can do all things through Christ which strengtheneth me," also "not I, but Christ who liveth in me," etc. Having the key to the church, I went in from time to time to pray.

My Call To The Ministry:

*On one of those occasions while praying at the Free Gospel Church, God gave me a vision of lost souls. He showed me an immense parade (of people) that terminated at the end of the block where I stood. I saw men and women dropping down in the flame by the thousands. I saw Christ standing with outstretched arms at the side of the road. But there was no one to turn their heads to Christ that they might be saved from Hell. God said, "What are you going to do about it?" I said, "Lord, I will open a mission. I will be the janitor if you will only put on the heart of any one of the talented persons in our assembly to come and preach. The Lord kept saying to me as I tried to convince Him as to whom He should send: "**What are you going to do about it?**" I said: "Lord, I cannot preach, I can only testify that you are real to me; I never spoke over five minutes in my life except on one or two occasions; Lord, I am not a preacher; I know nothing; there is no good in me." The Lord* said, *"All this I know, but if you will remain nothing I will use you."* **"What are you going to do about it?"** *This convinced me. I said: "Lord, here am I, send me."*

Led To Astoria:

On June 18, 1933, we opened our first church in a store on 42nd Street. God blessed us in this store and much fruit gathered there in the name of Christ Jesus still remains to this day; and we give the glory to Jesus. On March of 1934, we moved to a better location on Steinway Street. It was while we were here, that the first of our three summer tent meetings were held. However, in the middle of one winter, we got a notice to move as the building was to be torn down. We prayed, and God led us to put a small deposit on a lot on which to build a church. The Astoria church was a home missionary project built with money given by the people themselves. There was no solicitation for funds from any outside source. It was built in three different sections over a period of years by our own labor freely given to the Lord. Being a former builder, I was able to manage the job. After the first part of the church was completed, I thought if there was a parsonage, it would mean much toward the work if the pastor had a place to live. All had a mind to work and like Nehemiah's crew of the Old Testament we were led of the Lord to extend the church 20 feet with an apartment on the second floor in the back.

This is the site to which his grandson and family came in 1965. Over the years, many missionaries and ministers found refuge in this extension of the church, and have then been sent around the world as a result of Rev. William's work at 32-71 41st Street, Astoria, N.Y. He had tremendous impact on the Kingdom of God.

My Missionary Work:

While ministering in Haiti, I had a nice room and a clean bed

❧

but I also discovered some bugs and found they like people from America. I remembered the promise which states "no plague shall come nigh they dwelling," so I rebuked them in the name of Jesus and believe it or not the bugs departed. None troubled me the whole month I was there.

The following is an account and description of Rev. Williams' love for the mission field and his spiritual influence on others as rendered by his youngest son, Rev. Morris Williams:

My Father's Mission field:

As far back as I can remember, my father had a deep-seated concern for the mission fields of the world. And so in 1958 he embarked on a journey through the Caribbean, which took him to several islands including Haiti. The last three of his five trips to the Caribbean focused on Haiti. Here he built three churches and one parsonage. It was here also that he met Miss Consuelo Stephens, director of the Ebenezer Orphanage and Training School in Port-au-Prince. With her permission he built a small room on the second floor of the orphanage. This became both his home and headquarters whenever he was in Haiti. Immediately he began updating and improving the primitive facilities which housed almost 40 boys and girls.

On his third trip to Haiti, he showed that while he was a very generous man, he was also very frugal. It was his custom to bring with him clothing and supplies for distribution to the needy. But he lamented the high import duty he was required to pay. So this time, in order to circumvent the imposition of duty, he wore six suits. Strange sight he posed as he boarded a plane bound for the tropics! Upon his arrival, he proceeded to give away the suits to needy pastors . . . and saved the price of duty. While ministering in Haiti, he developed a respiratory problem and admitted himself to the hospital. Shortly after, a hurricane battered Haiti and extensively damaged the roof of the Orphanage. Hearing about this, he signed him-

self out of the hospital and walked several miles to check the plight of the orphans. They were safe, but drenched. The exertion and the drenching rain worsened his condition and he was admitted to the hospital again. Here, he passed away. He had often stated that he wanted "to die working for the Lord." He did!

His Life as we knew it:

We only know what we observed. He was not a lettered man, but through diligent self-effort he acquired a theological education. He lacked charisma, but he was a channel through whom the Holy Spirit moved people to commitment. He was not a theologian, but he built a theology into his parishioners that made them stalwart Christians. He never attended a seminary, and yet he provided many a minister-to-be with a pre-seminary education. Economically, he was on the bottom rung. Yet, as a good steward, he gave liberally and invested heavily in the securities of Heaven. While basically frugal, he was well known for his generosity. He loved people and many reciprocated that love. His life can best be summed up in one word . . . OTHERS!

AN ADDENDUM

Camp Bethel:

Rev. Williams also purchased a camp in Oldbridge, New Jersey:

Here we were led to purchase a seven-acre tract of land with fine drinking water, pine trees and a beautiful creek in which to swim. We laid part of the land out in lots, which were leased to some of our people for ninety-nine years.

I know that my husband has very fond memories of this camp that occupied their summer months. He often tells of how hard they worked to build a tabernacle and clear the land. This is where he learned most of his carpentry skills from his grandfather. They also had fun times. He and his twin brother had an old Model A Ford that kept them busy, remodeling and driving "crazily" through the campground. Also, our own children enjoyed many excursions to Camp Bethel while they were small. It was a refuge for many from the "cement city" we all lived in. Many camp meetings were also held on this property and hundreds were saved and blessed by Rev. Williams' vision for a camp.

His tenacity and faith were revealed during the building of the tabernacle where many worshipped. When the building was partially built, a fire broke out and destroyed the entire tabernacle. It was a sad day, for they had worked tirelessly to raise this place of worship for the Lord and now what? While the fire fighters were nearly finished extinguishing the remaining flames, Rev. Williams was no where to be found. Where was he? The family became concerned. Suddenly, he appeared carrying something in his arms. What was it?

He walked toward the remaining ashes, and there he placed a sign that read ROMANS 8:28: "All things work together for good." He said to his two grandsons: "Well boys, we'll just start over . . . God is still good."

Appendix B
Continuation of Accolades

For my husband's 70th birthday, by our son Steve:
"LIKE CEMENT"

Anyone that knows Pastor Johansson knows that he is a man of his word. What he says, he will do. It may not always be to the liking of others, but it WILL GET DONE. He has never gone back on his word and I can truly say that he practices what he preaches.

I can recall many times when he would come home with **cement** on his good suits and my mother would say: "Oh honestly, Rob! Can't you change your clothes before you do that kind of work?" My father would sort of chuckle and say, "We got it done Jan, we got it done."

Another memory that comes to my mind, is the time we were all waiting for a delivery of **cement** in front of the school. Somehow, the gate key had gotten misplaced. The key was nowhere to be found. The cement truck arrived, and still there was no key. My father said: "No key, no problem! Just hand me that sledge hammer." (WHACK.) I said: "Okaaay! No more lock and no more problem." To my Dad, problems were simply challenges to overcome.

Speaking of **cement!** When you work with cement, you don't just pour the cement on the ground and pray that it will become a sidewalk do you? No, in fact, any mason will tell you that the most important part of cement work is in the preparation of the forms. The cement takes the shape of its form and if you build a good form, you will lay a good slab of cement. My Dad, my Pastor, and my Friend, you have laid good forms . . . for your family and this church. Thank you!

Those of you sitting here today need to know, that those forms were laid with much sacrifice, and a clear vision by a skilled craftsman that loves you. A firm foundation it is, but there are still forms that need to be filled. You are the cement my friends. Take your rightful places in Christ and look for the empty forms that need to be filled.

Thanks Dad for being the **cement** that holds us together . . . for being the building block that we have built our own lives and families on. Like wet cement, you have left a lasting impression on us, such as how to persevere, be steadfast and especially, how to stay the course. You taught us how to "build the forms" and "pour the cement." Cement gets stronger with time, as do the impressions you have left on our hearts.

God Bless you this year in all you do.

— *Your son, Steve 1/4/06*

A BIRTHDAY MESSAGE TO MY FATHER
A birthday tribute by our son, Brian; 1998

I have wanted to write this letter to you for some time now. Your birthday seemed like a good opportunity to finally do so. My career has allowed me to work with many homeless men over the last several years and one common denominator seems to usually apply: THE LACK OF A GOOD FATHER. I had a man in my office the other day and he was telling me what it was like not having anyone there to guide him through life. I thought to myself: *I cannot identify with what this man is saying because God has given me a father who was and is involved in my life.*

The best analogy I can offer is the game of football. A good player goes through rigorous training, discipline and instruction under the watchful eye of a coach. Then, the "Big Game Day" arrives. The coach stands on the sideline, not allowed to go on the field (even though he would in a second if the rules would allow it). The best he can do is call in a play, encourage and watch. It is then, when the ball is snapped, that the coach will see what his player has developed into.

It is difficult watching his player get knocked down, but he taught him to get up. When the rain falls and the mud is thick, he taught his player to plod on. And when the game is over, regardless of victory or defeat, he taught his player to stop and thank God for the lesson.

Dad, as I go out onto the playing field of life every day, I thank God for a Father who is that coach, always ready to call in a play, and for a Mother who is always cheering me on from the stands. My desire is to make you both proud.

Thank you for always being there for me with advice, encouragement, wisdom and the occasional pep talk. I now appreciate those difficult lessons in hard work, problem solving and leadership . . . all of which I use every day! But most of all I thank you for deep roots which I can draw strength from. Your example to me is a treasure that I can pass onto my children and those I come in contact with every day.

I Love You, Dad.   *— Your son, Brian 1/4/98*

LIGHTHOUSE OF LOVE
Written and sung by our son, Stephen, at the Dedication Ceremony of the New Sanctuary June 6, 1999

In a lowly little store front room on 42nd Street
A man sat quietly praying for revival in this land.
With a vision in his eyes, and hope in his heart,
He put his faith and trust in God,
To carry out his part.

CHORUS
As we are building this lighthouse of love,
Let us join our hearts together,
Through rain and stormy weather,
And we'll shine the bea-con through the night,
On every ship that passes by,
Shine its bright and guiding light,
And light the way with truth to bring them home.

Now it's been a long hard journey, and we've given faithfully.
Now in this final sacrifice, we commit ourselves to be,
As Nehemiah, cried to God, "Strengthen our hands,"
As we carry out Your plan, Let us give both heart and soul
Of Your Amazing Love for all.

CHORUS
As we are building this lighthouse of love,
Let us join our hearts together,
Through rain and stormy weather,
And we'll shine the bea-con through the night,
On every ship that passes by,
Shine its bright and guiding light,
And light the way with truth to bring them home.

And in this very room, within these walls of love,
A foundation built by faith, each brick comes from above,
We dedi-cate our giving, so the vision keeps on living,
And we will sing a song of praise,
For the victo-ry's been wo-n.

CHORUS
As we are building this lighthouse of love,
Let us join our hearts together,
Through rain and stormy weather,
And we'll shine the bea-con through the night,
On every ship that passes by,
Shine its bright and guiding light,
And light the way with truth to bring them home.

❧

MY TRIBUTE
Father's Day Tribute by our daughter, Carolyn – June 20, 1999

I'm not the speaker in this family; I'll leave that up to my father and my mother (as you witnessed at the dedication). But, I feel it is only fitting to say a few words about my father, on this first Father's Day in this beautiful "pearl" of a sanctuary. My mother also mentioned in her speech, God chose wisely when He chose my father and so did she. Well, I consider myself even more blessed than my mother, because I didn't have to choose my father, God did that for me. *I could never have chosen a better father, even if I searched the entire world.*

I count it an honor when people say to me: "You're just like your father," because he has so many honorable traits. The trait that "sticks out" the most in my mind, is one that does not allow the word "can't" to be in our vocabulary. **I have never heard my father say, "I can't!" or "It can't be done!"** That word just doesn't exist to him. This trait is something that I have taken for granted my whole life. I never think twice about whether something can be done or not—I just do it! Daddy, today I want to say, "thank you" for instilling this trait in me. I also want to thank you for being an incredible example of selflessness. Your hours and hours of giving to others have been a model and guide to me.

There is a song written by Steven Curtis Chapman entitled "Burn The Ships," that *describes you and your courage.* God called you here on a mission, to be the Captain of Evangel. As Captain you have to make many important decisions, some not to everyone's liking, but always for the best of everyone. Listen to the words of this song about a captain and his mission:

In the spring of 1519, a Spanish fleet set sail. Cortez told the sailors, "This mission must not fail." On the Eastern Shore of Mexico, they landed with great dreams, but the hardships of a new life made them restless and weak. Quietly they whispered, "Let's sail back to the life we knew," but the one who led them there was saying:

"**Burn the Ships! We're here to stay!**
There's no way we could go back,
Now that we've come this far by faith,
Burn the Ships!
We're past the point of no return!
Our life is His, so let the ships burn!"[1]

— STEVEN CURTIS CHAPMAN

There was never a doubt in your mind that God called you here on a mission. When you came, you came with great dreams, and the many hardships that you faced made it seem like those dreams would never be fulfilled. **But you never gave up! You burned the ships and never looked back! You never said, "It can't be done!"** And, you have proven that God can do miraculous things with a life totally dedicated and yielded to Him.

It takes a very special person to be a Captain, a Father and a Friend. I want to say to you today: **"Daddy, I'm very proud of you, and more importantly, I know your heavenly Father is saying, "Well done, thou good and faithful servant."** I am honored to be your daughter and to have the privilege to work along side you.

I love you with all my heart,

— *Your daughter, Carolyn*

TO MY DEAR PARENTS:

My Father the mighty Oak,
My Mother, the gentle flower.
How can I thank you for all the time, for all the encouragement,
*   and for all the love?*
You have been a rock of courage, never wavering.
Your lives model true dedication and service to our loving Savior.
*Your unconditional love and constant striving for truth, created a **way***

❦

of life for me that would never include quitting or turning aside.

For when I would fail, you would always be there to comfort and guide. This I thank you for from the deepest part of my heart.

But, the thing I thank you most for, is introducing me to my Savior and Lord . . . for bringing me up in His Word. For teaching me, guiding me and for proving to me by your lives, that His Word is true. For this most Precious Gift of all . . . I thank you, and I only pray that I will be able to give to my own, as you have given to me.

— *Your loving daughter, Carolyn*

TO MY WIFE – MY LOVE – MY COMPANION AND THE WONDERFUL MOTHER OF OUR THREE CHILDREN
On the occasion of my 65th birthday celebration

It has been 42 years since we married, raised a family and made the service of the Lord our purpose and life's work. Kind words and awards have come *my way* for those things, which we have done *together!* And . . .

Tonight: I honor you!

You are God's gift to me and to the church.

Any honor that has been given to me, I shower upon you on this your 65th birthday. "This honor is long overdue."

You have remained dedicated to the Lord and loyal to me throughout our journey together. Because I seem to have the gift of finding impossible challenges—and get involved beyond what I planned which required "lots of time and lots of energy"—there was not much left over for you and the children. Yet, while caring for our family with warmth and order, you supported me in every project—even though there were outright attacks of Satan to hinder. Deuteronomy 32:30 states that: "one shall chase a thousand, and *two* shall put ten thousand to flight."

Every Saturday night, you set out all the children's clothes for Sunday. You *still* do that for me. While I was building a church, you were making a home. While I was building a church, you were building a temple—to teach, to protect and to bless our children. It was mostly you who read the stories to the children, tucked them in with prayers and was there to wake them for a new day. Whether you felt weak or strong . . . happy or sad . . . emotionally high or low, *you loved being a mother.* You made raising the children, your first responsibility and with God's help you have given them the inner strength that comes from unconditional love.

AND, you included me in your temple where I gained strength and love to go back again and again . . . to see the mountains removed!!!

AND, WHAT A BEAUTIFUL HOME YOU HAVE ALWAYS MADE. You are also artistic in music, the way you dress and in home decorating. Your gifts have blessed us . . . even though I, and the children continue to fall short!

When we came from Rochester to New York City in 1965 (38 years ago), someone said before we left: "Coming from a small village near Corning, New York, do you think Jan is strong enough to live in the city?" Well, we found out early on when we first came! You not only cared for the children; played the piano for church services; taught Sunday School classes; typed the Sunday bulletin at 2 AM on Sunday mornings; lived with dirt, plaster and cement for years while remodeling; cleaned the church and bathrooms; picked people up for church; lived in the church apartment in back of the church on 41st Street with the noise of vans and young people in the night hours; fed some young men who lived in the attic of the church and allowed them to use our shower until one could be built for them . . . *not only did you do all this and more, but you never gave up!!*

In fact, the person who wondered if you were strong enough to live in the city, visited us years later and said: "Jan has not only survived the city, she had thrived here."

When our children needed to be in Nursery School, and we had no money, you drove the old '53 blue Ford that was given us to pick up 6 children and take them home each day for several years. The money you earned, paid the Nursery School bill.

Then, after 25 years of church work and raising a family, you went back to college to get another degree. Before we married, you had earned a degree in Christian Education from Houghton College, but wanted to counsel Evangel's School Children. So, you earned a degree in Educational Studies and Counseling from the State University of New York. When you joined Evangel Christian School to counsel the children, it was the love you had given to your own children that you shared with the students.

New York City—Church Work—Expansion—Construction . . . how did you do it? Well, it is a mistake to think that your quiet, gentle, reserved and sensitive spirit are the whole package . . . you have inner strength and also determination. You have been a SOLDIER . . . a FIGHTER . . . serving your Lord, protecting your family and home by prayer and the courage of your faith. Even now, you have begun to write a book!

Today I honor you—"Your children rise up and call you blessed." You have brought me great joy! My hope is to continue our journey with more time for each other. Knowing that you are the writer, I looked back 4 years to see how you ended your words to me at the church dedication. Here they are:

"You and I have gone down many roads together and crossed many bridges . . . all of which have brought us to this very moment. And as I ponder on that, I am reminded of the verse God gave to us, separately, just before we were married. Ephesians 3:20 reads like this: 'Now unto him that is able to do exceeding abundantly above all that we ask or think, according to the power that worketh in us, Unto him be glory in the church by Christ Jesus, throughout all ages, world without end.' God has kept His promise. He has been more than faithful and He has done exceeding abundantly above all we could have asked or thought."

I LOVE YOU! YOUR FAMILY LOVES YOU!
YOUR CONGREGATION LOVES YOU!
WE HONOR YOU TODAY!!!

THE ANGELS KNEW
To my husband on the occasion of the 70th
Anniversary of the Church

The angels sang the day your were born,
And suddenly they began to blow their shiny horns.
For the angels knew, as God knew,
That earth had received a blessing—all dressed in blue.

The angels peeked their heads through the clouds,
And shouted in unison, "look out below"—real loud.
For the angels knew, as God knew,
That this one would cause, a real hullabaloo.

The angels "watched over" and protected you
The years you grew up,
Though ever so wearied from the task.
I know they never let up.
For the angels knew, as God knew,
That you were very special, that's why He made two.

The angels rejoiced the day you set out for Elim Bible School,
Even though, you were acting really, really cool.
For the angels knew, as God knew,
That to God's calling you would be true.

The angels applauded the day we were married,
For now by two, your burdens could be carried.
Out of this union came not two, but three,
And greater our joy could never be.
For the angels knew, as God knew,
The blessing our children would be to me and to you.

The angels have graced our lives these past 35 years,
They've shared our joys, as well as our tears.

I've been a recipient of your tenacity, your strength, your wisdom,
your courage, your commitment, your understanding, your patience,
your innumerable talents, and last but not least, your love.
For you know, as I know, these gifts are from heaven above.

The angels will be singing Hallelujah
The day we dedicate the new Evangel—and Behold!!!
They will be standing with you on the platform,
As your labor of love unfolds.
For the angels know, as we know, when God says to you "well done,"
That a very major victory . . . has now been won.

As His angels continue to look upon us, I trust you to His care,
And may your remaining days always be fair.
I believe in angels as I know you do too,
For heaven truly blessed us when we said, "I do."

He said He would give His angels charge over us
To keep us in all our ways as we trust.
May our remaining times reflect His love,
As His angels of grace and mercy bless us from above.

I love you so very much
JAN

WHERE GOD'S FINGER POINTS
To my husband—40 years at Evangel

Where God's finger points, there God's hand will make a way,
And because of this, there was really nothing we could say.
We packed our hearts, as well as our belongings,
And with two small children, we took up the challenge with nary
a backward longing.

We stepped onto the shores of a treacherous land,
We both said: "We shall surely need God's helping hand."
But since this is our Father's world, we chose to ne'er forget,
That though the wrongs seemed oft so strong,
God was our Ruler yet.

"New York, New York. But, dear God, are you sure?"
"Yes, my child, this is **MY** plan that is righteous and pure."
"Will you then breathe on us breath of God,
and fill us with Life anew,
That we may love what You love and do what You would do?"

We very soon found, we were in the very center of the will of God,
And like Moses of old, we knew God would give us
our very own rod.
It was to be a rod of heavenly grace to extend to a city sick with sin,
It has forever been our mission, and one we said we would win.

We climbed over and through mountains, crossed bridges,
swam a few rivers,
even fired some shots at the devil,
But the Lord always said: "I will never leave you nor forsake you,
and together, we will fight this evil."
Some hills have been excruciatingly steep,
but we've always been cheered along,
By those who have gone on before us, where we will one day belong.

We both said, "Master let us walk with thee,
in lowly paths of service free.
Tell us Your secret, help us to bear,
the strains of toil, the fret of care."

The Lord replied: "The heart that serves, and loves, and clings,
hears everywhere, the rush of angel's wings."

His angels have born us up on their wings when trouble came,
and given us a vision of why, when our hearts wanted to blame.

It seems we have always been building, expanding,
and enlarging our borders for Him,
For the Lord told us . . . one day, He plans to fill Evangel to the brim.
We expectantly wait to see that day fulfilled,
It will be a blessing from heaven, as He has willed.

Proverbs 4:12 says: "When thou goest, thy way
shall be opened up before thee step by step each day,"
Surely, He has given us a victorious journey, in every possible way.
His admonition has always been "Not by might, nor by power,
but by My Spirit, saith the Lord."
"Remember, Faith, Hope and Love is My three-fold cord."

One of our greatest joys is our children
and their love for God and for us,
It is truly a blessing that came to us, only through trust.
We gave them to Him many years ago for Him to hold,
And He has blessed us in return more than tenfold.

In all these things, we were made more than conquerors,
And we always want to remain His constant warriors.
The years have been good to us, the journey memorable,
Thank you Lord for enabling, equipping and making us capable.

So . . . let me just say, that it's been many Summers, Winters,
Springtimes and Falls,
Altogether, its taken 40 years to fulfill His call.
Not that it's over, there's still more to be done,
For in God's eyes, this work at Evangel has only begun.

THE CAPTAIN
Written and sung by our son, Brian,
at our 25th Anniversary at Evangel

The ship has left the harbor's side—Long, long time ago,
Set out on a voyage—true and faithful.
This tiny ship was built, by the Master Craftsman's hands,
So lovingly and sure—He set it out to sea.
Can it stand the waves, can it rough the stormy sea,
Nobody seems to care—except for a few.
One of those chosen few—is our Captain strong,
Looking o'er the bow—towards the west we sail.

CHORUS
Lord keep your eyes on this tiny ship we pray,
For we are surely sailing home,
Lord keep your hand on our Captain so dear,
And he will surely guide us—to port
ETERNITY

Can you see the Captain, he is standing on the deck,
He watches o'er the wheel—through the night we sail.
The wind blows through his hair, there is wisdom in his eyes,
His feet are firmly planted—in
RIGHTEOUSNESS.
A partner by his side, put there by the Lord we know,
To cheer and to hold—through all the stormy blasts.
Satan will surely try to bring this tiny ship to the bottom,
But we know the end—and the end is
TRUTH

CHORUS
Lord keep Your eyes on this tiny ship we pray,
For we are surely sailing home.

Lord keep Your hand on our Captain so dear,
And he will surely guide us—to port
ETERNITY

As you well can see—the Captain is your *Pastor,*
The ship is your *church*, and *you* are sailing home.
This Captain needs your prayers—by day and by night,
To survive the rough, and stormy sea.
Some call him *Pastor*, and some call him *Shepherd*,
Some call him *Captain*—but we just call
Him *DAD*

CHORUS
Lord keep Your eyes on this tiny ship we pray
For we are surely sailing home.
Lord keep Your hand on our Captain so dear,
And he will surely guide us—to port

ETERNITY

My husband's office is full of 50 or more plaques, awards from the city, recognition and citations from political figures, and honors from fellow pastors. Also, he was given a special show of respect and recognition as an exceptional Pastor by the City Council of Churches in New York City, has been written about in newspapers and magazines, and yet, he says: "I lay it all at the feet of Jesus. Without Him, I am nothing."

**YES LORD, WE LAY EVERYTHING AT YOUR FEET.
BE GLORIFIED!!**

*"Now to the King eternal, immortal, invisible, to God who alone
is wise, be honor, and glory forever and ever. Amen."*
I TIMOTHY 1:17

Bibliography

CHAPTER I - Obedience

1 "A Parable" (author unknown). Excerpted from *The Adventures of Discipling Others* by Ron Bennett and John Purvis (Colorado Springs, Colorado: NavPress, © 2003) 93-94. Used by permission.

2 John Piper quote. Excerpted from *Secrets of the Vine* by Bruce Wilkinson (Sister, Oregon: Multnomah Publishers, © 2001) 85.

3 "The Power of His Love" by Geoff Bullock (Brentwood, TN: Music Services, Inc. from Word Music, LLC Maranatha! Music, © 1992) Lyrics reprinted by permission, license # 407702.

CHAPTER II – Surrender

1 "God Answers Prayer" (author unknown) Excerpted from *The Pentecostal Witness in volume 4 #2 (Ashland, Kentucky,* © *Feb. 1948) 4. Reprinted by permission.*

2 "The Father and the Child" Excerpted from *Becoming A Woman Of Grace* by Cynthia Heald (Nashville: Thomas Nelson Publishers, © 1998) 117. Used by Permission.

3 Outline Headings excerpted from *Strengthening Your Marriage* by Wayne Mack (Phillipsburg, New Jersey: Presbyterian and Reformed Publishing Company ISBN 9780875523850, © 1999) 16-19. Used by Permission.

4 "A Baloney Sandwich" excerpted from *See You At The House* by Bob Benson (Nashville, Tennessee: Thomas Nelson Inc. © 1989) All rights reserved. Reprinted by permission.

CHAPTER III – Trust

1 "He Makes No Mistake," by A. M. Overton. (No publisher found after an exhaustive research).

2 Legacy Five Singers, "Trust His Heart," by Babbie Mason and Eddie Caswell. © 1989 May Sun Music (Admin. by Word Music, LLC). Word Music, LLC, Causing Change Music (Admin. by Dayspring Music, LLC) Dayspring Music, LLC. All Rights Reserved. License #PR120809-0. Reprinted by permission.

3 "The Missionary's Defense," by von Asselt taken from the book *Stories Worth Rereading* (Washington, D.C.: Review and Herald Publishing Assn. © 1913). (Reprinted by Angela's Bookshelf: Ithaca, MI, © 1992) 170-172. Used by Permission.

4 Legacy Five Singers, "The Storms I Never See" by Cindi Ballard/Twila Labar (Brentwood: TN, Music Services Inc., Christian Taylor Music/Hill Spring Music, © 2003) Lyrics reprinted by permission. License #408052.

CHAPTER IV – Abiding

1 "On That Great Day," by Jan Johansson. Inspired by the poem "Dear God" by Cheryl Kirking found in *Chicken Soup For The Christian Family Soul* (Deerfield Beach, Florida: Health Communications, Inc., © 2000) 100. Inspiration used by permission.

2 "A Child's Prayer" Excerpted from *Clippings From My Notebook* by Corrie ten Boon (Minneapolis, MN: World Wide Publications).

3 "The Pearl" Quote from *The Treasure Chest* by Charles L. Wallis, editor. (New York: Harper & Row, Publishers, 1965) 248. Used by permission.

CHAPTER V – Emotional Health

1 Max Lucado, *In The Grip Of Grace* (Nashville, Tennessee: Thomas Nelson Inc., © 1996) 155,157 All rights reserved. Used by permission.

CHAPTER VI – Mental Health

1 "A Stronghold" excerpted from *Keeping Your Balance* by Marilee Horton and Walter Byrd, M.D. © 1984. (Nashville, Tennessee: Thomas Nelson Inc.) 138 All rights reserved. Used by permission.

2 Vernon McGee, *Through The Bible* (Nashville, Tennessee: Thomas Nelson Inc., © 1983) 325.

CHAPTER VII – The Holy Spirit

1 Charles Stanley, *The Wonderful Spirit Filled Life* (Nashville, Tennessee: Thomas Nelson Inc., © 1992) 62.

2 "Fruit of the Spirit" Excerpted from *Fruit of the Spirit Bible, NIV Translation* (Grand Rapids, Michigan: Zondervan Publishing House, © 2000) 1400. Used by permission.

CHAPTER VIII – Love

1 Hannah Whitall Smith as quoted by Mary Tyleston, in *Daily Strength for Daily Needs* (London: Methuan & Co., © 1922).

2 "Calling Long Distance" by Barbara Johnson. Excerpted from *We Brake For Joy!* (Grand Rapids, Michigan: Zondervan Publishing House, © 1998). Used by permission.

3 Charles Swindoll, *Growing Strong In The Seasons Of Life* (Grand Rapids, Michigan: Zondervan Publishing House, © 1983). 310 Used by permission.

4 Quote from *The Message* by Eugene Peterson (Colorado Springs, Colorado: NavPress, © 2002) 2085 Used by permission.

CHAPTER IX – Joy

1 "In Praise of Teachers" by Mark Medoff, (Playwright, screenwriter, film and theatre director, author, actor, and professor). Most well known for his play: *Children of a Lesser God.* Used by permission of the author.

2 "Courage" by Charles Swindoll. Excerpted from *Growing Strong In The Season's Of Life* (Grand Rapids, Michigan: Zondervan Publishing House, © 1983) 368 Used by permission.

CHAPTER X – Peace

1 "Picture of Peace" Excerpted from *Friends With God* by Catherine Marshall (Ada, Michigan: Fleming H. Revell, a division of Baker Book House, © 1956) 239. Used by permission.

2 "Sweet Peace, the Gift of God's Love" by Peter P. Bilhorn, (1865-1936) (Grand Rapids, Michigan: Kregel Publications) Reprinted by permission.

CHAPTER XI – Patience

1 Oswald Chambers, *My Utmost For His Highest* by Oswald Chambers Publications, Ltd. (Grand Rapids, Michigan: Discovery House Publishers, © 1992) August 1.

2 "The Race" by Charlene Leach, Realife Ranch, (Rogers, Arkansas: Mountain Movers).

3 "Our Eyes On The Goal" by Carole Mayhal excerpted from *Lord Teach Me Wisdom* (Colorado Springs, Colorado: NavPress, © 1979). Used by permission. All rights reserved.

CHAPTER XII – Kindness

1 "A Brand New Pair of Shoes" by Graciela Beecher (Diocese of Fort Wayne, Indiana: *Today's Catholic Newspaper,* © 1999) Reprinted with permission from editor Tim Johnson of *Today's Catholic News* in Fort Wayne, Indiana.
2 "Chosen" by Marie Curling. Unable to locate author after exhaustive research.
3 "Look Alikes" by Linda Mango. Reprinted with permission from the April 1994 Reader's Digest. © 1994 by the Reader's Digest Assn, Inc.

CHAPTER XIII – Goodness

1 "The Sandwich Man," by Meladee McCarty. Excerpted from *A 4th Course of Chicken Soup For The Soul* (Deerfield Beach, Florida: Health Communications, Inc., © 1997) 73-75. All Rights Reserved. Reprinted by permission.

CHAPTER XIV – Faithfulness

1 "All The Way My Savior Leads Me," by Fanny Crosby from *Then Sings My Soul* volume I by Robert J. Morgan (Nashville, Tennessee: Thomas Nelson Publishers, © 2003) 195. Used by permission.
2 "When Christ Comes," by Max Lucado. Excerpted from *When Christ Comes* (Nashville, TN.: Word Publishing, © 1999) All Rights Reserved. Reprinted by permission.

CHAPTER XV – Gentleness

1 "Don't Quit" by Charles Swindoll. Excerpted from *Growing Strong in The Seasons Of Life* (Grand Rapids, Michigan: Zondervan Publishing House, © 1983) 48,49 Reprinted by permission.

CHAPTER XVI – Self-Control

1 "Consistency" by Charles Swindoll. Excerpted from *Growing Strong In The Seasons Of Life* (Grand Rapids, Michigan: Zondervan Publishing House, © 1983) 19 Reprinted by permission.

EPILOGUE

1 "The Refiner's Fire," (author unknown.) Excerpted from *Streams in the Desert* by Mrs. Charles Cowman (Grand Rapids, Michigan: Zondervan Publishing House, © 1925) 333 Reprinted by permission.

APPENDIX B – Accolades

1 "Burn the Ships," by Steven Curtis Chapman, and James Isaac Elliot (EMICGM, Christian Music Group, a Sparrow Record Production). Reprint license #501015. Lyrics reprinted by permission.

❧

Order Form

The Fragrance of His Grace by Jan Johansson

Quantity: _____ books x $12.99 ea. (discount price) = Subtotal: _____

Shipping & handling: Add 10% ($3.00 minimum): _____

Total: _____

Checks payable to Evangel Church. U.S funds only please.
(Mark your check "Books")

Name: _____

Address: _____

City, State, Zip: _____

Mail this completed Order Form together with payment to:
Evangel Church
Attn.: Fragrance
39-20 27th Street
Long Island City, New York 11101

_____

Direct comments to: RandJJohansson@gmail.com
For quantity discounts call Evangel Church at: 718-361-5454

Breinigsville, PA USA
27 October 2010
248125BV00003B/2/P

9 780615 364261